25/5/84

Hi Pussycat.

We were talking about
the Kennedy's this morning,
and what a coincidence
look what I found, and
on sale yet.

enjoy
Love
Henry

Jackie Oh!

An Intimate Biography
by Kitty Kelley

Jackie
Oh!

Photographs by Ron Galella

HART-DAVIS, MACGIBBON
GRANADA PUBLISHING
London Toronto Sydney New York

Published by Granada Publishing in
Hart-Davis, MacGibbon Ltd 1978

Granada Publishing Limited
Frogmore, St Albans, Herts AL2 2NF
and
3 Upper James Street, London W1R 4BP
1221 Avenue of the Americas, New York, NY 10020 USA
117 York Street, Sydney, NSW 2000, Australia
100 Skyway Avenue, Toronto, Ontario, Canada M9W 3A6
110 Northpark Centre, 2193 Johannesburg, South Africa
CML Centre, Queen & Wyndham, Auckland 1, New Zealand

ISBN 0 246 11113 5

Printed in Great Britain by
Richard Clay (The Chaucer Press) Ltd
Bungay, Suffolk

Author's Note

Writing a biography about someone who is still alive is difficult, especially when that someone happens to be the most famous woman in the world. Jacqueline Kennedy Onassis is a public figure, more so than any other woman, but there are many people who are reluctant to talk about her on the record for fear of being socially ostracized. More than 350 people were contacted in preparation for this book, including close friends and family members. Some were afraid to cooperate without her permission and others agreed to be interviewed only on condition that their names never be mentioned. So only a few people can be thanked here but I am grateful to all for their help and cooperation.

I made several attempts to interview Mrs Onassis herself but each of my letters and telephone calls went unanswered. Later I began writing and telephoning her secretary, Nancy Tuckerman, who informed me on each occasion that she could not cooperate in any way. So I relied on extensive personal interviews, plus secondary source material from books and articles.

The time and energy necessary to research this biography would have been formidable without the help of people like Leslie Helfer, Julia Kogut, Mary Haverstock, L. MacGregor Phipps, Keri Corcoran, Dick Leggitt, John Sullivan, Tom Wolfe, Philip Nobile, Barbara Raskin, Judy Klemesrud, Carey Winfrey, Paul Wieck, Al Maysles, Anne Chamberlin, Joel Oppenheimer, Silvia Koner, Jerry Anderson, Mervin Block, Betty Teitgen, Pat Tidwell, Joe Goulden, Jane O'Reilly, Don Uffinger, Terry Gwyn, David Michel, Steve Blaschke, Muffie Childs, Patricia Bosworth, K. T. McLay, Bob Clark, Priscilla Crane Baker and Frank Waldrop.

Liz Smith, whose column is syndicated in the *New York Daily News*, was especially helpful on the subject of Mrs Onassis, and the confidential interviews and notes she collected over the years, many of which have never been published before, were given generously and without reservation.

I am also grateful to newspaper librarians like William Hifner of the *Washington Post*, Dick Maschi of *Scripps-Howard* and Sunday Orme of the *New York Times* for their unfailing good humour and patience. Special friends like Tom and Heather Foley lightened the burdens of research and writing, and typing under deadline Cosette Saslaw and Irene King produced the manuscript in record time.

My deepest thanks to my husband Michael Edgley, my lawyer, Ian Volner, and my publisher, Lyle Stuart.

Kitty Kelley
Washington, D.C.
21 June 1978

TO MY HUSBAND AND MY PARENTS

'What makes journalism so fascinating and biography
so interesting is the struggle to answer that single
question: "What's he like?"'

John Fitzgerald Kennedy

'Throughout the world people love fairy tales and
especially those related to the lives of the rich. You
must understand this and accept it.'

Aristotle Socrates Onassis

Chapter One

High society began buzzing the day the wedding invitations arrived from Mr and Mrs Hugh Dudley Auchincloss announcing the impending marriage of Jacqueline Lee Bouvier to John Fitzgerald Kennedy. At that time the Auchincloss name had been part of American society for seven generations. Through marriage it touched such venerable families as the Rockefellers, Sloans, Winthrops, Saltonstalls, du Ponts, Tiffanys and Vanderbilts. By contrast, the Irish Catholic Kennedys were barely out of steerage.

Despite their fortune of $400 million, the boisterous Kennedys had never been accepted into the quiet drawing rooms of America's social elite. But now the doors of Anglo-Saxon, Protestant aristocracy would finally open and Newport's grande dames would take places alongside red-faced Boston pols.

Even in 1953 this marriage, which would unite the debutante daughter of high society and the junior Senator from Massachusetts, was being heralded as the wedding of the year, far surpassing the Astor–French nuptials of 1934 in public interest. This was going to be a marriage which would one day stretch into history, and no one wanted to miss it.

Ordinarily, the bride's family dictates the size and style of the wedding. Not this time. Not when the future father-in-law is the former Ambassador to the Court of St James, a man whose burning ambitions rested in the political future of his eldest living son. A big believer in marrying up, Joe Kennedy was delighted with this marriage which would finally bring his family the social acceptance it had always been denied. He was determined that the ancient rites uniting the grandson of a saloon-keeper and the daughter of American aristocracy would be played out with all the panoply of a coronation.

Too much was at stake to let the grand plan of such an occasion be left to the Social Register dictates of the bride's mother. After all, Janet Auchincloss was merely marrying off her daughter, whereas Joe Kennedy was introducing the country to its next First Lady. She was concerned with the propriety of the occasion; he was determined to produce an extravaganza worthy of the *New York Times*'s front page. So, leaving the details of rose-petal confetti and flowing champagne to the bride's mother, the future father-in-law started organizing everything from police lines to press coverage.

'Old Joe completely took over the whole show,' recalls a family member, 'and Janet was fit to be tied. Especially when he insisted on bringing in every Irish Catholic priest who'd ever been ordained to perform the nuptial Mass. Although both Jack and Jackie were born Catholic, they never attended parochial schools, and weren't exactly fervent about practising their religion. Since almost all their bridesmaids and ushers were Protestant, it was unseemly to Janet, an Episcopalian married to a Presbyterian, to make the wedding such a Roman ritual. But, by God, Joe got his way, starting with the old family friend Archbishop Cushing as celebrant and Monsignor Francis Rossiter of the Boston Archdiocese as an assistant.'

Actually, there were four priests assisting the Archbishop on the altar, plus a sanctuary filled with white-robed celebrants, including Bishop Weldon of Springfield, Massachusetts, the Very Reverend John Cavanagh, formerly president of the University of Notre Dame, and the Rev James Keller of New York, head of the Christophers. All were friends of Mr Kennedy, who insisted that each be given a starring role in his son's wedding.

The Ambassador selected Luigi Vena, a tenor soloist from Boston, to sing the 'Ave Maria', and asked a Mrs Maloney of Boston to play the organ. He arranged for Pope Pius XII to bless the bride and groom, and commissioned a bakery in Quincy, Massachusetts to bake a four-foot-high wedding cake.

Joe Kennedy recognized the political value of this

marriage, and his plans for his son to be the first Irish Catholic President of the United States could be seen in the guest list – prominent political columnists, society reporters, movie stars, members of Congress, and the Speaker of the House of Representatives.

While the groom was cavorting through Europe on one last fling, the bride was buying her trousseau through New York wholesale outlets and Janet Auchincloss was battling Joe Kennedy until every detail of the day was planned to precision.

Janet was the daughter of a self-made man whose family acquired its status in New York society late in life. Having achieved her lofty position through marriage, she understood the value of marrying well. But she had reservations about the Kennedys and would have preferred that Jackie marry into a more aristocratic family, as her sister Lee had done when she married Michael Canfield. Faced with a choice between impeccable social standing and great wealth, Janet made the decision of a pragmatic woman.

And she had been faced with just such a choice the year before when Jackie, at the age of twenty-three, became engaged to John G. W. Husted, Jr, the attractive young son of a New York banker. Although he came from the same social background, knew all the right people, lived in Westchester County, was graduated from Yale, and had sisters who went to school with Jackie at Miss Porter's in Farmington, he was not, in Janet's mind, financially suitable for her daughter.

'Her mother deemed me no great catch,' says Husted, still slim and attractive at fifty-one as a New York stockbroker with Dominick and Dominick. 'At the time Jackie and I were seeing each other and ready to be engaged, Janet asked me how much money I was making and I told her $17,000. My prospects for making more money were reasonable but not assured, and I had no great family fortune, at least not the kind she wanted for Jackie. Consequently, she was vehemently opposed to the match and did not approve of me at all. Janet Auchincloss is a most practical woman, and very ambitious for Jackie. Our engagement only lasted about four months.'

Sitting in his suite of offices forty-three stories above Wall Street, John Husted talks about the days when Jacqueline Bouvier was just a working girl in Washington who, despite her Auchincloss background, had very little money. 'During those days Jackie was driving a tiny used car and nothing about her life style indicated any money whatsoever. There was nothing elegant or opulent about her. I remember once we saw a painting, some fanciful thing of white horses, very impressionistic, and Jackie was quite taken with it but couldn't afford to buy it. She was a delight, though, very free minded, quite smart, and had a very good sense of humour.'

Recalling how they first fell in love, Husted reminisces about their whirlwind courtship. 'On our first date we went to the Dancing Class in Washington, which was a very proper, social thing to do in those days. I was immediately attracted to her, and we began seeing each other every weekend.

'I'd usually go to Washington and help her with her Inquiring Camera Girl business, which was an insipid little job but kind of fun. She was working then for the old *Washington Times-Herald* and had to go around asking people dumb questions and taking their picture. We had a lot of laughs doing that. We'd go to supermarkets and ask people stupid questions like, "Do you believe in husbands wearing wedding rings?" Then Jackie would write down their answers, take their pictures, and that would be her column.

'One weekend she came to Bedford to stay with my family and my mother offered her a baby picture of me or something foolish like that and Jackie declined, saying, "If I want a picture of John, I'll take my own." My mother was quite taken aback by her attitude, and they never got along very well after that. In fact, my mother hated her.

'But I loved Jackie and wanted very much to marry her. So I said, "If you meet me at the Polo Bar in the Westbury Hotel at a certain time on a certain day, that will be a signal that you agree." Well, the day came and it was snowing terribly. I went to the Westbury and waited and waited and waited, wondering if she'd ever show up. Finally, she walked in and we had dinner and agreed to be engaged.

'The engagement was announced in the papers and the Auchinclosses gave us a big party at Merrywood, their home in Virginia, where I presented Jackie with a sapphire ring with two diamonds that had been my mother's. Then I went back to New York and we began writing to each other and travelling back and forth.'

Husted hastens to add that their romance was 'very, very chaste'.

'Jackie took me to meet her father, and when I asked Black Jack for her hand in marriage he said, "Sure – but it will never work." He never explained and I certainly didn't push it. That was the first and last time I ever met him.

'Then Jackie and I started writing and at first her letters were very romantic, as were mine, but then I could tell that things were cooling. She'd write and say that her mother kept complaining that we were rushing into things, that we'd only known each other a short time, that maybe we ought to wait.

'I remember one letter Jackie wrote me, and I've still got them all, in which she said, "Don't pay any attention to any of the drivel you hear about me and Jack Kennedy. It doesn't mean a thing." Then I got another letter saying maybe our relationship would work better if we both waited six months before getting married. By this time, arrangements had already been made and Jackie had gone to talk to a priest about the wedding. Finally, I went down to Washington one weekend and she put the engagement ring in my pocket at the airport. There were no tears on her part, although I felt miserable.'

Jackie was relieved to have got out of the engagement so easily. Her mother was ecstatic and immediately began returning all the engagement presents while making sure an official retraction appeared in all the newspapers. This was something one did in those days to alert society that both parties were disengaged 'by mutual consent' and once again eligible.

Jackie's step-father, however, had genuinely liked young Husted and was all for the marriage.

'Hugh was a nice guy, a good friend of my father's, and I know he liked me and approved of the marriage. But Janet didn't, and that was that,' says Husted. 'After it was all over, he wrote me saying how sorry he was that it didn't work out. In that letter he quoted from Tennyson, saying, " 'Tis better to have loved and lost than never to have loved at all." Then he added, "P.S. And I ought to know." And he did know quite well because he'd been married at least two times himself before he married Jackie's mother.'

By this time Jackie was falling in love with the young congressman from Massachusetts, who had already confided to her that he intended to become President. Before that, of course, he had to beat Henry Cabot Lodge and be elected Senator. That took most of his time and energy during 1952. Between campaign stops throughout the state, however, he flew to Washington to take Jackie to the movies and to dinner.

Jackie found the pull of money and excitement of power that Kennedy generated more enticing than the quiet social status of John Husted and the conventional respectability of the Auchinclosses.

'Jackie got bored just interviewing people in supermarkets,' recalls John Husted. 'She wanted to meet bigger names and started after congressmen and senators and people like that.'

The free-wheeling life style of a multi-millionaire politician was a natural attraction for a young woman whose life had been governed by financial restraints although she was raised in luxury. While working, her spending money was limited to $56.27 a week she earned from her job, $50 a month allowance from her father, and occasional largesse from her mother.

Jackie's maternal grandfather, James Lee, hated Jack Bouvier so much that he wanted to ruin him after the divorce from his daughter and to deprive Bouvier's children of any claim to his fortune. So he forced Jackie and her sister Lee to sign documents swearing they would never lay claim against his money. Being disinherited from their grandfather's estate taught both Bouvier children early: if they were ever going to be financially secure, they would have to marry well.

'Essentially Jackie was motivated by money,' says Nancy Dickerson, the television commentator who later bought Merrywood. 'Though she grew up in the midst of luxury, extravagant amounts were not spent on her, and early on she had vowed to marry someone "richer than Uncle Hughdie", her step-father.'

Gore Vidal, who lived at Merrywood when his mother was married to Hugh Auchincloss, agrees. 'Jackie and Lee and I had no money, contrary to what people think. Mr Auchincloss was very rich and our step-brothers and sisters were rather well looked after. But we were not, and we had to survive out there in the world. That's why I had to work and Jackie and Lee had to marry well. But Merrywood was so remote from the Depression that the girls never knew what real life was like.'

Recognizing that with Jack Kennedy she'd have it all, Jackie confided to a newspaper friend that 'What I want more than anything else in the world is to be married to him.' To that end she devoted her time and attention, tolerating what she would later call 'a spasmodic courtship' and ignoring the other women who always would be a part of his life.

A politician whose father was a social outcast in Boston was not exactly an ambitious mother's dream husband for her daughter but, considering the bankroll behind the young man, Janet Auchincloss enthusiastically announced the engagement on 25 June 1953, a week after the *Saturday Evening Post* ran an article entitled 'Jack Kennedy – The Senate's Gay Young Bachelor'.

At the next opportunity the future mother-in-law took the groom aside and said, 'Please, Jack. Let's have a nice wedding. No press, no pictures, just a discreet notice in the Newport papers.'

Kennedy laughed at Mrs Auchincloss. 'Look,' he said, 'your daughter is marrying a public figure, a United States

Senator, a man who may one day be President. There are going to be photographers whether we like it or not. So the idea is to show Jackie off to her best advantage.'

Blessed with good looks, Kennedy was usually nonchalant about his personal appearance, frequently showing up in rumpled suits, frayed shirts, and unmatched socks. But for this wedding he allowed himself a certain amount of vanity. He ordered his formal attire from the Rockefeller tailor at H. Harris & Co. and paid his barber to fly up from the Sherry-Netherland Hotel in New York to do his hair.

Meanwhile, the guest list kept getting longer and longer. Kennedy invited the entire United States Senate, and his father included business contacts from his days in Hollywood. Watching the list grow from a few hundred to a cast of thousands, Mrs Auchincloss became upset and insisted that Jackie call the Kennedy office in New York and speak to Kay Donovan, who was handling the invitations for the Ambassador.

Miss Donovan immediately called Washington and talked to Evelyn Lincoln, Kennedy's personal secretary in the Senate. 'Jackie thinks the list is getting too long,' she said. 'Can we take some names off?'

The message was relayed to Kennedy, who, according to Mrs Lincoln, merely ignored it 'and went right on adding more names'.

Then the arch-Republican mother began ramming heads with her future Democratic in-laws over details of the occasion. She fretted that the senior Kennedy might slip his longtime friend, Gloria Swanson, onto the guest list, causing more gossip than she could tolerate for a wedding which she wanted to be perfect, proper, and unquestionably upper class. Even Jackie's aunt, Michelle Bouvier Putnam, was incensed by the hoopla. 'The whole Kennedy clan is unperturbed by publicity,' she said. 'We feel differently about it. Their clan is totally united; ours is not.'

By the morning of 12 September, the sunken gardens and rose beds surrounding Hammersmith Farm, the rolling country estate of Hugh Auchincloss, had been spaded and pruned to perfection for the reception. As the blue gravel driveway curving between hay fields and orchards was raked for the arrival of 1,200 reception guests, a battalion of caterers set up a huge canopy for Meyer Davis and his society orchestra. To complete this pastoral setting, Janet Auchincloss had parasol-topped tables placed on the sloping lawns, which were surrounded by meadows with romping ponies and a decorative herd of grazing Black Angus cattle.

Inside the Victorian mansion overlooking Narragansett Bay, soft-slippered servants and maids in black taffeta uniforms pattered through the rooms arranging flowers and the display of hundreds of wedding presents, all of which had been catalogued and numbered by Joe Kennedy's office in New York. The day before, the family's seamstress finished sewing fifty yards of flounces on the bride's ivory tissue silk taffeta gown. Upstairs, cradled in a box, was the heirloom veil of rosepoint lace worn by generations of Lee brides.

A reservation at the Munchener King Hotel was being held for Senator Joseph McCarthy, the close Kennedy friend and Communist-chasing demagogue from Wisconsin, who called to say he would attend 'if official Senate investigation duties permit'.

The senior Kennedys were staying at the Newport mansion of Robert Young, who frequently entertained the Duke and Duchess of Windsor and would now host Westbrook Pegler, Morton Downey, Bernard Gimbel, Marion Davies and their wedding guests.

Jackie's little silver picture frames with her initials and the date of the wedding were wrapped and ready to give to her twelve bridesmaids, along with the fifteen black silk umbrellas with silver monogrammed handles the groom was giving to his ushers.

Meanwhile, the valets at the Viking Hotel were pressing knife-edged creases into the striped trousers of John Vernou Bouvier III, the bride's father, who, despite his hatred for the Auchinclosses, had come to Newport to give his daughter away.

Although his marriage to Janet Lee had ended in bitter divorce years before, he continued to dote on his two

children with fatherly pride while referring to their pros-
perous step-father as a 'dull and graceless oaf'. Both men
were stockbrokers, about the only thing they had in common
apart from Janet. Upon her remarriage in 1942, Jack
Bouvier started a saying on the floor of the New York Stock
Exchange which would soon become a Wall Street joke:
'Take a loss with Auchincloss.'

That saying would seem prophetic years later when the
Washington brokerage of Hugh Auchincloss fell on hard
times and his widow was forced to sell his beloved Hammersmith Farm for $150,000 below asking price. But, at the
time, Jack Bouvier suffered the greater loss because, with
Janet's remarriage, he lost his daughters to a man with two
huge estates and a ready-made family.

Never remarrying himself, he continued to see his
children as often as possible, supporting them, paying for
their education, and giving them monthly allowances, charge
accounts and horses to ride, all the while courting them more
as a suitor than a father to keep their allegiance and loyalty.

Known as Black Jack because of his dark swarthy looks,
he was dashing and Jackie adored him. 'Jack told me she
had a big father crush,' says George Smathers, the Florida
Senator who ushered in Kennedy's wedding. 'He pointed
out her dad to me at the rehearsal dinner, saying, "There's
Black Jack with the blue balls." Bouvier had bluish-black
skin from some disease he had, but his features were quite
handsome. He was very striking, and Jackie was just crazy
about him.'

Jack Bouvier's virility attracted men as well as women.
He was rumoured to be bisexual, and to have once enjoyed
an intimate relationship with Cole Porter, who had graduated with him from Yale in 1914. 'I'm just mad about Jack,'
Cole told his close friends at the height of his relationship
with Bouvier. The dalliance between the two men soon
dimmed, but Cole Porter and Black Jack remained on
amicable terms the rest of their lives.

Because he was flamboyant and adventuresome, with
great style and extravagant whims, Jackie and Lee adored
their father. They never forgave their mother for the divorce,

which was an emotional wrench for both of them. Jackie was only thirteen at the time, and moving to Merrywood with her step-father and his three children meant leaving New York and the frivolity that only her father could provide.

'I was the ogre,' says Mrs Auchincloss, 'the one who had to teach them manners, tell them to sit up straight and brush their teeth. He just indulged them.'

Feeling stifled by her new environment, Jackie lived for her visits with her father and the colourful family reunions with the Bouviers in East Hampton, where she was born.

'Jack Kennedy was the closest Jackie could ever come to duplicating her dad,' says her cousin. Although Black Jack was a conservative Republican and Kennedy a Democrat, the two men got on famously and had a great deal in common, beginning with their fickle, self-indulgent attitude towards women. Neither identified with the stolid virtue of fidelity. Neither could make the transition from freewheeling bachelor-about-town to monogamous husband. Nor was either hypocritical enough to try.

Both were witty and openly intolerant of dullards. They shared a certain sophistication and worldliness born of extensive experience with women. Both enjoyed sports, suffered from bad backs, and relished living well. Of course, by the time they met, Jack Bouvier at fifty-three was on the downslide of his life; he had squandered most of his money and was waging a losing battle against alcoholism. Jack Kennedy, at thirty-six, was in his prime, had just been elected to the US Senate, and was heading for the Presidency.

Jackie recalls their first meeting: 'They were very much alike. We three had dinner and they talked about politics, sports and girls – what all red-blooded men like to talk about.'

Having to make this trip into Auchincloss territory was difficult for a man of Black Jack's vanity, but he arrived like a visiting maharajah, sporting a magnificent tan and an elegant wardrobe with a cutaway made to order, a pearl stickpin, and a new pair of grey suede gloves. He was going to walk down that aisle in glory, making Jackie proud of him and Jack Kennedy, too, plus all the other Bouviers and Kennedys gathered for this grandiose occasion.

This was the part of the day that Janet Auchincloss secretly dreaded. Having to tolerate the presence of her former husband was difficult at best. Having to watch him grandstand through the wedding in his inimitable style – hearing all those Newport socialities, whom she had so carefully cultivated, whisper 'That's her first husband, the one who played around so much and finally walked out on her' – was more than she could bear.

She had suffered through Lee's wedding to Michael Canfield a few months before when Jack showed up to do the honours as the father of the bride. She had hated every minute of it and was determined not to go through it again, especially in the public glare the Kennedys attracted. In an icy telephone call, she told Jack Bouvier not to come, saying that his presence would ruin the day and that if he really loved Jackie he would stay away. Besides, Janet felt it wasn't fair to Hughdie, who had rescued her from a forlorn life as a divorcee, to be shunted to the side like hired help on this important occasion when he had actually given Jackie and Lee more than they ever would have received had she remained married to their father.

And it galled her to think of the invidious comparisons which would be made between the debonair, swashbuckling Bouvier and the doughty, balding Auchincloss, who was racked with emphysema. Still, when Jackie insisted that her father be there to give her away, all her mother could do was grin and go along, trying to be as gracious as possible. Janet Auchincloss was nothing if not a lady.

To everyone's relief, the wedding day dawned clear and bright with a crisp breeze blowing off the water. Even Joe Kennedy could not have arranged more magnificent weather. As the early morning sun streamed through the old stained glass windows of St Mary's Church, throngs of people gathered outside where the socially prominent friends of the Auchinclosses and Bouviers would finally meet the entourage of senators, congressmen, mayors, and Massachusetts ward-heelers who had arrived en masse to pay homage to the Kennedys.

Yes, it was going to be a glorious wedding. Soon a beautiful bride, preceded by a bevy of bridesmaids rustling in pink taffeta, would float down the aisle of an historic church to meet her handsome groom.

But an hour before the church bells tolled, the elegant façade began to crack. As Rose Kennedy slipped into her couture blue lace dress and the Ambassador cinched his cummerbund, the phone rang a few miles away at Hammersmith Farm. While Jack Kennedy played touch football with his brothers and got pushed into a rosebush, the animosity which had festered for years between Janet Auchincloss and Jack Bouvier exploded, scalding their daughter with humiliation and shame.

The first call was from a Bouvier cousin, reporting that the bride's adored father was dead-dog drunk in his hotel room, slobbering all over his frock coat. A few minutes later the phone rang again. This time it was Black Jack himself, threatening to storm the church door, drunk as he was, to walk his daughter down the aisle.

'You can imagine the bedlam that broke loose then,' recalls John Davis. 'Janet was ready to die and Jac-Leen was absolutely heartsick.'

Turning on her daughter in fury, Janet screamed: 'I knew your father would do something like this to ruin the day. I just knew it. Why you insisted he be here to do this to us, I'll never know.'

Jackie fled to her room, sobbing that she wouldn't walk down the aisle without her father. Janet came in to plead with her, but Jackie insisted that the wedding be delayed so her father could make it. But in the event he was too drunk to get to the church.

When Jackie finally appeared at St Mary's, carrying her bouquet of pink and white spray orchids, she was rushed by a crowd of well-wishers who had been standing for hours outside the gothic church waiting for her arrival. She looked so lovely that few people beyond her closest friends and relatives paid much attention to the fact that she was on the arm of her step-father. Joe Kennedy took it upon himself to tell the *New York Times* that her father had come down with the flu at the last minute and couldn't give her away.

19

The crowds outside pressed forward again as the bride and groom left the church, stopping briefly to pose for photographers, Senator Kennedy with a great grin on his face and Mrs Kennedy looking a bit startled.

Surrounded by twelve bridesmaids and fifteen ushers, the glamorous young couple stood in the receiving line in the long fireplaced living room of Hammersmith Farm for two and a half hours while the dowagers of Newport danced and the Boston pols watched.

Finally Jackie threw her bridal bouquet and went upstairs to dress for the flight to her Acapulco honeymoon. She appeared minutes later in a grey going-away outfit, still wearing the diamond pin she had received from her father-in-law and the diamond bracelet that was a wedding present from her husband – her first real pieces of jewellery.

As Jack Kennedy kissed his mother goodbye and escorted his bride outside, Jack Bouvier was rolled into an ambulance to be driven back to New York. His daughter, the sun and moon and stars to him, left to enter her orbit in a world which would one day make her the most celebrated woman of the twentieth century.

Chapter Two

'I really don't want to go into my relationship with John F.,' says the pretty silver-haired woman as she sips her wine. 'After all, he's dead now and what I have to say will serve no good purpose, but I can tell you – and I'm very proud of this fact – that I bullied him unmercifully into marrying Jackie. You see, he was having an affair with her the same time he was having an affair with me.'

With that little bon mot, Noel Noel curls her long, thin legs up on the chair like a kitten. Even at fifty-four, she still retains some of the prettiness that first attracted Kennedy to her years ago. The bedroom walls of her apartment are covered with photographs of herself as a young woman looking like a stunning version of Vivien Leigh in *Gone With the Wind*. Thick dark hair falls down her shoulders, displaying a perfectly chiselled face of exquisite features with wide eyes, a full sensual mouth, and high cheekbones. She was, unquestionably, a beauty.

'I aged terribly when I hit forty,' she says, almost apologetically. 'That was when Philip died, and he was the love of my life for fourteen years. My hair turned in a period of three days.' She takes another sip of wine and lights a cigarette.

Noel, who lives in Washington and works nights in a law firm, explains that Philip Graham, then publisher of the *Washington Post*, was the number one love of her life and John F. Kennedy was her number one playmate.

'Philip killed himself in August 1963 and John F. was shot three months later, and I couldn't come back to this town for many years because they were both gone. Washington was filled with too many ghosts for me. Now, well ...' She shrugs.

Enough time has passed so that the memories are not quite so painful. A huge picture of Philip Graham still hangs on her bedroom wall, and in the kitchen there is a small snapshot of John F. Kennedy on a bulletin board next to a reminder to feed her cat Sweet Vittles and phone numbers of her hairdresser and the local liquor store.

'He was such a delight,' she says, recalling her affair with Kennedy. 'I got on so well with him. Not because he was so great in bed, although he wasn't bad, but because he had such a great sense of fun. He loved sex but he was not an affectionate man and didn't enjoy hugging and kissing at all, but oh, such fun.

'I remember one day after we made love and he went to sleep. He had taken off his back brace, and I just happened to have some pink lace lying around, so while he was sleeping I grabbed his girdle and sewed lace all over it. You should have seen his face when he woke up and went to put it on. He didn't laugh out loud but his eyes danced. He put that back brace on, completely ignoring the fact that it looked like some harlot's corselet, and never said a word. He had such good humour.

'Once, during the days he was sleeping with Jackie and me at the same time, I gave him a red moustache for Christmas so he could disguise his comings and goings and not be recognized. What else do you give a man who has everything money can buy?'

With a little more wine Noel Noel explains how she 'bullied' Jack Kennedy into marrying Jackie. 'We were in Europe together, and after we made love in Italy I told him I was going to send him home to propose to the girl he should marry. I told him Jackie was young and pretty and social and, by a wonderful coincidence, Catholic, which would be ideal for him. He had to marry someone like that if he was going to be President, and we both knew he was going to be President one day.'

At that time, in 1952, Jackie, living with her mother and step-father, began pursuing Jack Kennedy in the most ingenious ways she could devise, always being available for his last-minute calls for movies and dinner. She once spent hours translating and summarizing a dozen French books about Indo-China for him, labouring late at night to finish the task in the cramped little rafter room she shared with her sister at Merrywood. 'He has got to ask me to marry him after all I have done for him,' she told a friend. She bought books for him all the time, brought lunches to his Senate office, and used her newspaper column to catch his attention with such whimsical questions as: 'What do you think of marriage?' 'What's your idea of the perfect mate?' 'Do you consider a wife a luxury or a necessity?' 'Can you give any reason why a contented bachelor should get married?'

And then there were the questions Kennedy was sure to appreciate, incorporating quotes from his favourite writers: 'Noel Coward once said, "Women are like gongs and should be struck regularly." Do you agree?' 'Winston Churchill once said, "For a happier marriage, each spouse should breakfast alone." Do you agree?' 'The Irish author, Sean O'Faolin, claims the Irish are deficient in the art of love. Do you agree?'

Years later there would be many women who could answer that question about Kennedy because, like the fanciful Noel Noel, they knew him intimately before and after he met Jacqueline Lee Bouvier. Coping with the fact of these women would become one of Jackie's hardest adjustments, because she was marrying a man much like her own father, who was unable to devote himself exclusively to one woman.

Sadly enough, in a way she was prepared for this. Never having been the favourite of her mother and being separated from her father, Jackie grew up lonely, feeling like an outsider in the snobbish Auchincloss family and always having to take a back seat to her younger sister, a sparkling child of rare beauty.

'Lee was always the pretty one,' sighed Jackie years later. 'I guess I was supposed to be the smart one.'

The disintegration of her parents' marriage was so devastating to her that shortly after the divorce her Bouvier relatives began to notice her tendency to withdraw into a private world of her own. She became distant and aloof, a child-like camouflage for the humiliation and shame she felt.

Throughout it all, though, she adored her father, the most

enchanting figure in her young life. Despite the hateful comments of her mother, who condemned Jack Bouvier's extravagant life style, ranted about his 'cheap affairs' with other women, and ridiculed his good looks and elegant manners, Jackie continued to love those very things about her father. The picture of him she painted for friends was of a dashing buccaneer absolutely irresistible to women. One photograph in the family album thoroughly delighted her, and she took great glee in displaying it to her friends. It shows her parents standing with a gorgeous woman named Virginia Kernochan. Janet, dressed in riding clothes, is perched on a fence while Black Jack, resplendent in a European-cut suit, complete with an elegant pocket hand-kerchief, stands next to the exquisite Miss Kernochan with his hand cupped over hers, holding it to her breast.

John Husted remembers the picture well. 'Jackie showed me that one of her dad holding hands with another woman in full view of her mother, and absolutely roared her head off with laughter. She loved it.'

Another friend recalls Jackie relating her father's affair with another woman on his honeymoon. 'Jackie told me that within forty-eight hours after Jack walked down the aisle to marry Janet, they were aboard ship on their honey-moon and he spotted a gorgeous creature, pursued and conquered her within minutes, and continued the affair for the duration of the cruise. Janet found out about it, was absolutely devastated, and years later told Jackie in an obvious effort to discredit her philandering father, but Jackie loved the story and told it to all her friends.'

Years later according to this same friend, when more than two hundred spicy letters written by her paternal grandfather to his mistress in the 1940s were discovered and put up for sale, Jackie merely smiled as if enchanted. The letters from the late John Vernou Bouvier, Jr, a retired New York attorney then in his seventies, were adorned with naughty limericks, original love poems, and amusing speculations on the nature of love, sex, marriage, and female attire. In the letters was mention of 'the fragrant Jacqueline', who at eighteen in Mr Bouvier's estimation was 'one of the most charming and beautiful young girls, quite aside from her alert intelligence, that I have ever encountered'.

Along with her grandfather, Jackie romanticized her father as a man who would eventually return from his philanderings to hearth and home, where he always was forgiven because he never neglected his children nor forgot to lavish them with love and affection.

For the rest of her life she would use him as a measure of every man she met, always being attracted to older men who showed her father's qualities and, like him, would make her feel like a little girl again.

She never completely outgrew her lonely childhood despite the luxuries of growing up on Park Avenue and summering in East Hampton. By the time she met Jack Kennedy, her insecurity was noticeable to friends who still remember her from those days.

'Jackie was very sweet but rather shy,' recalls the wife of a Senator friend of Kennedy's. 'She was so in love with Jack, although he barely paid any attention to her and was always making fun of her because she was so flat-chested and had to wear padded bras. It was quite obvious to us then that she wanted to marry more than he did, although he was thinking about it and asking his friends what they thought he should do. He was so darned ambivalent about it that we kidded him and said he should put the matter before the Senate for a vote.

'When he finally got around to proposing to her, Jackie was ecstatic, and I don't think it was just because she was so crazy about Jack. She would also be getting out from under her domineering mother, who criticized everything she did. I don't think her mother ever forgave Jackie her idolatry of her father. Once, when Jackie and Lee were teenagers, they secretly managed to get him out of a hospital where he was drying out, and Janet was furious because in her eyes things could never get bad enough for Black Jack Bouvier.

'Anyway, once Jack proposed, Jackie immediately quit her job and started concentrating on getting married. But the wedding pressure became too much for him and, soon after the engagement was announced, Jack took off for Europe with his Harvard roommate, Torby MacDonald, to charter a yacht and go sailing off the coast of France. We were all afraid he'd never come back.'

A Newport friend of Jackie's, who was also close to JFK, remembers being with Kennedy at a party the evening before the engagement announcement appeared in the papers. 'He went out to dinner with my wife and myself, got very drunk, and later took a woman home and spent the night with her. But before that we were together for about three hours and he never once mentioned the engagement announcement coming out the next day, which you've got to admit doesn't sound like a man in love and looking forward to getting married.'

Still, Jackie felt secure with Kennedy, who was twelve years her senior and possessed an immense amount of self-confidence at times bordering on arrogance. He was the most eligible bachelor in the country, rich, famous, handsome, and Jackie was ecstatic. 'I'm the luckiest girl in the world,' she said. She especially relished the fact that her mother was scared to death of him. As she told one friend, 'Mummy is terrified of Jack because she can't push him around at all.' For his part, Kennedy maintained a polite relationship with his formidable mother-in-law and, even after years of marriage, referred to her only as Mrs Auchincloss.

'By the time Jack met Jackie he was thirty-five and had just been elected to the Senate,' recalls Betty Spalding, a long-time friend of the Kennedys, 'and his chariness or fear of marriage was being superseded by the political need for a wife. That's why he married her. He was going to be President, and he certainly couldn't take an actress like his friend Angie Dickinson to the White House with him. Jackie fit the bill.' She also broke Jack Kennedy's lifelong pattern of being attracted only to beautiful models, voluptuous starlets, and Copa girls who had no formal college degrees, no intellectual inclinations whatsoever, and no social standing. Fully aware of his previous involvements, Jackie would say in a puzzled, touching way, 'But I'm so different from the kind of girls Jack usually finds attractive ...' From his father, Jack Kennedy had learned how to draw a shrewd line between women for mistresses and women for marriage. Jackie was the wifely type.

'Jackie was pretty enough, but she certainly didn't have the luscious beauty of some of Jack's other women, like Anga Arvad, Angela Greene and Flo Pritchett,' recalls one of JFK's Navy buddies. 'But she was very well educated and had impeccable social credentials. And don't forget, she was Catholic, too. Jack could never have married outside the Church and still become President.'

Such reminiscences from close friends indicate that Jack Kennedy's political ambitions motivated his marriage proposal to Jackie as much as anything. He was attracted to her, yes, but it was not the romantic involvement of a young man desperately in love that was propelling him down the aisle. There was a definite design in his selection of a wife who was schooled at Miss Chapin's, Miss Porter's and Vassar, who spoke French fluently, who was Catholic, and who came from a securely established family. It was a more refined decision than a butcher makes selecting a slab of beef, but it had the same deliberate overtones.

'I once asked him if he'd ever fallen desperately, hopelessly in love,' recalls James Burns, 'and he just shrugged and said, "I'm not the heavy lover type." '

Having grown up with a father who would blatantly flaunt his mistresses, bringing them home for dinner with his wife and children and travelling with them openly on family vacations, Jack Kennedy naturally grew up with a distorted view of marriage. In contrast to his philandering father, his mother played the role of the perfect wife, ferociously religious, and seemingly content with raising the children and supervising the corps of maids, cooks and butlers, much like a general dispatching troops.

'To Jack's way of thinking, women were there to serve men,' says Betty Spalding, 'and any wife of his would be there to do for him the same way Mama Rose did for Big Joe, with the right food, good clothes laundered and cleaned, meals on time, and the house running smoothly so he could attend to business and not worry about the domestic side of life when he came home.'

This was completely compatible with Jackie's way of thinking as she viewed her primary role of wife and mother.

Even as First Lady, her intention was to create a home, to distract and amuse her husband in the evenings when he was torn by the pressures and problems of his job. This was all she ever really wanted, all she ever knew.

Being the product of a broken home, her own vision of marriage was marred by the cold and passionless relationship between her parents, their six-month separation, their abysmal reconciliation, and finally their bitter divorce which shattered any emotional security she had ever known. While developing a strong fixation for her father, she watched her mother marry a man of wealth and position, who by high society standards was considered a good provider. Growing up in a subculture where women must marry well in order to survive and prosper, Jackie understandably gravitated to John F. Kennedy, who fitted into her scheme of the world as she knew it.

As one of her friends from Newport said, 'During those days our future was to marry well. That's all we'd ever really been trained to do and that's what we did, just like our mothers did before us. Jackie deviated only by taking a job after college – a very daring thing to do in those days – but in the end she used that job to meet interesting people and snare Jack, and once that was accomplished she married like the rest of us.'

This particular friend, who grew up with Jackie and made her debut at the same time, remembers Jackie lolling about the family cabana at Bailey's Beach in Newport, flying with Steve Spencer in his private plane, playing tennis with Bin Lewis, and swimming with John Stirling. 'But for all of that she was never really popular with boys in the way Lee was. Steve and Bin and John were all part of our Newport crowd and Jackie got along very well with all of them, but she wasn't really pursued. Maybe it was because she was so aloof and not vivacious like her younger sister. In those days we were all very superficial and didn't really know how to communicate. We spent all our time just having fun and waiting to get married.'

Jackie waited longer than most of her friends. Even in high school she wondered if she would ever find a husband.

'I just know no one will ever marry me,' she told a friend at Miss Porter's School, 'and I'll end up as a house mother at Farmington.' Later, not many men were interested in her. Aside from her step-brother, Yusha, who was very much in love with her, she had few dates.

One man, now living in Washington, remembers being forced to take her out by his mother, who was a good friend of Janet Auchincloss. He recalls: 'I was in the Navy then and stationed in Newport, and my mother kept pushing me to call her, saying she would be a nice girl for me to date. So I finally asked her out and we went to a few parties and dances. We must have gone out six or seven times, but it was a dreadful experience each time. She wasn't very pretty. In fact, she was what we used to refer to as a real wallflower. She was so introverted and shy that it was almost painful to be with her. Her parents liked me, though, and encouraged me to take her out. They even proposed me for a private membership in Bailey's Beach so I felt rather obligated then to date her, but Jackie was so insecure and complicated that it was never any fun.'

Always uncomfortable in Newport, Jackie found it difficult to make friends easily. The resentment she felt towards her mother was transferred to women in general, so that she had few girl friends as a youngster, and as an adult never established strong friendships with women other than her sister. During those years she preferred pets to people and was happiest when out riding alone.

Zsa Zsa Gabor recalled meeting her on a plane flying back from the coronation of Elizabeth II in 1953, when Jackie was a wandering photographer and dating Jack Kennedy: 'Twenty-four hours on the plane she kept asking me – it was no joke – "What do you do for your skin?" And I never bothered to ask her name. She wasn't the most glamorous nor the most beautiful woman. She had kinky hair and bad skin.

'When we arrived at the airport, Jackie said, "There's a young man who's going to propose to me." And I was taken off the plane before her, and Jack stood there. And Jack says, "My darling sweetheart, I was always in love with you." Jack used to take me out quite often ... and he was a sweetheart. He lifted me up in the air. Jackie came off the plane and saw Jack do that to me. After twenty-four hours of pestering me, asking about this cream and that lotion, she didn't say hello to me. So Jack Kennedy said to me, "I want you to meet Miss Bouvier." He didn't say "my future wife". And I said, "Oh, my God! We spoke twenty-four hours together on the plane. She's a lovely girl." '

Before Jack Kennedy came along, Jackie tried to enjoy the parties and dances her mother insisted she attend. 'They were okay,' she said later. 'But Newport – when I was about nineteen, I knew I didn't want the rest of my life to be there. I didn't want to marry any of the young men I grew up with – not because of them but because of their life. I didn't know what I wanted. I was still floundering.'

The vivacious Lee – three and a half years younger than her sister, tinier, prettier, more feminine and not so floundering – beat Jackie down the aisle by marrying Michael Temple Canfield in April 1953 when she was twenty. Like her sister, Lee attended Chapin School and later Miss Porter's in Farmington. Like Jackie, Lee was Debutante of the Year when she made her debut in 1950. But it was Lee who received full-page coverage in *Life* magazine plus a movie offer from a Hollywood talent scout. Instead of following Jackie to Vassar, Lee went to Sarah Lawrence for two years, where she dabbled in design and took parts in school plays.

After taking voice lessons in Italy for a few months ('My mother thought I had a beautiful voice'), she came home to marry Canfield, the socially prominent son of publisher Cass Canfield.

A Harvard graduate and Marine combat veteran of Iwo Jima, Canfield was working for his father's publishing house in New York. He later took a job at the American embassy in London as private secretary to Winthrop Aldrich, the US Ambassador to the Court of St James and he and Lee soon became part of international society.

Considered the outsiders in the Auchincloss family, Jackie and Lee clung to each other. But Jackie, always having to take care of her younger sister, resented Lee, especially when she stole the spotlight. In later years it would be Lee who would flounder around, trying first to establish herself as an actress, then, once demolished by the drama critics, giving up the stage to become a writer. After the dismal failure of her first book, *One Special Summer*, in which she recounts her schoolgirl adventures with Jackie in Europe, she gave up writing, too. She tried television but failed to excite any interest as a talk show hostess, then worked as an interior designer. Although she would eventually become a princess with a royal title and immense wealth, Lee always felt beaten in life by Jackie's success as First Lady.

The sisters' childhood rivalry for their father's affection made their adult relationship extremely complex and at times explosive. Both gravitated to the same type of man when they grew up. Jackie resented the attention that Kennedy paid to Lee, and she hated the fact that when she was out of town or unable to accompany her husband he would proudly take her younger sister on state trips abroad. It was Lee, not Jackie, who stood at the President's side in Germany when he made his famous 'Ich bin ein Berliner' speech. Again it was Lee, not Jackie, who accompanied Kennedy on his sentimental journey to Ireland.

'Lee is so dippy about Jack it's sickening,' Jackie once complained to a friend. But the grating resentment came because Kennedy was just as fond of Lee, and always looked forward to her visits and the gossipy little stories she would bring him about who was sleeping with whom in London and Paris. 'I used to store up anecdotes to amuse him,' said Lee. 'He was interested in everything – that kind of life-enhancing vitality was very much part of him. He would remember the littlest unfinished detail and ask about it next time.'

Although it was customary then for the oldest daughter to marry first, no one was at all surprised when Lee had the first wedding. 'She was a sexy little thing while Jackie was more of a tomboy and into horses,' says a woman who knew both sisters very well.

'Virginity, considered a middle-class virtue in the 1950s, was something we all wanted to get rid of then, and I'm sure Lee did that first, too,' she says, 'Jackie was just not as advanced as her sister in those areas, although she certainly tried hard enough. She used to say she liked before and after sex better than during, and we all laughed about the story, probably more apocryphal than authentic, of her deflowering, and Jackie, blunt as ever, exclaiming afterwards, "Oh! Is that all there is to it?" '

Hardly a bashful virgin, Jackie tried to be discreet about her affair with Jack Kennedy before her marriage. Once, on the night train from Newport to Washington after a weekend at Hammersmith Farm, JFK sat on a berth talking to a friend who was preparing for bed. As the friend tells the story, Jackie walked down the aisle, saw the two chatting, and headed off without so much as a smile or a nod of recognition.

'Kennedy laughed out loud, grabbed her by the hand and said, "Jackie, come back here and stop acting so silly. So-and-So knows all about us." I was Jack's age and married but having my own affairs at the time, which he knew all about. He obviously felt Jackie was being a little too prissy to try to pretend in front of me that they weren't sleeping together.'

New York autograph dealer Charles Hamilton recalls an exchange of letters he found between Black Jack Bouvier and his daughter when she was in college. 'Jackie tried to explain to her father why she had stayed out all night with a young man. Her excuse for the all-night escapade was specious. However, her father wrote back a beautiful letter saying that a woman could have wealth and beauty and brains, but without a reputation she was lost. It was a tender letter that did not censure her – only tried to tell her to take care of herself.'

Sexually experienced but emotionally immature, Jack and Jackie were unable at first to relate to each other in terms of husband and wife. Each self-centred, they did not know how to share themselves with each other, and, having only communicated on a superficial social level all their lives, neither was prepared to deal with the intimacies of living together.

'I think that was one of the things that was so difficult

for Jack when he finally married Jackie,' says Betty Spalding. 'Both of them were emotionally blocked. She had the same emotional blocks and panics that he had. And their relationship was extremely stormy in the beginning because their psychosexual emotional development had been retarded. Jack used to tell me how hard constancy was for him, and showing emotion. "I just can't do it," he'd say, and neither could Jackie. Nor could Jack really talk to her with the same ease and fluency, however superficial, he had with other women.

'In their strangulated way they loved each other, but neither was able to relate to the other, and there was never any affection between them at any time. He was always quite diffident towards her.'

The extremely self-conscious young woman who married John Fitzgerald Kennedy in 1953 was light years away from the woman she would eventually become. At that time she was vulnerable, tentative and shy, always worrying about her appearance, fretting over her clothes and what she should wear to make the right impression. Once, when she accompanied Jack to Hyannis Port for a weekend before they were married, she showed up for dinner terribly overdressed and he teased her, saying, 'Where the hell do you think you're going?' Jackie was humiliated by the incident, especially when his sisters, elbowing each other in the ribs, laughed at her.

'I first met Jackie at one of their engagement parties on the Cape when I was married to Chuck, and I liked her very much,' says Mrs Spalding. 'She was not at all the kind of girl Jack had been seeing before. She had a certain amount of polish. We got on very well together, and she told me that I was the only one of Jack's friends she could really talk to, confiding in me then how terrified she was of marrying into that Irish stronghold of Kennedys.

'The thing that worried her most was handling the family, and God, they were an overbearing bunch, always charging around, busting into the room constantly, interrupting you, dropping in unannounced, having their own private jokes, ganging up to make fun of someone and then holding the poor fool up to noisy ridicule in front of everyone else. The Kennedys were like the family in Tolstoy's *War and Peace*, but with none of the polish and intellect. All their energies were thrown into sports and politics. It was a culture shock for Jackie, who was absolutely stupefied about how to cope with such an Irish picnic.'

'Competition – that's what makes them go,' Joe Kennedy once described his family. 'They're all competitive, including the girls. In fact, Eunice has more drive than Jack or even Bobby. If she had balls, she'd probably be President herself.'

This raucous family of over-achievers, each trying to pummel the others athletically, was anathema to a woman who hated competing at team sports. In the beginning Jackie tried valiantly to play the Kennedys' roughhouse games, but after Teddy broke her ankle by falling on top of her in a game of touch football she retired to the sidelines.

'Just watching them tires me out,' she once said publicly. Privately, she was telling Lee what gorillas they all were, romping and stomping each other like a bunch of baboons suddenly let loose. After one family siege at Hyannis Port, Jackie returned to Washington black and blue with bruises, and told her sister: 'They'll kill me before I ever get to marry him. I swear they will.'

Jackie admits to more than a little apprehension about her first meeting with the entire family, including Rose, whom she always refused to defer to, considering her autocratic and self-centred and mimicking her as 'the grande dame mother'.

'I'd met Jack in Washington when he was in Congress, and he used to come to Bobby and Ethel's house, so I knew him with Bobby and Ethel well, and I knew Eunice, but I'd never seen the whole group together. Obviously, if you really liked the elder brother and were rather shy, you might have been a little nervous.'

And she was more than justified in being a little nervous, because behind her back the Kennedy sisters were beginning to question their brother's taste in women. While Jackie and Lee giggled to themselves about the Kennedy women, calling them 'the Rah Rah girls', the sisters disparaged Jackie, calling her 'The Debutante', and making fun of what they termed her 'babykins voice', which was whispery and soft.

They even mimicked her for pronouncing her name Jack-Leen. 'She says it rhymes with queen,' Ethel told her sisters-in-law. When Jackie told Ethel her secret ambition had once been to be a ballet dancer, Ethel yelped with laughter. 'With those clodhoppers of yours?' she screamed, pointing to Jackie's feet. 'You'd be better off going in for soccer, kid.'

Ethel would soon find her brash humour no match for Jackie's rapier wit. Confiding in her sister, Jackie described Ethel as 'the type who would put a slipcover on a Louis Quinze sofa and then spell it Luie Cans'.

Jackie's devotion to fox-hunting, French, and fine antiques automatically put her at odds with the Kennedy women, who, like Jack, Bobby and Teddy, cared only for the rough and tumble of politics and winning, winning, winning. 'They even compete with each other in conversation,' said Jackie, 'to see who can say the most and talk the loudest.'

For a woman who treasured privacy and needed solitude, the tightly-knit, boisterous Kennedys were wearisome en masse. Jackie refused to attend the nightly family dinners at Hyannis Port where they would all gather to argue politics. 'Once a week is great,' she said, 'but not every night.' Though she found their ravenous appetite for power perplexing, it was the continual political discussions of the clan that completely baffled her. She had been raised in a family so Republican that all through her childhood she confused Franklin Delano Roosevelt with the devil. For as long as she could remember, her father blamed his Wall Street misfortunes on the Securities and Exchange Commission which Roosevelt established in 1934 to regulate the nation's stock market.

When Joseph P. Kennedy took over the SEC, he forced Jack Bouvier and other stock brokers to curtail their buying and selling, allowing them to purchase stocks only on the downswing. As a result, Black Jack suffered a $43,000 trading loss in one year and developed a teeth-grinding hatred of FDR's New Deal, the SEC, and, in particular, Joe Kennedy. So strong were his feelings that, according to John Davis, 'Jack's tan would momentarily fade at the mere mention of Kennedy's name.'

Yet it was the old man, a paterfamilias in the grand tradition, running his family like a tribal chieftain, who alone would truly appreciate Jackie's worth. Accustomed to his aggressive daughters and the equally bombastic Ethel, he was confused at first by Jackie's quiet ways. But she slowly won him over by standing up to him and displaying the kind of character the elder Kennedy could respect.

Once, during a rare lull in a family conversation, Jack turned to Jackie and asked, 'A penny for your thoughts?' Jackie smiled sweetly and said softly, but loud enough for everyone else to hear, 'But they're my thoughts, Jack, and they would not be my thoughts any more if I told you, now would they?' The lull in the conversation became a deafening silence as the rest of the family looked at each other, wondering about this peculiar creature who insisted on being so private and evasive. Finally, old Joe started laughing uproariously.

'By God, Jack, she's got zipperoo,' he said. 'Jackie's a girl with a mind of her own – a girl just like us.'

'You betcha she is,' said Jack, grateful to his father for salvaging the awkward situation.

In such little ways did Joe Kennedy pave the way for Jackie, giving her his imprimatur, which did not necessarily require the rest of the family to embrace her but merely to accept her as he did – despite her differences. Jackie identified with her father-in-law, saying she was more like him than anyone else in the family, including his own children. She enjoyed teasing him, or 'giving me the needle', as Joe Kennedy described it, and once painted a water colour for him, showing a crowd of young Kennedys on the beach looking at the sun. The caption read: 'You can't take it with you. Dad's got it all.'

This proud, domineering man who was determined to put

his son in the White House naturally took an active interest in the women Jack was dating. During the days he was involved with Inga Arvad, Joe Kennedy did all he could to break up the relationship. Inga was a Scandinavian beauty who had known Adolf Hitler in Berlin. She even accompanied Der Führer to the 1936 Olympics. When she came to the United States and began working for the *Washington Times-Herald*, she was immediately placed under investigation by the FBI on suspicion of espionage.

Word about the FBI files being kept on Inga leaked to Joe through his political network, and he furiously tried to persuade his son to stop seeing her, knowing that such a dicey relationship would ruin Jack's political career.

Inga Binga, as Jack fondly called his lover, was not only suspected of being a Nazi spy but was also at the time a married woman. While Joe Kennedy could afford to buy an annulment, he refused to do so, knowing that his money could never pay for the ugly scandal which would inevitably result.

Years later, the private files of J. Edgar Hoover would indicate yet another woman John Kennedy was involved with who was allegedly paid $500,000 to drop a lawsuit claiming that Kennedy jilted her in 1951.

The late FBI director's files contain a 1963 memo sent to Attorney-General Robert Kennedy, noting an article in the Italian weekly magazine, *Le Ore*, which stated that a woman identified as Alicia Purdom, then the wife of actor Edmund Purdom, said she had been engaged to marry John F. Kennedy. The magazine said the engagement was broken off in 1951 after strenuous objection from Joseph P. Kennedy concerning the woman's Polish and Jewish ancestry.

According to the FBI files, the alleged lawsuit filed prior to Kennedy's Presidency was sealed by a judge in New York when Robert Kennedy managed to settle the matter out of court by paying the woman half a million dollars.

The FBI memo to the Attorney-General reads in part: 'In addition to the bill of particulars, letters were exhibited which mentioned John F. Kennedy as an associate of this woman ... When this suit was filed in New York just prior to

37

the President's assuming office, you [Robert Kennedy] went to New York and arranged for a settlement of the case out of court for $500,000. All papers relating to this matter, including the complaint, allegedly were immediately sealed by the court.'

Unquestionably, Joe Kennedy had the power to quash the matter and quietly arrange a pay-off in a way that could never be traced back to him or politically damage his son. One man close to the Kennedys says, 'Old Joe was too smart to cave in to blackmail but, when faced with a lawsuit that might explode and ruin Jack's presidency, he would definitely pony up with whatever it took to keep the matter quiet, and $500,000 to him was nothing but a good investment to protect his son. I'm sure the FBI files are accurate, but what the hell difference does it make now? Joe put Jack into the White House, and that's all that ever mattered to him.'

During 1962 there were unsubstantiated reports circulating that President Kennedy had been married and divorced before his marriage to Jackie in 1953. The reports stemmed from an obscure genealogy published in 1957 as *The Blauvelt Family Genealogy*, by Louis L. Blauvelt, who died at eighty-two, a year before publication of his book.

The questionable entry in the book reads: 'Durie (Kerr) Malcolm. We have no birth date. She was born Kerr, but took the name of her step-father. She first married Firmin Desloge, IV. They were divorced. Durie then married F. John Bersbach. They were divorced, and she married, third, John F. Kennedy, son of Joseph P. Kennedy, one-time Ambassador to England. There were no children of the second or third marriages.'

Reporters trying to check out the story never found the records of any marriage licence being issued or any marriage certificate or divorce proceedings pertaining to the reported marriage of John Kennedy to Durie Malcolm. The only document found in the files of the compiler of the genealogy was an old clipping from a Miami gossip column reporting that Miss Malcolm and Mr Kennedy had been seen together in a restaurant soon after World War II.

Miss Malcolm later, in 1947, married Thomas Shevlin of

Palm Beach and Newport, ten years before publication of the genealogy. Shevlin was once married to Lorraine Cooper, wife of the then Senator from Kentucky, John Sherman Cooper, a close Kennedy friend.

Records show that this woman was unmarried, and thus technically in a position to marry Kennedy, only twice in her life – once between the summer of 1938 and January 1939, when he was a junior at Harvard, and once between January and July of 1947, during his first six months in Congress as a member of the House of Representatives.

Kennedy refused to issue a public denial which would have given added circulation to the story. When his close friend, Bed Bradlee, then working for *Newsweek* magazine, asked him about the marriage, Kennedy was quite amused and replied, 'You have met her. You remember one day we played golf at Seminole and we went into the pro shop and there was this girl on the sofa and a guy standing next to her? Well, that was Durie Malcolm and that was Shevlin. She was a girl friend of my brother Joe and I took her out a couple of times, I guess. That's all.'

Bradlee says Kennedy then said, 'You haven't got it, Benjy. You're all looking to tag me with some girl and none of you can do it, because it just isn't there.'

Being his father's son, Jack Kennedy was naturally a womanizer. 'He comes by it honestly,' Joe Kennedy once joked. The father's concern was that Jack should not do anything to damage his political career. He relished his son's escapades with beautiful women at the Everglades Club in Palm Beach and teased him about 'the broads' he took to El Morocco in New York. On occasion, Joe even tried to seduce the same woman himself. But when it came to marriage he was adamant that his son make a calculated choice in picking a wife, one that, as he said, 'is not related to the groin'.

In Jackie, Joe saw the perfect wife for his son. She was a woman who had 'class', one of his favourite words, and she had enough of it automatically to elevate the family socially. Most importantly, she was Catholic, which was the number one requirement if he was going to put his son in the White

House. Marriage to a Protestant or a divorcee would be out of the question if Jack Kennedy was to break the barriers of bigotry which had existed since Al Smith tried and failed for the Presidential nomination in 1928. Being a French Catholic made Jackie, in Joe's mind, an aristocrat in comparison with Boston Irish Catholics.

Throughout their marriage Jack's father would be the one person Jackie would always turn to for protection and support. So close was their relationship that Jackie once said, 'Next to my husband and my own father, I love Joe Kennedy more than anyone else in the world.' Strong as he was, Joe was not able to shield her from all the internal strains clawing at her.

Chapter Three

'Jack told me once that Jackie teased him about doing to her on their honeymoon what her father had done to her mother, lightly taunting him not to let his "better part" get the best of him,' recalls a Navy chum. 'He loved that irreverent wit of hers and the way she could seem so ladylike and yet sound so ... uh, not whorish, but you know, rather playful and teasing in a sexual kind of way.'

Jackie didn't have to worry on her honeymoon because for the first few weeks in Acapulco she had her husband all to herself but, as she later said, recalling their idyllic days in a pink villa overlooking the Pacific Ocean, 'That honeymoon was so short. It all went so fast.'

From Mexico she wrote her father a letter forgiving him for failing to walk her down the aisle on her wedding day. Jack Bouvier was so moved by his daughter's note that he cried and showed it to his partner, who termed it one of the most touching, compassionate letters he had ever read, 'one that only a rare and noble spirit could have written'.

Before returning home, Kennedy took his bride to California to visit his old Navy friend Red Fay and his wife, Anita. Then he and Jackie drove with the Fays from the Monterey Peninsula to Palo Alto to visit another Navy chum, Tom Casey. Things were a bit strained because Jackie and Anita, thrown together to entertain themselves, did not get along as well as their husbands, and Jackie would have preferred spending those last few days alone with Jack in Acapulco. Kennedy, thoroughly enjoying himself, was oblivious to the friction, and on their last day decided to accompany Fay to a football game, leaving his new bride to be shown the Bay area by his shipmate's wife.

Upon returning to the East Coast Jack and Jackie headed for the Kennedy compound at Hyannis Port, where Jack decided they should stay until they could find a house in

41

Washington. He said he had so much to do in the Senate after a month's absence that he wouldn't have much time to spend with her, so she could stay with his family at the Cape where he would visit her on weekends.

'It will give you time to write all those thank-you notes you have to write,' he said.

During that time Jackie, who had won *Vogue* magazine's Prix de Paris contest in 1950 by writing an essay, began composing a poem for her husband inspired by 'John Brown's Body'. As a youngster she had authored a steady stream of little books in manuscript form as special gifts for her family, frequently taking a poem like 'The Midnight Ride of Paul Revere' and making up her own rhymes. This time she patterned her verses on a poem by Stephen Vincent Benet.

Jack Kennedy was so delighted by his wife's poem that he wanted to have it published, but Jackie refused, telling him that it was as private as a love letter and 'too personal' to ever be shown. However, Kennedy did show it to his family, and to a few close friends. Years later Rose Kennedy had it published with her own memoirs, admitting then that while there were doubts about Jackie 'among one or another of Jack's brothers or sisters or cousins at first', they were immediately resolved when they read 'that marvellous poem'.

During his younger years Kennedy filled a loose-leaf notebook with his favourite quotations and later, when he ran for office, he would give speeches quoting from memory Goethe, Swift, Bismarck, and even Queen Victoria. When they returned from their honeymoon, he read Jackie a poem he liked and she memorized it. Later she recited it for his pleasure. The poem was Alan Seeger's 'I have a Rendezvous with Death', and his favourite lines were:

> It may be he shall take my hand
> And lead me into his dark land
> And close my eyes and quench my breath ...

> But I've a rendezvous with Death
> At midnight in some flaming town,
> When spring trips north again this year,
> And I to my pledged word am true,
> I shall not fail that rendezvous.

Within a matter of months Kennedy would begin his own rendezvous with death, and barely escape the dark land. Plagued by a congenitally bad back, exacerbated by encroaching Addison's disease, he began having excruciating pain which forced him to use crutches to walk.

When his weight plummeted from 175 to 140, and his sister Eunice noticed how thin he had become, he tried to joke about it at first, saying, 'Don't worry. It's nothing serious – just a result of Jackie's cooking.'

Finally the pain became so unbearable that he made an appointment for X-rays at the New York Hospital for Special Surgery, where he was given the stark alternatives of living in continual pain or undergoing surgery for spinal fusion which might take his life.

He was told at the time that his chances for surviving such an operation were 50-50 because of the inefficiency of his adrenal system. Still, he decided to take the risk. 'I'd rather be dead,' he said, 'than spend the rest of my life on these goddamned crutches.'

So on 21 October 1955, Jackie accompanied her husband to New York for the operation which, as expected, was a failure. Staphylococcus infection set in, making Kennedy so delirious that he slipped into a coma and was placed on the critical list. His family was alerted at midnight to come to the hospital immediately, where he was given the last rites of his church in preparation for death.

Chain-smoking around the clock, Jackie clung to Joe Kennedy for support. 'It was the first time in my life I really prayed,' she later told a friend.

Earlier, Jackie had planned to attend a charity fashion show in Boston, but because her husband was so sick she decided not to go.

When Kennedy began to rally, his father decided to fly him to Palm Beach for the Christmas holidays so he could relax in the comfort of familiar surroundings. The family hoped the warm climate would revive his spirits.

Years later, when Jackie could joke about that Christmas, she said, 'It was horrible. We spent the whole time hovering around the heir apparent.' At the time, though, it was traumatic for everyone, and she spent her days trying to cheer him up.

Six weeks later, still wracked with pain and suffering terribly, Kennedy decided to go back to New York for a second operation to remove the metal plate which had left a gaping hole in his back. This time the operation was successful, but there followed months of convalescence with the family worried that he might never resume his Senate duties.

Recuperating at the Kennedy home in Palm Beach, Jack had a room off the patio beside the swimming pool and Jackie stayed in the room next to it. This was the hardest time for her because there was little she could do to help him. 'I think convalescence is harder to bear than great pain,' she said, watching her husband grow restless and frustrated.

Stretched flat on his back, unable even to use a pillow, Kennedy could sleep for no more than one or two hours at a stretch. He began reading to research a magazine article which would eventually grow into *Profiles in Courage*, the book that won the 1957 Pulitzer Prize for biography.

'This project saved him,' said his wife. 'It helped him channel all his energies while distracting him from pain.'

It also kept a constant stream of people coming in and out of the waterfront estate. Letters and memos and dictabelts went from the sickbed to the Senate office requesting more than two hundred books, journals, and magazines from the Library of Congress which were immediately flown to Florida. Stenographers went back and forth transcribing dictation, while Theodore Sorenson and other aides laboured rewriting the rough drafts.

Through it all, Jackie worked with her husband, reading aloud to him when he was too tired to hold a book, taking copious research notes, and writing memos to his secretary in Washington for further books and articles.

Living under the same roof with her rigid mother-in-law, who got up at dawn to attend daily Mass, was difficult for Jackie. When she wasn't at her husband's bedside she went off by herself to stroll through the stores on Worth Avenue. Shopping became a luxurious escape for her from the unpleasantness and tedium of the real world.

During this time, Kennedy needed the company of his political cronies more than ever to help him pull out of his severe depression. Jackie shared Jack's waking hours with men like Red Fay and Dave Powers, who were summoned to Palm Beach by the Ambassador.

Powers, a warm, genial man who once described himself as a 'three-decker Irishman', meaning that he came from a neighbourhood of three-flat tenement houses in the poor waterfront district of Boston, was Jack Kennedy's closest friend. Jack liked to have him around as much as possible. Expertise in Democratic party politics, an incredible memory for polling statistics and voting figures, and a repertoire of ribald anecdotes made him a delightful companion. He was a source of constant entertainment to Kennedy. Knowing this, Joe Kennedy insisted Powers spend the first two months with Jack after he got out of the hospital.

Jackie, although she was twenty-four years old when she married, had never voted. She did not understand this fascination for politics, but she accepted Dave Powers because he had such a tonic effect on her husband. The rest of the politicos surrounding Kennedy she accepted with less enthusiasm. For the most part she mockingly referred to them as 'Jack's flunkies' and considered them grubby, back-slapping, cigar-smoking cretins.

Her husband, she felt, was not one of them. In her eyes, Jack's taste, charm, wit and sophisticated appeal made him more a statesman of the order of Lord Melbourne than a back-room politician.

Jackie quoted Shakespeare to describe her husband: 'His delights were dolphin-like; he showed his back above the element he lived in.' She did not see him as a hard-bitten politician fuelled by expediency in all things. She even refused to see him as pragmatic. 'He's an idealist – without illusions,' she said. The same held for Bobby, her brother-in-law. 'Sometimes I wish Bobby was an amoeba so we could breed him to himself,' she said.

But Jackie was merciless in mocking others in the Kennedy entourage, terming them 'boring and boorish'. Still, she was savvy enough to know that her marriage would crack if

45

her husband was ever denied his consuming passion for politics. While he immersed himself, she remained totally apolitical.

'I can't understand it,' said Kennedy. 'She breathes all the political gasses that flow around us but she never seems to inhale them.'

Knowing his overriding ambition to be President, yet aware of his precarious health and deepening depression, Jackie worried that he might not be physically capable of achieving his goals. During that painful convalescence she once asked Ted Sorenson if he thought Jack would ever make it to the White House. Seeing him bedridden and almost cadaverous, she wondered how he would ever pull through. Sorenson assured her that Kennedy should be and could be President but would probably have to settle for the Vice-Presidency first.

Barely able to feed himself, let alone get out of bed and walk, Kennedy began mapping his campaign to secure the second spot on the Democratic ticket in 1956. His biggest concern then was not his health but rather what to do with his wife, whom he frequently described as having 'a little too much status and not enough quo'.

'How to make Jackie, the fox-hunting, French-speaking socialite, palatable to voters was the subject of many family conferences,' recalls Betty Spalding. 'We were visiting them once in Palm Beach and discussing the matter when Jack said, "The American people just aren't ready for someone like you, Jackie, and I don't know what we're going to do about it. I guess we'll just have to run you through sub-liminally in one of those quick flash TV spots so no one will notice."

'That was like a slap in the face to Jackie, who burst into tears and ran out of the room, sobbing hysterically. Jack was absolutely mortified by the whole thing and couldn't understand what he'd said to upset her so. He was accustomed to his sisters, who would have shot back with something like "Stick it up your own subliminal." But Jackie was not like Eunice and Pat and Jean. She was crushed by the comment. Though accustomed to being ignored by the rest of the family, she was terribly hurt when Jack treated her in a similar fashion.

'Jack couldn't demean himself by running after her to apologize, so I felt it was my duty to get her and bring her back to the group,' Betty Spalding recalls. 'I felt a little self-conscious myself because I was always defending Jackie in those tribal councils, saying she would be a great political asset and then getting the living hell beat out of me for suggesting such a thing. They were terribly cruel about it, and made me feel awful, too, but I went to get her and bring her back.

'When she stopped crying and we walked back in the room, Jack said, "I guess I should have said that a little better, huh?" Of course, he couldn't come right out and say, "I'm sorry," because he really didn't know how to apologize, but that was an apology of sorts for him, and Jackie recognized it as such. No more was said about it that day.'

But there were other Kennedy conferences on the subject of Jackie, who by this time was developing such a dislike for the prospect of a big political campaign that she wouldn't even discuss the matter. Rose, Eunice, Ethel, Jean, and Pat were rearing to go again and begin stumping with a series of Kennedy tea parties. Jackie, however, shrank at the thought of shaking hands and making small talk with strangers or, worse yet, making some public *faux pas* in front of Jack's sisters. She also despised the Irish Mafia strategists surrounding Kennedy. They in turn resented her, feeling she would be a detriment to their hopes and might prevent their man from reaching the top. They tried to tell her she was so pretty she would make the female populace envious, but Jackie knew what they were really thinking, and hated them for it. The Ambassador himself, her own ally, finally said, half in jest, 'Well, Jackie, if you want out, you'd better get yourself pregnant.'

Years later, when Kennedy won the Presidency and Jackie was showing signs of panic about the official duties of First Lady, she told a friend, 'I'll get pregnant and stay pregnant. It's the only way out.'

After eight months, Kennedy was fully recuperated and

his book finished. He threw away his crutches and returned to the Senate while Jackie began house-hunting. Hordes of cheering tourists, reporters, photographers, and television camera crews awaited him at the Capitol. Looking at the news coverage later, Jackie teased him: 'God, it was like recording the Crown Prince taking his first baby steps.'

Within days Jackie found a rambling white-brick Georgian house called 'Hickory Hill'. Located across the Potomac River in McLean, Virginia, it was not far from Merrywood, where she had grown up. Hickory Hill had been the home of the late Supreme Court Justice Robert Jackson and had once been used as General George McClellan's headquarters during the Civil War.

While Jackie spent her days fixing up the house, Jack immersed himself in his work and launched a speaking schedule which would keep him on the move until fall. Then he and Jackie left on an official trip to Europe which included an audience with the Pope and a visit behind the Iron Curtain to Poland. Thanksgiving was spent with the Kennedys at Hyannis Port and, a few weeks later, Christmas with the clan at Palm Beach. The following year Jack's schedule was even more intense as he tried to bolster his chances for the Vice-Presidency.

'I was alone almost every weekend while Jack travelled the country making speeches,' says Jackie. 'It was all wrong. Politics was sort of my enemy as far as seeing him was concerned, and we had no home life whatsoever.'

Jackie made no effort to take an active role in her husband's political planning. 'Jack wouldn't – couldn't, just couldn't – have a wife who shared the spotlight with him,' she said, acknowledging her secondary position. Consequently, her political role became one of mere decor and then only under duress. 'I show up and smile,' she said of her campaign activities then, 'and sometimes I might say a few words, but that's all Jack says I really have to do.' Usually those words took the form of little speeches delivered in whispery French or Spanish, depending on which ethnic group the Kennedys were trying to impress.

From the time Jackie met Jack she knew that he was

determined to become President and that if she married him she might become First Lady. Indeed, his certain ambition and the romance of marrying a United States Senator played a large role in her attraction to him, but she was naive about the realities of being a political wife. When asked by a reporter whether life with a Senator had been what she anticipated, she replied honestly, 'I just didn't know what to expect.' She later admitted she had to learn it all the hard way.

'One morning the first year we were married, Jack said to me, "What food are you planning for the forty guests we are having for luncheon?" No one had told me anything about it. It was 11 am, the guests were expected at one. I was in a panic.'

One Senate wife, whose husband was a close friend of Kennedy's, remembers Jack bringing Jackie to dinner shortly before they were married and saying, 'Okay, now tell her what she's in for as the wife of an up-and-coming politician.'

'I told her that a Senator belongs to his constituents and doesn't have time for his family,' the wife recalled. 'As his wife you don't see your friends because you're too busy with his, spending all your time helping him get re-elected. Jackie kind of giggled and said it was oh, so exciting. She could hardly wait. And then, a few months later, she came to me and said, "My God. You told me what it would be like but you really didn't tell me everything. You only told me half." '

Another problem was Kennedy's schedule. 'It was most difficult our first year of marriage,' said Jackie. 'Being married to a Senator, you have to adjust to the fact that the only routine is no routine. He is never home at night before 7:45 or 8, often later. He's away almost every weekend, making a speech somewhere. No, I don't go along. I stay home. And he's usually so tired that only about once a week are we able to go out – or have someone in.'

Other areas of incompatibility made marriage hard for Jackie. While Jack thrived on large crowds of people and going to gaudy musicals, she preferred to give small but elaborate dinner parties at home, where she could have occasion to use her elegant silver and Sèvres china. Jackie liked to sip daiquiris and linger over candlelight at the table, talking about foreign films or art. Kennedy preferred to drink beer and talk politics all night after a simple meal of steak and mashed potatoes.

'She was not an easy dinner partner,' says columnist Marquis Childs. 'Her close friends described her as shy, reserved; her conversation was her own shorthand of the hunting field, the ballet, Baudelaire, the people she had known, *always* in the correct places. With a husband so self-centred, so ambitious, the centre of a jealous, protective clan, she found her role circumscribed.'

Another friend from the early days says, 'At their dinner parties we always had to play those silly games like Categories that the Kennedys loved so much. Jackie was best on couturiers and Jack always won with Civil War generals and Davis Cup teams. It wasn't much fun for the rest of us.

'When she would serve cheese and fruit for dessert, he would go into the kitchen and come back with a huge dish of vanilla ice cream and chocolate sauce. If we ever strayed too far from politics and started talking about something else, which Jackie always tried to do, Jack would get bored and go upstairs to bed. He could be atrociously rude that way and was actually something of a pig at the dinner table when he ate, but Jackie improved his manners considerably after a while, and was always telling him to eat more slowly. Before he married her he used to show up in wrinkled suits with the lining hanging out, but she spruced him up there, too.'

After a nomadic life of shuttling back and forth from Washington to Boston, from Newport to Palm Beach, living off and on with both sets of parents, Jackie hoped that Hickory Hill would give them a home in the true sense of the word and be a place where her father could spend quiet weekends and her husband relax. She spent months buying furniture, shopping for antiques, and planning the decor for their new house.

She gave special emphasis to a nursery because she was expecting a baby in October.

Perhaps fearing a second miscarriage – she had had one the

first year of the marriage – she kept her pregnancy secret as long as possible. By the time of the Democratic convention in Chicago that August, however, she was excited and full of anticipation.

Because of her pregnancy, she stayed with the Shrivers at their apartment rather than sharing a suite with Kennedy and his campaign aides at the Conrad Hilton Hotel.

Chicago was miserably hot that summer. Socked in by humidity, the stench of the stockyards hung over the city like a noxious cloud. Waves of nausea hit her every time she stepped outside, but Jackie managed to accompany her husband to the breakfast for the New England delegates at the Palmer House and the Perle Mesta champagne fest at the Sheraton Blackstone the next day.

Jackie, as her mother says, has a long memory and never forgets a snub, especially when directed at her husband. At the same time, she never grasped the reality of politics – that your enemy today will be your intimate tomorrow. When her husband would come home irritated by some political colleague, Jackie would conclude that the man was an enemy and glare across the room the next time she met him, refusing to speak. Later Jack would say something agreeable about the man and Jackie, dumbfounded, would exclaim, 'Why are you saying nice things about that rat? I've been hating him for three weeks now.'

'He would tell her that in politics you rarely had friends or foes – only colleagues,' said Arthur Schlesinger, Jr, 'and that you should never get in so deep a quarrel as to lose all chance of conciliation; you might need to work with the other fellow later.'

Kennedy tried to explain how politics was played, admonishing Jackie not to get her feelings hurt. 'You can't take politics personally,' he said. 'It arouses the most heated emotions, and if you are sensitive to what people are saying, you'll always be upset.'

Jackie could never understand this facet of political life. Her naive loyalty to her husband led her to adopt an us-and-them outlook towards opponents and to ignore the in-betweens and undecideds.

Consequently she always resented Eleanor Roosevelt. At the time Kennedy was seeking the Vice-Presidency, Mrs Roosevelt announced she would not endorse him unless he declared his opposition to Senator Joseph McCarthy and his anti-Communist tirades. This demand was hard on Jack, however, because the Irish Catholic Republican from Wisconsin was a close personal friend of the Kennedys and a frequent visitor at Hyannis Port. When he met Mrs Roosevelt he dodged the issue, saying he would make his views clear when the occasion presented itself.

Eleanor insisted he make the occasion himself and clear up the matter. Kennedy refused to do so, and as a consequence Mrs Roosevelt refused to support him.

Politically, Eleanor Roosevelt was using legitimate tactics which Kennedy recognized, but Jackie felt she was being 'pigheaded, mean and spiteful', and refused to speak to her. Even when she was First Lady, Jackie would not soften and insisted on leaving the White House when her husband brought Mrs Roosevelt in for a tour of the family quarters.

As First Lady, Eleanor Roosevelt travelled the world as her crippled husband's trusted representative. She joined a labour union, wrote a newspaper column, held press conferences, met coal miners, and pacified White House pickets. Her death moved the country to national mourning. But Jackie Kennedy was not moved.

Patricia Peabody Roosevelt remembers her at the funeral. 'Jackie Kennedy sat regally on a couch nearby, listening with cool unconcern to the scraps of talk floating about her. With an elegant gesture, Jackie took a cigarette from her purse and held it for a light ... Elliott's sons were too mesmerized to react. They stared. Jackie balanced her unlit cigarette, waiting. At last, with a resigned sigh, she drew a match from her purse and lit it herself.'

When the Kennedy family and political entourage stampeded Chicago early in the week, they began making the rounds of delegates to drum up support for their candidate. As co-hostess of the Chicago Women's Hospitality Committee, Eunice corralled her sisters and Ethel into total participation, while Sargent Shriver and Bobby Kennedy worked the floor, moving from delegation to delegation trying to rally Southern votes. Meanwhile, Papa Joe was on the trans-Atlantic phone from France, trying to buttonhole party leaders for his son. During these long hours of campaigning Jackie spent most of her time in the Shrivers' apartment and barely saw her husband. He was usually sprawled on his hotel bed in shorts, analysing the action with his political aides.

Soaking in a tub in the Stockyard Inn, Kennedy watched the turbulent floor action on television while his wife waited inside the convention hall for the balloting to begin. On the first roll call, Kennedy polled 304 votes, trailing Tennessee's Estes Kefauver but still very much in the running. When his name shot ahead on the second ballot, outdistancing Kefauver 618 to 551½, Jackie started yelling, waving her Adlai-Stevenson-for-President placard enthusiastically from the Kennedy box where she sat with other members of the family. Kennedy only needed 68 more votes for the nomination, and Jackie was sure he would make it.

On the third ballot, he got 30 more votes and the Massachusetts delegation began stamping their feet. The chairman pounded his gavel for order as delegates waved their standards for recognition. Then Missouri dashed all Kennedy hopes by throwing its votes to Kefauver, who in a matter of moments went over the top.

When Jack Kennedy walked into the convention hall a few minutes later and moved that Kefauver be nominated by acclamation, his wife began crying, knowing how bitterly disappointed he was to have come so close to winning.

Accepting defeat with a forced smile, Kennedy left the platform as the band swung into 'The Tennessee Waltz'. He would return triumphant fifty-four months later to receive the Democrats' top price, but at that point he was a defeated man, tired, bitter, and disillusioned.

He met Jackie and his friend, Senator George Smathers, and returned with them to his hotel room to phone his father on the French Riviera. 'We did our best, Dad,' he said. 'I had fun and didn't make a fool of myself.' Then he hung up the phone and began rehashing his disappointing loss.

'I've never been to an Irish wake before,' said Smathers, 'but I guess maybe this was it. The three of us just sat around the hotel room glum, none of us saying very much. We were there about an hour and a half, and all Jack could think of were all the different things he might have done that might have made the difference. He was hurt, deeply hurt. The thing is, he came so close.'

Kennedy was determined to leave for France the next day with George Smathers to vacation with his parents, despite Jackie's pleas to stay with her and go to Newport. She hated flying, especially now that she was pregnant. Rather than be by herself, she decided to stay with her mother and step-father at Hammersmith Farm.

'Jackie was so bitter about Jack's leaving her that she said she didn't care about the baby,' recalls a friend who was with her in Newport. 'She really did, of course, but she was so upset by his taking off like that she turned herself inside out, letting it eat away at her; and on top of being so strong out from that convention with all those crowds and the noise and everything, she finally ended up in the hospital.'

A week after she arrived at Hammersmith Farm, Jackie began to haemorrhage and experience severe cramps. She was hospitalized and underwent an emergency Caesarean operation. The foetus – that of a girl – was stillborn. Summoned by Mrs Auchincloss, Robert Kennedy flew to Newport Hospital to be with his sister-in-law while Eunice tried desperately to locate her brother in the south of France.

The next day the *Washington Post* carried a front page story headlined: 'Senator Kennedy on Mediterranean Trip Unaware His Wife Has Lost Baby'.

'Jack was so damn mad when he read that story later, but Jackie said he deserved it. "What else do you expect," she yelled at him,' reports a friend.

The newspapers said 'nervous tension and exhaustion as a result of the Democratic convention' caused the miscarriage. Jackie blamed Jack.

Three days passed before Kennedy, cruising off Capri in a chartered yacht, found out what had happened. When finally reached by ship-to-shore radio, he took the news calmly and decided to continue his vacation after learning that Jackie was all right. Only the insistence of George Smathers persuaded him to return.

'If you want to run for President, you'd better get your ass back to your wife's bedside or else every wife in the country will be against you,' said Smathers. ' "Why the hell should I go now?" he asked. I told him I was going to get him back there even if I had to carry him. Joe Kennedy agreed, so we went back together.'

Emotionally and physically drained, Jackie remained in the hospital while her family arranged a memorial service for the little girl who did not live long enough to be christened. Years later a tiny coffin bearing the name 'Baby Kennedy' would be reinterred alongside two other Kennedy graves at Arlington's National Cemetery.

Kennedy spent only a few days with his wife in Newport before taking off again to campaign for the Stevenson–Kefauver ticket, making 140 public appearances in twenty-six states. When he returned, he and Jackie stayed a few days in New York seeing plays and then came back to Washington. At that time he told his secretary, Evelyn Lincoln: 'I don't think we will be living at Hickory Hill this coming year. You know that Jackie spent so much time fixing up the nursery, and she doesn't want to go back there. She's terribly upset about the baby.'

Chapter Four

Eisenhower was returned to the White House with a landslide victory. Kennedy reflected on the fact that it was just as well he had lost the chance to be Vice-President. Had he been Stevenson's running mate, the Democratic defeat might well have been blamed on his Catholicism, and any subsequent chance he might have had for higher office might have been ruined.

Remembering his elder brother who died in World War II, Kennedy said: 'Joe was the star in our family. He did everything better than the rest of us. If he had lived, he would have gone on in politics, and he would have been elected to the House and Senate, as I was. And, like me, he would have gone for the Vice-Presidential nomination at the 1956 convention, but, unlike me, he wouldn't have been beaten. Joe would have won the nomination. And then he and Stevenson would have been creamed by Eisenhower, and today Joe's political career would be in shambles, and he would be trying to pick up the pieces.'

Jack Kennedy said this with a certain amount of satisfaction. He was in complete control of his political future. At the age of forty, he was nationally known as the handsome young Senator who gave the Stevenson nominating speech at the Democratic convention, and people were already beginning to mention him as a possible Presidential contender even before he received the 1957 Pulitzer Prize for *Profiles in Courage*.

Joe Kennedy leaned heavily on his close friendship with Arthur Krock, the *New York Times* columnist and member of the Pulitzer board, to make sure his son received this prestigious prize for, as he told Krock, 'You would be surprised how a book that really makes the grade with high class people stands you in good stead for years to come.'

The Pulitzer Prize elevated the Senator's intellectual

status and he began charting his political future. First he started an incessant round of barnstorming with a view to being re-elected by the largest majority in Massachusetts history. From there on he drove himself mercilessly to the Presidency.

For the next three years his wife would try to hang on in his wake, clutching at a marriage that was, in her words, 'wrong, all wrong'.

'It's not the right time of life for us,' Jackie said. 'We should be enjoying children, travelling, having fun.'

Rumours had circulated in Washington that the Kennedys were having marital problems, and it was no surprise to see them out at night without one another, each going separate ways. There were even published reports that their marriage was over, including a story in *Time* that Jackie had threatened divorce and Joe Kennedy had made a million-dollar deal with her at New York's River House to stay with his son.

This story, which had no basis in fact, started shortly after Joe Kennedy was publicly proclaimed the 11th richest man in the United States, worth 400 million dollars. His fortune was based primarily on the manipulation of stocks, the production of low-grade Hollywood movies, and the importing of liquor immediately after Prohibition. He certainly was in a position to offer his daughter-in-law a great deal of money, but there was no such transaction. However, Joe Kennedy did talk to Jackie at length about her marriage, reassuring her that despite evidence to the contrary her husband loved her very much. He impressed on her the importance of staying together to make things work, saying that the thing Jack needed most to settle him down was a child.

Concerned about the gossip swirling around his friend's marriage, Red Fay finally asked Kennedy about the rumours. He recalls putting the question like this: 'The sister of the wife of one of my closest friends, who supposedly travels in the same set in New York as Jackie and Lee, has circulated the story that Jackie is staying with you only until you are nominated or the election is over, and then is going to divorce you. She claims she got the information from one of Jackie's closest friends. I want the rebuttal directly from you, so I can kill the story if it is false, but I wouldn't feel all that confident about killing it if I were you. People who spread stories like that don't want to accept a denial. I think I know the girl in New York who is spreading that report. She and Jackie go to some of the same parties and, amazingly enough, Jackie says she is always very friendly.'

Jackie was aware of the rumours. But, as a passive person with no taste for confrontation, she remained private and guarded, confiding her loneliness only to intimates. Still, she tried to be independent, and started seeing men like Walter Sohier and Philip Carroll as often as she could.

'Believe it or not, Jack was jealous of Jackie seeing any other man,' says Betty Spalding, 'even a pal like Bill Walton, because he was convinced that she was doing the same things he was doing. It upset him to be envious that way because it threatened his macho image of himself as a husband and a man who must be all things to his wife and every other woman in the world. In Jack's mind his other women were always separate and apart from his responsibility to his wife. Compulsive womanizers feed something they need deep inside themselves to reinforce their own sexuality, and that has nothing to do with the women they're married to.'

Jackie frequently played on this jealousy in retaliation for Kennedy's affairs and felt pleased and reassured when he responded. As First Lady, she took Caroline on a trip to Italy, and the newspapers were filled with pictures of her with Fiat tycoon Gianni Agnelli. When Kennedy saw the photographs and heard all the embassy gossip, he dispatched a cable to her via diplomatic pouch, saying, 'A little more of Caroline and a little less of Agnelli'.

'Jackie did have a lot of male friends because she got along better with men than women,' says Mrs Spalding, 'which, I'm sure, stemmed from the fact that she never got along well with her mother. But she was not flirtatious at all, and there was absolutely nothing seductive or sensual about her. She was too guarded.'

Still, there were rumours about Jackie, too, and she was well aware of the gossip prevalent about her own affairs. She told Robin Douglas-Home, 'What can I do? I have dinner with someone, dance with someone for more than one dance, stay with someone, get photographed with someone without Jack – and then everyone automatically says, "Oh, he must be her new lover." How can you beat that?'

When Home asked her about one particularly well-known friend of hers, and why the story of their love affair had stuck so persistently for so long, Jackie said, 'Do you know why? Because every time he is going to see me, he rings up the three biggest gossips in New York beforehand and says casually in the course of conversation, "Oh, by the way, I'm going to nip down and see Jackie – she's asked me and she's desperately lonely and needs me – but, of course, you won't tell a soul, *will* you, because you know how embarrassing it would be for *her* if it got out ..." '

Home felt that Jackie looked on her husband's powers of attraction as a challenge to be all the more attractive and desirable and essential to him as a wife.

Another friend says, 'The other woman business was foremost in her mind. Sometimes she could be very adult about Jack's little flings and other times she would retreat and thrash herself and mope for days, becoming very aloof from everyone and being glacially cold to him. That's when she would go on shopping binges and spend hours visiting Walter Sohier in his Georgetown house. Then there were times she would actually tease Jack about it. I remember once when we had all gone swimming, she came back to the house and said to him, "You'd better get down there fast. I saw two of them you'd really go for."

'There was frequent bantering between Jack and Jackie on the subject of sex and who was sleeping with whom and what they did in bed. They both loved to gossip about that sort of thing all the time. Jackie's sexual curiosity about low doings in high places was just as great as Jack's. They could shovel stuff about other people's affairs for hours.'

One woman remembers visiting Jackie in the White House shortly after a state visit of the Shah of Iran. 'We laughed about the Shah who was so stuffy and stern and his new young wife who was so pretty and vibrant. Jackie was quite curious about their marriage and said it couldn't possibly have been

59

a love match. She wondered if he ever went to bed with his wife. We had a wonderful time gossiping about that sort of thing.'

Another time, as First Lady, Jackie wandered into a White House party for the astronauts and broke them up by asking if they knew Sigismund Von Braun, Werner's brother, who had figured so heavily in the messy divorce case of the Duke of Argyll.

While she had a delicious sense of humour about the sex lives of other people, she wasn't always as casual about her own husband's. 'The only indication I ever had that Jackie knew about all of Jack's women was when they were in the White House and she asked me if I knew if he was having an affair with Pamela Turnure,' says Betty Spalding. 'I said I didn't know, and even if I did I wouldn't tell her. It was a matter between her and Jack, and one that I had no right to be involved in. It distressed her that there might be an ongoing affair with an employee she had to see every day and deal with. That bothered her more than the fact that Jack might have been sleeping around.'

That particular affair, which began when Miss Turnure was a secretary in Kennedy's Senate office, could have been an obstacle to his Presidency. If he had experienced the same press scrutiny prevalent after Watergate, he probably would not have made it to the White House. Even his press secretary, Pierre Salinger, admitted as much when he said in 1977, 'Why, if Kennedy had been in office today, we'd have been thrown out after six months for some of the things we did.' However, when Kennedy was a candidate he did not have to contend with a press corps which investigated the private lives of public men.

During the summer of 1958, when Jackie was in Hyannis Port, he made a late-night visit to his pretty twenty-one-year-old secretary, who was renting an apartment in the Georgetown home of Mr and Mrs Leonard Kater.

'We were up late one night, and heard someone outside throwing pebbles at Pam's window about one am,' recalls Mrs Kater. 'We looked out and saw Senator Kennedy standing in our garden, yelling, "If you don't come down,

I'll climb up your balcony." So she let him in.

'My husband and I were so intrigued by the whole thing that we set up a tape recorder on the kitchen cabinet and another in the basement to pick up the sounds from the bedroom. The next time Kennedy came over we turned on the tapes and listened to their conversation in the living room, and when they went in the bedroom we heard the unmistakable sounds of love-making and intercourse.

'I can assure you that he was not a very loquacious lover,' says Mrs Kater, who claims the verbatim conversation in the living room had the Senator saying, 'Are you ready for it?' and his secretary replying, 'Whenever you are ready for it.'

Mrs Kater recalls having trouble with her young boarder and finally asking her to leave when she refused to empty her garbage.

'When I kicked Pam out, JFK arranged for her to move into Mary Meyer's house in Georgetown for the summer and continued seeing her there. I was so enraged that this Irish Catholic Senator, who pretended to be such a good family man, might run for President that I decided to do something about it. I was very innocent and naive in those days and had no idea of the power I was going up against. I knew no one would believe my story unless we had actual proof, so in addition to the tape recordings, we decided to get a photograph.

'On the night of 11 July 1958 – it's funny I can still remember the date after all these years – my husband and I drove to 34th Street where Pam was then living and saw Kennedy walk up to the house and watched the two of them leave together in her white Alfa Romeo. She recognized our car and so we went back and rented a smaller one, and waited in the dark for them to return. You don't know how eerie this was. The leafless night and the one footfall of the next President of the United States.

'Kennedy came out about one am and my husband was waiting for him on the sidewalk. He called out, "Hey, Senator," and Kennedy turned. When he saw my husband with his camera, he hid his face with his hand. Then he said, "What in the hell are you doing here? How dare you take my picture!"

'I jumped out and said, "How dare you run for President under the guise of a good Christian?" I told him I was an Irish Catholic myself and after thirty years we could do better than have a lecher in the White House. I handed him a book called *The Irish and Catholic Power*, and he jotted down our licence number on the book.

'The next day I called Joe Kennedy. He was an unctuous, urbane, soothing man. He said he was leaving for Europe and he didn't think what I had to say was important.'

A few nights later the Katers got back in their car and drove to Kennedy's Georgetown house on N Street, where they sat and waited. 'The Senator came out, walked to the car, looked at the licence, and walked back in,' Mrs Kater recalls. 'Then he came out a second time with some man and said to my husband, "I want you to know that I know all about you and your job. You're doing very well, so why don't you keep it that way. If you ever bother me or my father again, I'll see to it that you never work in Washington as long as you live."

'I jumped out of the car and yelled at him, "I have a tape recording of your whoring. You are unfit to be the Catholic standard bearer for the Presidency of this country." I thought a rather horrified look came over his face right then, and he turned and left.'

When JFK walked away from the car, Mrs Kater said to her husband, 'That man is walking away from the White House and I'm going to get him. It would have been okay to punch you in the nose, but it's not fair to threaten your job like that.'

Before Mrs Kater began her one-woman campaign to discredit Kennedy she received a call from Ambassador Kennedy's attorney, James M. McInerney, formerly with the Criminal Division of the FBI. According to Mrs Kater, McInerney, now deceased, asked them to hand over the photograph and tape recordings and forget the whole matter. 'He told me if I went public with my information it would be political suicide for the Senator and economic suicide for my husband.

' "Every Catholic in the country will hate you," he said,

"and your husband will be of no use to his company." ' By this time the Standard Register Company had received several calls regarding Kater's employment.

Discussing the matter between them, Mrs Kater says she and her husband told the attorney that they loved art and had always wanted to own a Modigliani to add to their collection, and that if they got the painting they would forget the incident. McInerney never produced the painting for them but did continue his visits.

'He visited us about nine times, and then I called Joe Kennedy about the Senator's affair and told him what I thought about it. He told me not to "get in a stew over it" and that he would like to see me after a trip we were making to California. He asked me when we would be back in Washington, and I told him. He said that it coincided perfectly with a trip he planned to make to Washington. He said he would be glad to see me anywhere I suggested, and so I suggested my home. He asked me if I would like to have special studio passes when we would be in Hollywood, and I said I would not. He said he heard I was "quite a character" and he looked forward to meeting me soon. His attitude was that I was a silly prude.

'I then called Cardinal Cushing in Boston for an appointment and got it, and went there with all my evidence of Senator Kennedy's moral unfitness to be President of the United States. I told Cardinal Cushing that if Senator Kennedy would not withdraw from the Presidential race I would do everything in my power to publicize his lechery. The Cardinal said he was shocked by my story but had no influence and couldn't do anything about it.'

Mrs Kater then began sending copies of the photograph to journalists and politicians around the country, but no one paid any attention to her until she showed up at one of Kennedy's political rallies carrying a placard of the enlarged photograph and loudly asked, 'Why are you hiding your face in this picture, Senator?'

A photographer from the *Washington Star* took a picture of Florence Kater shoving her poster towards Kennedy, who was grinning at her. The photo ran in the paper the next day.

Minutes after the home edition appeared, Robert Kennedy called Bill Hill, the *Star*'s managing editor, and said that if the picture was not withdrawn immediately there would be a lawsuit.

'Kennedy said the picture was not his brother, and if we didn't yank it he'd own the paper by nightfall the next day,' recalls Hill.

The *Star* immediately started investigating the incident. Its top reporters and photographers were sent to Georgetown to locate the house Kennedy was photographed leaving. Meanwhile, campaign aides spread stories that Mrs Kater was a religious fanatic who had been pursuing Kennedy throughout the country. 'They even said I'd spent time in an insane asylum,' she says.

Having assembled enough information to defend themselves in court should the Kennedys bring suit, the *Star*'s editors decided not to pursue the story because of its personal nature. Although the reporters found Mrs Kater eccentric, they did not doubt her story.

When she realized the paper would ignore the matter, she donned her hat and coat and took to the streets to picket the *Star* and later the White House with a placard showing the now famous Kennedy photograph and bearing the following message:

This is a picture of Senator Jack Kennedy of Massachusetts leaving his girlfriend's house at 1:00 in the morning. Take a long look at Senator Kennedy's left hand as it hides his face. Can you see that same hand on the Holy Bible next January 26th taking the oath of highest office? Is the country ready for Senator Kennedy? Is this the picture of a President of the United States?

For taking this picture, Senator Kennedy planned to deprive my husband of his job. Failing that, his lawyer, James McInerney (a former assistant attorney general) spent 5 months trying to intimidate us and thus keep this matter from the public.

Last May 14th at a rally at the University of Maryland I confronted Senator Kennedy with this placard and asked him about it. I was escorted away by the police. After the rally Kennedy aides said the man on the placard was not Senator

Kennedy, that it was a contrived picture made by religious fanatics in Arizona. This picture of Senator Kennedy was taken in Georgetown in Washington, DC.

I am an Irish American Roman Catholic Florence Mary Kater (Mrs Leonard), 2733 Dunbarton Avenue, NW, Washington, DC 20007.

I will give my $10,000 Renoir painting to anyone who can prove this recent picture a fake or altered in any way.

No one ever challenged Mrs Kater or claimed her painting. 'No one could ever prove that I was lying,' she says. 'I had told the truth but no one would listen to me. The press wanted Kennedy to be President and that was that.

'After he became President, he called me and said the trouble with me is that I needed a good lay. Then he called me five or six times more from the White House just to be nasty. Once he called and said he was going on a campaign trip and couldn't decide which tie to wear. "You're a very smart woman, Mrs Kater, so you tell me what the most sincere type of tie would be. Striped or solid?" He got his kicks out of stuff like that, I guess. I don't know. I never could figure it out.'

The painful perplexities of living with such a man were Jacqueline Kennedy's. She had come to grips with them early in her marriage by ignoring what hurt and accepting what she understood only as a basic male drive, a masculine need that had to be satisfied. She recognized this compulsion in all the men she truly loved. Her father, her grandfather, and her father-in-law had all been susceptible to women. While they rarely denied themselves a dalliance, they had such a strong sense of family that they would never disrupt their homes.

The stories of Jackie threatening divorce were not only untrue but out of character for a woman who knew innately that a casual liaison without any emotional involvement could never threaten her marriage. This is not to say that she was immune to the hurt of Kennedy's affairs, because she was not. But in her mind they had nothing to do with him as her husband. They were all part of the political man, and to Jackie politics were power and power was promiscuous, part

65

of a game little boys must play when they are vulnerable.

'I separate politics from my private life,' she said, 'maybe that's why I treasure my life at home so much.'

A pragmatic woman, she also realized that her future as a divorcee, despite generous alimony and child support, would be severely limited. And, having suffered through the ugly divorce of her parents as a youngster, she would never knowingly subject her own child to the same trauma.

'In this business there's always going to be flare-ups about something,' she said. 'And you must somehow get so it doesn't upset you. I think I always was fairly good at it. I can drop this curtain in my mind.'

That mental curtain allowed her to overcome pain, avoid reality, and live in her own insular world – safe, protected, and unharmed.

'Her reaction, later to become so familiar, was simply to pull some invisible shade down across her face and cut out spiritually,' says Ben Bradlee. 'She was physically present but intellectually long gone.'

Still, Jackie knew what was happening and became quite cynical about marriage. 'I don't think there are any men who are faithful to their wives,' she said. 'Men are such a combination of good and bad.'

Chapter Five

The Kennedys actively entered the field of mental health in 1946 by establishing the Joseph P. Kennedy, Jr Foundation. A memorial to Joe and Rose Kennedy's eldest son, killed in World War II, the foundation was the first in the United States to direct benefits solely to the mentally retarded. Born of remorse and guilt, this philanthropy was the family's means of making amends.

Until 1962, when Eunice Kennedy Shriver wrote a *Saturday Evening Post* article entitled 'Hope for Retarded Children', few knew that Joe and Rose Kennedy had a retarded child who had been institutionalized. There were rumours during his Presidential campaign that something was not quite right with one of Jack Kennedy's sisters, but the family insisted that she was merely the quiet one who had decided to devote her life to the Sisters of St Coletta by helping the handicapped. They could not bring themselves to admit the painful reality of her condition. They even allowed stories to circulate that she had attended her brother's inauguration with the rest of the family, when in fact she never appeared publicly in Washington during his administration and never entered the White House.

Rosemary Kennedy, the third of nine children, has been living at the St Coletta School in Jefferson, Wisconsin, since she was twenty-one years old. She was placed in the religious institution because her mental faculties were so impaired that she could no longer function in the real world. The stigma of mental retardation in those days caused the Kennedys to hide this daughter. They mentioned her condition only to her doctors.

From the time of her birth in 1918, her mother says, Rosemary was extremely slow and had difficulty in learning to walk and talk. Later, Mrs Kennedy said that her eldest daughter's retardation was the result of a genetic or birth accident. The family kept hoping that she would improve in the competitive atmosphere of the home, surrounded by her precocious brothers and sisters.

So determined were they to make Rosemary appear normal that they presented her to the King and Queen at Buckingham Palace when her father was Ambassador to the Court of St James. When the family returned to the United States that summer, Rosemary became hyperactive. She threw violent temper tantrums, hitting people and breaking things. She was taken to the best doctors available, and they diagnosed her rages as neurological disease. Distressed by her extreme behaviour, the Ambassador and his wife finally decided to take a drastic, irreversible step. In 1941, they submitted their daughter for a prefrontal lobotomy.

Prefrontal lobotomies were first performed on human beings in 1935, after experimental surgery on chimpanzees had indicated that certain neurotic symptoms could be modified by cutting some of the nerve fibres. This surgery was considered a radical treatment for mental illness. The operation causes irrevocable damage to the brain for the purpose of altering undesirable behaviour. The Kennedys were so desperate that they were willing to try anything. They conferred with several doctors and then secretly arranged to have Rosemary hospitalized for the surgery.

During the operation, holes were drilled in the skull and surgical incisions made in the white matter surrounding the frontal lobes of the brain. The procedure was intended to make her more tractable. Unfortunately, Rosemary's prefrontal lobotomy left her with minimal use of her faculties. Today, doctors would prescribe psychoactive drugs for her hyperactive condition rather than resorting to such mind-altering surgery.

To this day the family has not divulged the exact nature of the operation performed on Rosemary. In her memoirs Rose Kennedy alluded only to a certain form of neurosurgery that was tried after consulting the most eminent medical specialists in the country. 'The operation eliminated the violence and the convulsive seizures,' she wrote, 'but it also had the effect of leaving Rosemary permanently incapacitated ... She functions on a child-like level but is able to have excursions in her motor car, and to do a little personal shopping for her needs – always with an attendant – and to enjoy life to the limit of her capabilities. She is perfectly happy in her own environment and would be confused and disturbed at being anywhere else.'

Sister Paulus, the nun who accompanies Rosemary, admits that the fifty-nine-year-old woman now at St Coletta's institution was indeed lobotomized. 'It's so very sad,' she says, 'but I don't think they had tranquillizers in those days like they do now. The lobotomy wasn't necessary because with medication Rosemary would have been just fine. But she's very sweet and is taken good care of where she is.'

Eunice Kennedy Shriver is especially close to her retarded sister. As director of the Joseph P. Kennedy Foundation, she has devoted herself to the field of mental health. Annually she opens her estate in Rockville, Maryland, to an Olympics sports event for the handicapped, and throughout the year she makes frequent speeches on the subject of mental retardation, stressing the need for more research and re-habilitation. She also visits Rosemary regularly and brings her to the Kennedy compound in Hyannis Port every summer. These visits are hard for Rose Kennedy, who has never conquered the awful guilt she still feels about the lobotomy. She admits to suffering terrible anguish over her eldest daughter. 'I asked myself endlessly why this had to happen to her,' she said. 'I felt it was so unfair for her to have so many handicaps and the others to be so blessed. The more I thought, the clearer it became to me that God in His infinite wisdom did have a reason, though it was hidden from me, and that in time, in some way, it would be unfolded to me.'

Joe Kennedy's overbearing personality left its mark on all the Kennedy children. They were reared to excel and never to admit defeat. 'We soon learned that competition in the family was a kind of dry run in the world outside,' said Jack Kennedy. In such a large family, the younger children were frequently deprived of their parents' time and attention. Bobby Kennedy acknowledged the emotional handicap of being the seventh child in a competitive family.

'When you come from that far down you have to struggle to survive,' he said. 'What I remember most vividly about growing up was going to a lot of different schools, always having to make new friends, and that I was very awkward. I dropped things and fell down all the time. I had to go to the hospital a few times for stitches in my head and my leg. And I was pretty quiet most of the time. I didn't mind being alone.'

Growing up was even harder for the daughters, who had to compete with their brothers for a place in their father's sun. As an adult, Jean Kennedy Smith complained to her mother about the lack of time she received as a youngster. 'I was shuffled off to boarding school at the age of eight,' she said.

'Well, what was I to do?' retorted Rose Kennedy. 'Your father was always gone, or we were giving dinners and parties at the Embassy. So I had no time to spend with the children.'

'That's why I'm still trying to get my head screwed on straight,' replied her eighth child.

Eunice Kennedy Shriver, the fifth child, emerged as the strongest, toughest member of the family, as hard-hitting and driven as her father.

As a child Eunice displayed ferocious energy, competing with her brothers in sailing, swimming, and touch football. In later years, when she had a stroke at Hyannis Port during the summer of 1977, the fact was hushed up and kept a family secret. She refused to be hospitalized, insisting that she could take care of herself. Self-sufficiency had become such an obsession with her that she would not tolerate physical infirmity.

The men and women who married into this family became subjected to the Kennedys' overwhelming drive and ambition as much as the children. Steve Smith and Sargent Shriver each assumed a position running the family fortune. Later both helped mastermind the political campaigns of their brothers-in-law but never managed to achieve the same success for themselves, although both tried to run for public office. Peter Lawford became the family's Hollywood link to celebrities, providing Jack with access to starlets and socialites.

'The rough-and-tumble of a large, gregarious family was completely foreign to me,' said the British actor, 'and thus I became – by marriage – an outsider in an almost over-whelming situation ... Actually, it took two years of exposure to the Kennedy family esprit before I began to get the message that the secret was participation.'

Partaking in the family's affairs was mandatory for each of the men who married Joe Kennedy's daughters. None was per-mitted to lead his own life or allowed completely to support his family. Emasculated by their domineering father-in-law, they were beholden to him and his money. Their wives continued sending their bills to the Kennedy office to be paid and never let their husbands forget their financial dependence.

The Ambassador frequently went into tirades about the family finances, chastizing his spendthrift children for the extravagances he himself encouraged in them. Over dinner one night he said, 'I don't know what's going to happen to this family when I die. There is no one in the entire family except for Joan and Teddy who is living within their means. No one appears to have the slightest concern for how much they spend. I don't know what is going to happen to you all after I am gone.'

Turning to his daughter Jean, he said, 'And you, young lady, you are the worst. There isn't the slightest indication that you have any idea what you spend your money on. Bills come in from all over the country for every conceivable item. It is utterly ridiculous to display such disregard for money.'

Seeing his wife burst into tears and run out of the room, Steve Smith spoke up. 'I think you have made your point,' he said. Minutes later he brought his wife back to the dinner table where everyone, including Jackie, was subdued and tense. Jack Kennedy looked up at his sister and smiled.

'Well, kid, don't worry,' he said. 'We've come to the conclusion that the only solution is to have Dad work harder.'

Following in father's footsteps, each Kennedy son married a woman more socially prominent than himself. Besides bringing a certain social status to the marriage, these women were required to be happy helpmates devoted exclusively to their husbands' careers. They were expected to produce children, heirs, Kennedys with regular effortless-ness. The wives of Kennedys were relegated to second place, dominated by the ambition of their husbands. They were expected to suppress their own personal identities by enthusiastically supporting the ambitions of their single-mindsd husbands and making them their own.

This was an impossible role for Jacqueline Bouvier Kennedy. In the beginning she tried very hard, but she could never change her basic personality. 'My natural tendency is to be rather introverted and solitary and to brood too much,' she said.

As a child she was so aloof from her classmates that they began calling her Jacqueline Borgia. Even as an adult, it was easier for her to give someone a luxurious present than to give of herself.

She sees friends intermittently, every six to eight months or so, because she cannot sustain constant companionship. 'Everyday life is really more of a burden for her than it is to most of us,' says one friend. 'Just as she can respond to the dramatic occasions but can't bring herself to deal with ordinary happenings, she isn't up to close friendships with the weekly phone calls and lunches, the effort and the intimacy they entail. Jackie is capable of being capriciously, intermittently involved with people but she can't sustain anything.'

Paul Mathias, a French reporter for *Paris Match* and a good friend of Jackie's, says, 'There can be a period when she would call and see me or someone else and be charming and delightful and sweet, and then there may be a period when she doesn't see you for a year. She doesn't want to let herself go with people and when she does, she sometimes resents the person for having listened to her. She is not capricious but she hurts people very much, then consoles them afterwards. She is fighting herself all the time.'

She was also given to extreme moodiness prompting her husband to draw this illustration of their relationship:

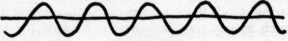

He said that he was the straight, solid line, and indicated that his consistently even temperament was the foundation supporting his wife's volatile mood swings. Jackie agreed with the assessment. 'He is a rock,' she said, 'and I lean on him in everything. He is so kind. Ask anyone who works for him. And he's never irritable or sulky.'

Once Kennedy was asked to describe his wife with one word. He paused a moment to think and then smiled. 'Fey,' he said. Most people assumed he was referring to a Celtic penchant for imaginative fancies that contrasts sharply with stolid matter-of-factness. 'Fey', meaning 'elfin' and 'ability to see fairies', was a charming way for a hard-hitting Boston politician to describe his ethereal wife.

Jackie's black moods were noticeable to anyone who spent much time with her. Although outwardly calm and composed, she had a habit of biting her fingernails. She never wore nail polish for fear of calling attention to her hands.

Norman Mailer described her as 'a lady with delicate and exacerbated nerves.' He added: 'There was something quite remote in her – not willed, not chilly, not directed at anyone in particular but distant, detached as psychologists say, moody and abstracted the novelists used to say ... She had perhaps a touch of that artful madness which suggests future drama.'

'She is not a happy person,' said Paul Mathias. 'She is so complicated. She is erratic. There are also moments when she is out of control with herself. They might aggravate the imbalance that is in her.'

The splintered personality she developed as a child became more fragmented as she grew up. When she married Jack Kennedy, powerful pressures pulled her in various directions. The indignities she suffered trying to contend with the other women in his life only exacerbated her raging conflicts. She resented her sisters-in-law and their constant hymn of praise for the family and its money and power. She felt superior to them but she was also dependent on them.

'Jackie did not get along with Rose and Rose did not like Jackie,' said Smathers. 'And Jack's sisters were unbelievably overbearing. God, those women were always talking about how much money they had, how influential Joe was, and how much power the family possessed. They'd drive you crazy with that kind of talk. All of them were that way, except for Pat, who was more female than the rest. I think it really got to Jackie after a while.'

Chapter Six

During 1957, Jackie made several trips to New York to visit her ailing father, but never mentioned that she was pregnant. Thus it was with confused feelings of surprise, delight, and pique that Black Jack learned from the newspapers he was going to be a grandfather in November.

Jack Bouvier was dying that summer. While Jackie celebrated her twenty-eighth birthday at Hammersmith Farm, he took a turn for the worse and was rushed to Lenox Hospital. No one told him he had cancer of the liver, and, although Jackie knew her father was sick, she was unprepared for the shock of his death a week later.

Deeply shaken, she flew to New York to arrange the funeral. Staying at Joe Kennedy's apartment, she sent her husband to pick out a casket while she went to see one of Black Jack's female friends to obtain a photograph for the obituary. She carefully composed the text, stressing his family background, and insisted that her husband personally deliver it to the managing editor of the *New York Times*. The newspapers neglected to use the photograph.

At the funeral home she stood beside the coffin and looked at her father – the first dead person she had ever seen. She impulsively unfastened the bracelet Black Jack had given her as a graduation present and placed it in his hands. Then she kissed him good-bye and cried.

For the rites in St Patrick's Cathedral, Jackie ordered garlands of daisies in white wicker baskets, saying, 'I want everything to look like a summer garden.' Despising stiff floral bouquets and solemn wreaths, she covered the casket with bachelor's buttons and surrounded the altar with gay meadow flowers.

Sadly, only a few friends joined the Bouvier family and his nurse Esther for the dashing *bon vivant*'s funeral. His former wife, Janet Auchincloss, received the news aboard

74

the *Queen Elizabeth*, on which she, her husband, and her young son Jamie were bound for a European vacation.

Jackie wept with regret that her father did not live to see his first grandchild. 'He would have been so happy,' she said, 'so happy. Promise me, Jack, that whether it's a boy or a girl, we will give the baby the name of Bouvier.'

The unadorned headstone in St Philomena's Cemetery at East Hampton bore only the initials J.V.B., but Jackie made sure before she left it that the graveside looked like a country garden.

Black Jack's will bequeathed his desk to Lee and 'a picture of Arabian horses by Shreyer' to Jackie. In addition, each daughter received approximately $80,000.

Back in Washington, Jackie brought out the letters her father had written to her at school and asked her secretary, Mary Gallagher, to type them in duplicate and send a copy to Lee in London.

At that time Jackie was getting ready to move into a house in Georgetown, having sold Hickory Hill to Bobby and Ethel Kennedy. She had decorated the house in her mind months before. Knowing there was no room for the painting her father left her, she sold it, along with several wedding presents including a silver cigarette box from Jack Kennedy's ushers engraved with their names.

A few months later Caroline Bouvier Kennedy was born. Within three weeks the Kennedys moved into their new house accompanied by a personal maid, a cook, a houseboy, a chauffeur, and a British nanny, Maud Shaw, to take care of the baby. Despite the servants, Jackie frequently described herself as 'an old-fashioned wife'. Like a nineteenth-century chatelaine, she saw her role as lady of the castle, mistress of the château. Her yearbook profile from Miss Porter's School noted that her ambition in life was 'not to be a housewife', and she never was.

'I think the best thing I can do is be a distraction,' she said. 'Jack needs that kind of wife. He lives and breathes politics all day long. If he came home to more table thumping, how could he ever relax?'

She watched her husband's diet and made certain that he

took his prescribed medications and ate three meals a day. Often she sent a hot lunch to his Senate office.

'I brought a certain amount of order to his life,' she said. 'We had good food in our house – not merely the bare staples that he used to have. He no longer went out in the morning with one brown shoe and one black shoe on. His clothes got pressed and he got to the airport without a mad rush because I packed for him. I can be helpful packing suitcases, laying out clothes, rescuing lost coats and luggage. It's those little things that make you tired.

'The thing that gives me the greatest satisfaction is making the house run absolutely smoothly so that Jack can come home early or late and bring as many unexpected guests as he likes. Frankly, this takes quite a bit of planning.'

When Jackie was first married, a friend compiled for her a housekeeping manual detailing the operation of a gracious home. Instructions ranged from how a maid should make a bed to tips for keeping iced beer mugs ready for all-male gatherings. With this guide, Jackie briefed her staff so that everything ran according to schedule, allowing her time to paint and read and play with Caroline.

Organized to the point of compulsion, she spent hours arranging her wardrobe, checking her schedule well in advance to ensure that the right outfits and accessories would be ready. She always planned a season ahead for her wardrobe. She paged through fashion magazines, clipping designs she liked, and sent them to Paris, where every fashion house had a Jacqueline Kennedy dummy. Then she would spend hours on alterations, making sure that each hem hung perfectly and that she had extra perspiration shields for dresses she wore on campaign trips. She gave the same care and attention to her husband's clothes, organizing his closet by colour and lining up his shoes to match his suits.

One woman who visited her during those days in Georgetown says, 'I was amazed when she opened her closets because there were rows and rows of beige shoes, and at least twenty-five lipsticks in a gold lipstick holder on her dresser. She could spend a whole afternoon in front of the mirror with a lipstick brush and make-up. She had a drawer for short gloves and a drawer for long gloves and special lingerie bags for nylons, and catalogues and scrapbooks for everything. She lived quite regally in a regulated way. She had a standing appointment to get her hair done every week and a massage, and usually took an afternoon nap every day.

'She hated to be surprised or taken unawares, even to the point of having neighbours drop in unannounced, so she made sure she was always prepared for company with enough food and liquor on hand at all times. In fact, she had her chef cook and freeze gallons of that fish chowder Jack liked so there would always be plenty for him and she wouldn't have to worry.

'With all that household help to do the big things for her, Jackie concentrated on niggling little details like picking out the right shade of off-white paint for her dining-room walls, painting stencils on the floor, selecting the frames for her paintings and rearranging the furniture, which she seemed to do constantly.

'She didn't have many friends because she preferred it that way and once, when I asked her why she spent so much time alone, she laughed and said, "I need to sulk."

'Moodiness was very much a part of her, which Jack simply wouldn't tolerate, so she spent a good deal of time by herself. That's when she'd read what she called her trash, which was every bestseller she could get her hands on.'

'Mummy thinks the trouble with me is that I don't play bridge with my bridesmaids,' said Jackie, who enjoyed spending time by herself and shuddered at the thought of joining women's groups or doing volunteer community work. 'I guess that's very un-American of me because in this country people love to congregate and join. I don't know whether the men started joining and the women followed them or what ...'

Having a baby seemed to complete Jackie's life, giving her a feeling of being needed and useful. 'That child made all the difference in the world to her,' says a Georgetown friend. 'She had tried so hard to have a baby before and had taken such good care of herself to insure a safe delivery with Caroline that I think she would have had a nervous breakdown

77

if anything had gone wrong. It also gave her more acceptance with the rest of the Kennedys, who produced children so effortlessly and thought seriously that something was wrong with Jackie because she always had so much trouble.'

In those days Jackie lived by her concept of the well-brought-up young lady, being 'a bit' interested in the arts, learning the vintage years of great wines, giving little dinner parties, taking care of the gentlemen's cigars, and riding to the hounds. But any participation in Jack's political career was a drudgery that sapped her energy and interest. Unlike her husband, she did not thrive on frenetic activity and saw no point in wearing herself out shaking hands with strangers and asking for their votes.

Even posing for pictures seemed to weary her, and she begged off as many stories as possible, explaining once in a letter to an editor how tiresome it was for her.

Jackie saw the Presidential campaign as a horrendous monster ready to gobble her up and spew her in little pieces across the landscape. 'God, I dread it,' she told one woman. 'Just thinking about it makes my stomach heave. He'll be going, going, going constantly and I'll be absolutely worn out just trying to keep track of him.'

More than once during those days, Jackie confided to a friend how lonely she was. At one point she said: 'Even when he *is* here, the damn phone rings so much we can't even get through dinner together. I've got an unlisted number but if I tell him not to answer it or try to take it off the hook, then we fight. I tell him I feel like I'm running a boarding house and he doesn't understand. He'll just look at me in that way of his and say, "You seem to be doing okay to me."'

So driven towards a single goal was he that Kennedy seemed oblivious to his wife's need for attention. Jackie, unable at times to cope with her own frustrations, would either fly off the handle with pent-up anger or retreat inside herself, misunderstood, helpless and miserable. Often, when Jack started talking politics with someone, she would leave the room.

With few strong friendships or loyalties, Jackie would strike out, making fun of everyone around her with a biting wit. Not even her huaband was safe from her barbs. Once she complained to a neighbour: 'He fills the house with people who are the ages of my mother's friends, or else political jackals who drive me up the wall.'

One friend recalls: 'She was always making fun of her mother, saying in a sing-song voice, "Mummy this" or "Mummy that". It was always behind her back, of course, but it was quite unnerving. Even when she was married to JFK, she would mimic him when he wasn't around and make fun of him, imitating his pronunciation of "Foah moah years". It was immensely amusing but discomforting because it concealed a real hostility. She had a way of picking up snatches of people's conversation and then aping them unmercifully. She was very funny, but you always knew she was doing the same thing to you behind your back in front of others.'

Robin Douglas-Home once admitted that it took him a long time and several conversations with Jackie before he felt comfortable alone with her – 'without the nagging fear I had had in our previous talks that that razor brain suddenly, on a whim, would be turned on me, her silent listener; the fear that the merciless mockery she could direct at other people and customs and protocols and institutions would be suddenly flung in my own eyes, like gangster's ammonia. Perhaps the ability to arouse that fear was a quintessential part of her fascination.'

Her personal secretary of six years recalls: 'Jackie was happiest when her sister was around because Lee was the one person with whom she could relax and pour out her feelings. They were like school girls together, sharing confidences and telling how some frustrating or dense person "drove me up the wall – screaming and knocking everything over". Or how someone had "a knack for being interested in and remembering the dullest details".'

JFK's political entourage got the brunt of Jackie's wither-ing sarcasm, being variously labelled 'flunkies', 'lackeys', 'jackals', and 'imbeciles' behind their backs, while to their faces she managed a smile and soft chit-chat.

As much as she dreaded another campaign, she had no

79

choice but to go along. 'If Jack didn't run for President,' she said, 'he'd be like a tiger in a cage.'

By this time Kennedy was criss-crossing the country, making over a hundred speeches in a hundred cities a year, touching base with party leaders, taking polls, collecting names of precinct workers, delegates and volunteers, and building a powerful political machine which would see him through the primary states. At the same time he was putting as much public distance as possible between himself and his father, whose conservative views and controversial image conflicted with Jack's political strategy. Joe Kennedy withdrew from public notice during the campaign and did not even appear in a newspaper photograph with his son until the day after the election.

At the time of his run for the Presidency Kennedy was only forty-two years old. At first his candidacy was not taken seriously; his legislative record in the Senate was undistinguished and his religion was considered a handicap. Thus he was frequently asked if he would accept second place on the ticket. Irritated, he would respond: 'I am not going to accept the Vice-Presidential nomination. I shall support the Democratic ticket, I will work hard for it, but looking at the history of the last sixty years, I don't recall a single case where a Vice-Presidential candidate contributed an electoral vote.'

Jack's father agreed. Joe, who invested more than seven million dollars to put his son in the White House, declared: 'Not for chalk, money or marbles will we ever take second place.'

Jackie also was adamant on the subject, despite her dislike of politics. One night when Bill Attwood, a Stevenson aide, was dining with the Kennedys at the Georgetown house of Ben and Tony Bradlee, Kennedy asked Attwood what Adlai was up to. Jack wanted Stevenson's endorsement at that time and was appalled when Attwood said that if the convention chose Stevenson, it would draft Kennedy for second spot.

'I wouldn't take it,' Jack said in a flat, hard voice. 'I'm campaigning for the Presidency, period.'

Jackie, who had taken no part in the political exchange, spoke up with feeling. 'Let Adlai get beaten alone,' she said. 'If you don't believe Jack, I'll cut my wrists and write an oath in blood that he'll refuse to run with Stevenson.'

Jackie's pregnancy spared her from the most gruelling aspects of the campaign, but initially she accompanied her husband to each primary state and spent a few days campaigning before returning home. 'Thank God, I get out of those dreadful chicken dinners,' she said. 'Sitting at head tables where I can't have a cigarette and have to wear those silly corsages and listen to some gassy old windbag drives me up the wall. Poor Jack.'

Jackie agreed to help out in the Wisconsin and West Virginia primaries, where Kennedy faced his toughest opposition from Senator Hubert Humphrey. The Minnesota senator, overwhelmed by the invasion of Kennedy kin, complained: 'They're all over the state. They all look alike and sound alike so that if Teddy or Eunice talk to a crowd, wearing a raccoon coat and a stocking cap, people think they're listening to Jack. I get reports that Jack is appearing in three or four different places at the same time.'

Shunning the housewife teas held by Rose and Jean and Pat and Ethel throughout Wisconsin, Jackie had her own ideas about campaigning and often carried them out without consulting anyone. One day in Kenosha she walked into a busy supermarket and, after listening to the manager announce bargain sale items over a loudspeaker, she located the microphone and in a breathy voice began talking. 'Just keep on with your shopping,' she whispered, 'while I tell you about my husband, John F. Kennedy.' She talked briefly about his service in the Navy and in Congress and then closed with, 'He cares deeply about the welfare of his country – please vote for him.'

In Fort Atkinson, the wife of a Lutheran minister was waiting outside the Blackhawk Hotel with her twelve children, eager to meet Kennedy. After he came out and shook hands with the beaming mother, he told Dave Powers, 'Get Jackie and bring her over here.' Powers escorted Jackie across the street and Kennedy made the introduction:

'Shake hands with this lady, Jackie. Maybe it will rub off on you.'

When Kennedy left Wisconsin to return to Washington for a day, Jackie filled his speaking engagements, then stayed up through election night waiting for the results. Jack won the primary with over 56 per cent of the vote, and Jackie flew to Washington and then to Palm Beach to recuperate. She promised her husband she would campaign again in Indiana, Nebraska, and West Virginia if he promised to take her to Jamaica for Easter. 'She'd never show up unless she got a vacation afterwards,' said an aide.

The West Virginia campaign was brutal, with the rich Kennedy machine rolling over Humphrey. The Minnesota senator couldn't compete against the supporters Kennedy assembled to canvass the state. One of them, Franklin D. Roosevelt, Jr, would hold up two fingers tightly pressed together and tell coal miners: 'My daddy and Jack Kennedy's daddy were just like that.'

The Kennedy women staged hot dog roasts and barbecues in the mining towns and attended country club receptions in the big cities. But Jackie often was accompanied only by a driver as she visited miners' wives in their ramshackle houses. She was shocked by the poverty and remembered it. Subsequently, as First Lady, she ordered tulip-shaped champagne glasses for the White House from the Morgantown (West Virginia) Glassware Guide.

'That glassware was advertised and sold everywhere as the White House wine glass – it only cost something like six dollars a dozen,' she said, 'but I didn't mind that at all, as I thought it was nice to help West Virginia and nice that people should see that those simple glasses were pretty enough for the White House.'

Later, when she was offered a donation of costly glassware, she turned it down and wrote a memo to her decorator, Sister Parrish, explaining why. 'The whole problem is still West Virginia – it still is NO – and will be until they aren't poor any more. It is funny – but in all the places we campaigned – and sometimes I was so tired I practically didn't know what state we were in – those are the people who touched me most –

The poverty hit me more than it did in India – Maybe because I just didn't realize that it existed in the US – little parched children on rotting porches with pregnant mothers – young mothers – but all their teeth gone from bad diet – I would practically break all the glasses and order new ones each week – It's the only way I have to help them –'

The night of the West Virginia primary the Kennedys were in Washington, dining and seeing a movie with Ben and Tony Bradlee. Back at their N Street house, they got a victory call from Bobby and immediately ordered up the *Caroline*, their private campaign plane, to fly them to Charleston.

'Once in West Virginia for the victory appearance, Kennedy ignored Jackie, and she seemed miserable at being left out of things,' recalls Bradlee. 'And this night she and Tony stood on a stairway, totally ignored, as JFK made his victory statement on television. Later, when Kennedy was enjoying his greatest moment of triumph to date, Jackie quietly disappeared and went out to the car and sat by herself until he was ready to fly back to Washington.'

By July, when Kennedy arrived at the Democratic convention in Los Angeles, his nomination was sealed with 761 hard-won delegate votes. As he watched the demonstration for Adlai Stevenson on television, he reassured his father: 'Don't worry, Dad, Stevenson has everything but delegates.'

Moments before he walked into the convention hall to accept the nomination, Jack called Jackie in Hyannis Port. 'It's a good thing you didn't come out here,' he said. 'There's too much pandemonium. You can watch me on TV in a few minutes. I'll call you later to see how you like it.'

To strengthen his chances for election, Kennedy picked Senator Lyndon Johnson of Texas to be his running mate, despite outcries from campaign aides, labour leaders, liberals, and civil rights activists who were pushing for Stuart Symington, Henry Jackson, Orville Freeman, and Adlai Stevenson. His brother Robert, who was his campaign manager, was dismayed. But one supporter applauded the choice. Joe Kennedy told his son: 'It's gotta be Lyndon.'

That night there was a huge victory celebration at Pat and

Peter Lawford's California house. The participants – including Angie Dickinson, Pierre Salinger, Bobby Kennedy, the Lawfords, and the next President of the United States – got drunk and went skinny-dipping in the pool, splashing and howling until the small hours of the morning.

'They were making so much noise that the neighbours called the police, who arrived with sirens and hauled them all into the station ready to book them on public drunkenness and disorderly conduct,' recalls an aide. 'None of them had any identification because they weren't even fully dressed when they were thrown in the paddy wagon, so they had one hell of a time trying to explain who they were. But when the cops realized who they had in tow, they released them immediately and said, pointing to Jack, who was sopping wet and laughing his fool head off, "You better get this guy out of here fast." '

During this time Jackie was in Hyannis Port working on a painting for her husband which depicts him sitting at the helm of his sailing boat, *The Victura*, wearing a Napoleonic hat and surrounded by relatives, with cheering crowds on the shore. The impressionistic water colour, executed with a technique suggesting a cross between Grandma Moses and Raoul Dufy, shows Jackie on the dock with both arms raised, next to Caroline and her pets, while the British nanny, Maud Shaw, enthusiastically waves the US flag and the Union Jack. A plane flies overhead carrying a banner. Across the band playing on the dock is a sign: 'Welcome back, Mr Jack.'

Meeting reporters that day, Jackie said, 'I suppose I won't be able to play much part in the campaign but I'll do what I can. I feel I should be with Jack when he's engaged in such a struggle and if it weren't for the baby, I'd campaign even more vigorously than Mrs Nixon. I can't be so presumptuous as to think I could have any effect on the outcome, but it would be so tragic if my husband lost by a few votes merely because I wasn't at his side and because people had met Mrs Nixon and liked her.'

Interest in the two candidates' wives was becoming so intense that newspapers ran front page stories on their hair styles and wardrobes, comparing the amount of money each spent on her personal appearance. Jackie became irate when she read reports that women resented her because she spent too much money on her clothes.

'That's dreadfully unfair,' she said. 'They're beginning to snipe at me about as often as they attack Jack on Catholicism. I'm sure I spend less than Mrs Nixon on clothes. She gets hers at Elizabeth Arden and nothing there costs less than $200 or $300.'

Months before, when reporters asked Jackie where the Democratic national convention should be held, she replied brightly, 'Acapulco'. Then, when asked why she didn't like to campaign, she said candidly, 'I simply don't like crowds.' Again her husband hit the roof.

When criticisms kept building about Kennedy's Catholicism, Jackie retorted, 'I think it's so unfair of people to be against Jack because he's a Catholic. He's such a poor Catholic. Now, if it were Bobby, I could understand it.'

Kennedy told reporters: 'When we were first married, my wife didn't think her role in my career would be particularly important. I was already in the Senate and she felt she could make only a limited contribution. Now, quite obviously, that I'm in a very intensive struggle – the outcome uncertain – she plays a considerable part in it. What she does, or does not do, really affects the struggle. Since I'm completely committed, and since she is committed to me, that commits her.'

Privately, he insisted that Jackie meet reporters on occasion and try to cultivate good relations, stressing that she remain as uncontroversial as possible. 'Just smile a lot and talk about Caroline,' he advised. He also reminded her not to smoke in public.

Kennedy insisted that Jackie appear with him on certain television programmes. Later in the campaign Dorothy Schiff, publisher of the *New York Post*, told him she thought Jackie had been very good on a recent telecast. 'He said that she was much better than in personal interviews,' recalled the publisher. 'He was utterly cold in his remarks about her, and I had a feeling he had very little interest in her except as she affected his campaign.'

Jackie was only at ease with established journalists like

Joseph Alsop, Arthur Krock, and Walter Lippmann, whom she considered her equals. She privately referred to the women reporters assigned to cover her as 'the slobs' and resented 'their stupid little questions'. Nancy Dickerson noticed that when she went from radio to television Jackie, who had known her for years, suddenly began treating her like a celebrity while scorning reporters she considered inferior and beneath her.

'Early in 1961 she gave a White House luncheon for women of the press,' recalls Mrs Dickerson, 'and everyone was dazzled by her. Just ahead of me in the reception line was Doris Fleeson, the highly respected political columnist. On seeing her Jackie said, "Oh, Doris, what in the world would you be doing here with these others?" – a dig at everyone else within hearing distance. As we walked away, Doris whispered, "That young woman has a lot to learn!" '

Jackie felt that reporters who were personal friends had no right to ask Kennedy tough questions or push him hard on the issues. Once when she accompanied him to an appearance on 'Face the Nation', she slipped notes onto the desks of journalists she knew, saying, 'Don't ask Jack mean questions.'

Forced by her husband to talk to the women reporters covering her, Jackie barely restrained her condescension. When asked her views of issues, she replied, 'I shouldn't talk about politics.'

'Why not?' inquired one woman.

'I don't like to speak for my husband.'

'Then just speak for yourself.'

'Why are you all here?' she snapped. 'Because I'm his wife, that's why. My opinions are his, but he can express them better himself.'

When asked if she would continue writing her weekly column, 'Campaign Wife', which was distributed by the Democratic National Committee, Jackie said: 'Well, that depends on how it goes.'

'Do you have a ghost writer?' she was asked.

'Listen – I won't sign my name to anything I don't write myself.'

'Will you continue to go out shopping without hose or

86

wearing Capri pants if your husband is elected President?' asked a woman accustomed to seeing Jackie dressed casually and walking barefoot through Georgetown.

'Oh, God. Of course I wouldn't,' she said. 'I never leave the house until I think I'm suitably dressed.'

Later, when Jackie complained about the reporters and their 'rude questions', a friend said, 'Well, when you are First Lady you won't be able to jump into your car and rush down to Orange County to go fox-hunting.'

'You couldn't be more wrong,' said Jackie. 'That is one thing I won't ever give up.'

'But you'll have to make some concessions to the role, won't you?'

'Oh, I will,' she replied. 'I'll wear hats.'

Towards the end of the campaign, she frequently admitted nervousness and expressed doubts about the outcome. This irritated her confident husband. So sure was he of beating Richard Nixon that four months before the election he told Jackie to start looking for a White House social secretary and someone to handle press relations.

The morning of election day, Jack and Jackie flew to Boston to vote, then returned to Hyannis Port to watch the results on television. During lunch, Jackie told Arthur Schlesinger, Jr, 'I cast only one vote – for Jack. It is a rare thing to be able to vote for one's husband for President of the United States, and I didn't want to dilute it by voting for anyone else.'

Later the Kennedys ate dinner with Bill Walton and Ben and Tony Bradlee, then congregated at Bobby's house with the rest of the clan to tabulate the voting returns. At 3 o'clock in the morning, when a weary Nixon appeared on television with his tired wife on the verge of tears, Jackie turned to her husband and said, 'Oh, Bunny. You're the President now.'

Kennedy shook his head. 'No, not yet,' he said. Then, with the results still far from certain, he walked off by himself to go to bed.

The record turnout in 1960 gave the Kennedy–Johnson ticket a narrow margin of 118,550 votes. When a reporter commented that only 24,000 more votes in five states would have put Nixon in the White House, Joe Kennedy snorted: 'Well, what the hell. Did you expect me to pay for a landslide?'

That morning, while the Kennedys played touch football. Jackie walked out of her house in a raincoat with a green knitted cowl collar and low-heeled shoes, heading for the beach to be by herself. Secret Service men were already surrounding the Kennedy compound, and newsmen called out their congratulations to her.

'Do you think you ought to say that?' she said. 'Is it really certain?'

Assured that it was, she kept walking past the seaside cottages where photographers were gathered, yelling their good wishes. She did not acknowledge them, but turned her head so they wouldn't see her tears. The prospect of being First Lady was too terrible for anyone else to understand.

Chapter Seven

Jackie was so confused and unhappy by the time she got back to Washington that she couldn't cope with the activity bristling in her Georgetown house. Eight months pregnant and suddenly overwhelmed by the responsibility of becoming First Lady, she was terrified and at times depressed to the point of tears. While she was proud of her husband's victory, she took no joy from it herself. Having suffered through campaign criticism of the way she wore her hair and the clothes she bought, she now would have to live in a strobe light where every public action would cause comment and each chance remark would be magnified. The separate identity she had fought so hard to attain would be impossible to continue as a public person, she felt, and any attempt to lead a private life would be scrutinized and publicized.

'I feel as though I have just turned into a piece of public property,' she said. 'It's really frightening to lose your anonymity at thirty-one.'

Accustomed to a quiet routine in the privacy of home, she suddenly was overrun by campaign aides, new appointees, Senate staffers, Secret Service agents, squads of reporters and television newsmen, and secretaries.

New security telephone lines had been installed and the phones rang constantly, but never for her. All activity centred on Kennedy, who was buoyant and jaunty as he appeared on the steps of his house to make pre-inaugural announcements to reporters standing in the snow.

Jackie was infuriated by the cheering crowds of tourists who milled in front of the red brick house hoping to catch a glimpse of her and Jack. Having her husband 'underfoot all the time', as she put it, conducting business at home and jumping up to wave from the window at gaping strangers, exasperated her.

Huge sacks of mail arrived along with a deluge of gifts for

the soon-to-be-born baby. Packages of crocheted booties, crib blankets, coverlets and rompers cluttered Jackie's French drawing room. Finally, she directed her secretary to clear out the unwelcome presents.

'God, just put them in your car when you leave and get rid of them,' she said.

To her husband, who was thriving on every exciting minute, she said, 'I can't stand this chaos, Jack. It's driving me crazy.'

'Oh, for God's sake, Jackie. All you have to worry about right now is your inaugural ball gown. Let Tish do the rest.'

Letitia Baldrige, a lifelong Republican who preceded Jackie by two years at Miss Porter's School and at Vassar, had been selected as White House social secretary. The day after her appointment was announced, reporters asked about the responsibilities of her new job.

'I shall probably just stand in the background and hand out copies of the new baby's formulas,' she said.

The remark, obviously meant to be humorous, nettled Jackie, who was fiercely determined to guard her children's privacy 'in that awful place', as she was then calling the White House.

Tish was a blonde, bombastic woman who had previously worked as social secretary to Ambassador and Mrs David Bruce in Paris, private secretary to Ambassador Clare Booth Luce in Rome, and public relations director for Tiffany's in New York. Kennedy, impressed by her energy and expertise, had suggested that Jackie contact her during the summer to take the White House position. Only after Miss Baldrige arrived in Washington to hold her first press conference did he want to change his mind.

Wearing a Dior suit and a leopard hat, the new social secretary met reporters at the Sulgrave Club. She began by defining Jacqueline Kennedy as 'the woman who has everything, including the next President of the United States'.

She said Mrs Kennedy would make the White House a showcase of great American art and artists. 'She plans to make the Executive Mansion a place of current as well as historic interest. She plans to seek out paintings by prominent artists either on a loan basis or as permanent gifts.'

'Well, where will she hang them?' inquired one reporter. 'There certainly isn't much empty wall space – at least on the first floor.'

'That's a problem the First Lady-designate and her staff will have to face,' said Tish. 'They won't throw out portraits of Presidents and First Ladies already on the walls, but we will find a place even if it means hanging paintings in front of other paintings.'

Then, in answering a question about all the clubwomen who would try to meet the First Lady, she said, 'Mrs Kennedy was thinking about what to do with those big, vast hordes which want to be entertained at the White House – I mean those large groups of very interesting ladies.'

Without pausing, she went on to say she was going to scrape the White House dining room panelling to see what lay under the green paint. 'I'll just get my little knife out the first day and see what it looks like.'

When asked if Mamie Eisenhower had invited Mrs Kennedy to see the living quarters, Tish said, 'The invitation has not been extended yet – but we certainly hope it will be.'

The next day, when Kennedy read the interview, he stormed out of his Georgetown study clutching the newspaper and waving it in the air. 'Jesus Christ, Jackie,' he shouted, 'what in the hell is going on here? Can't you even manage your own goddamned social secretary? Have you seen what this woman has done to us?'

With the *Washington Daily News* thrust under her nose, she stared at the bold-type headline: 'JACKIE ISN'T DISTURBED ABOUT MISSING INVITATION'.

Kennedy bolted from the room and ordered one of his secretaries to 'shut this goddamned woman up before she opens her mouth again'. Then he came back to Jackie, saying that he had not received that much coverage on all of his cabinet appointees. 'There will be no more press conferences by Letitia Baldrige. Is that clear?' he bellowed.

Later, little Caroline wandered into the room and asked her nanny, 'What did that goddamn lady do to make Daddy so mad?'

Outside the house on N Street there was an exhilaration in the air as crowds continued to gather. People throughout the country were excited about this young man they had chosen as President. Even the press corps was pulled into the whirlpool of adulation.

'Reporters who stood outside the house on N Street hour after hour, day after day, waiting for tidbits of news, were caught up in the excitement,' said Helen Thomas of United Press International. 'We were numb with cold but we knew we were recording a fascinating period in history, and from a privileged vantage point.'

But inside the house tension mounted between the President-elect and his wife. A few days before, Kennedy had brought former President Truman into their home and was irritated because Jackie was still upstairs in her robe and couldn't come down. Later he complained to a friend: 'The Empress managed to lean over the banister to say hello. Christ, you'd think she was the one who had a government to run and I was just the prince consort.'

Kennedy left for a week at the LBJ ranch in Texas and then went to Palm Beach to relax with his parents. He returned to Washington to have Thanksgiving dinner with Jackie and Caroline but insisted on returning to Florida that evening.

'Why can't you stay here until I have the baby and then we can go down together?' Jackie asked. She resented the fact that he would bask in Palm Beach sun while she remained in ice-packed Washington. Kennedy refused to change his plans. When Jackie walked him to the front door with Caroline to say good-bye, she looked as if she had been crying and barely managed a smile to hide her distress.

An hour after he left, Jackie was resting in her second floor bedroom when she suddenly called for Caroline's nurse.

'Can you come quickly, Miss Shaw?'

The nanny rushed in and instantly knew that the baby that wasn't due for another four weeks was arriving prematurely. She hurried to call the obstetrician, Dr John Walsh. Within fifteen minutes Jackie was en route to Georgetown University Hospital, where she underwent an emergency Caesarean operation. At the same time frantic messages were being radioed to Kennedy, who was finishing a drink aboard his private plane.

Startled by the news and stricken with guilt that he was not with his wife, he said, 'I'm never there when she needs me.' As soon as he landed in Palm Beach he boarded the press plane to return to Washington and insisted on staying in the pilot's cabin to get further reports. At 1:17 am the news came over the radio earphones that John Fitzgerald Kennedy, Jr, had been born. The reporters in the back of the plane applauded wildly.

The moment Kennedy landed in Washington he went directly to the third floor of the hospital to visit Jackie and peek at his son through the nursery window.

'Now that's about the most beautiful baby boy I've ever seen,' he told reporters. 'Maybe I'll name him Abraham Lincoln.'

A few days later the Ambassador flew Luella Hennessey to Washington so the Kennedy nurse could tend Jackie as she had all the other Kennedy mothers. The chief duty of this cheerful New Englander was to ease the mother's post-partum depression. While Miss Hennessey ministered to Jackie, Maud Shaw looked after Caroline and Elsie Phillips arrived to take care of the new baby, who spent his first six days in an incubator.

One day as Jackie sat on the hospital's sun roof, wrapped in a long black suede coat, another patient wandered by and stared at her.

'You're Mrs Kennedy, aren't you?' she gushed. 'I recognize you from your pictures.'

'I know. That's my problem now,' replied Jackie as she immediately got up to return to the privacy of her room.

The day of the baby's christening, Kennedy arrived at the hospital to push his wife in a wheelchair to the chapel. Seeing a group of reporters and photographers at the end of the hall, he slowed down. Jackie gritted her teeth.

'Oh, God. Don't stop, Jack,' she pleaded, 'Just keep going.'

But Kennedy, aware that this was the first baby ever born to a President-elect and his wife, smiled broadly and allowed the photographers to take a few pictures.

Over at the White House, Mamie Eisenhower summoned the Chief Usher, J. B. West.

'I've invited Mrs Kennedy for a tour of the house at noon on 9 December,' she said. 'Please have the rooms in order, but no servants on the upstairs floors. And I plan to leave at one-thirty, so have my car ready.'

'Mrs Kennedy's Secret Service agent phoned from the hospital this morning,' the usher replied. 'She asked that we have a wheelchair for her when she arrives.'

'Oh, dear. I wanted to take her around alone,' said the First Lady, drumming her well-manicured fingernails on the night table. 'I'll tell you what. We'll get a wheelchair, but put it behind a door somewhere, out of sight. It will be available, if she asks for it.'

On the morning of 9 December Jackie arrived home from the hospital. A few hours later she slipped out of the back door to avoid reporters and was driven in a green station wagon to the White House. There she was escorted to the second floor to meet Mrs Eisenhower, who shared Jackie's dread of this traditional housekeeping briefing.

An hour later – after they had toured the thirty rooms of the private quarters where Jackie was horrified by the stiff bouquets, the cheap reproduction furniture, and Mamie's gold plastic fans in front of the fireplaces – the two women appeared in the North Portico and posed a few minutes for photographers.

'I think that's enough,' said Mrs Eisenhower, in a hurry to play bridge. She shook Jackie's hand and said, 'Good-bye.'

'Good-bye,' whispered Jackie. 'Thank you so much for all you've done. You don't know how much I appreciate it.'

'I was very happy to do it,' said Mrs Eisenhower. 'Good luck. Have a nice time going south.'

And in Mrs Kennedy's low voice came her parting words, 'Bye-bye, dear.'

By the time Jackie got back to the N Street house, she was sobbing hysterically.

'Oh, God,' she cried. 'It's the worst place in the world. So cold and dreary. A dungeon like the Lubianka. It looks

94

like it's been furnished by discount stores. I've never seen anything like it. I can't bear the thought of moving in. I hate it, hate it, hate it.'

In Palm Beach she called her friend Jayne Wrightsman to tell her about Mamie's tour, complaining that she wasn't even offered a cup of tea. 'God, it was so awful, it almost sent me back to the hospital with a crying jag.'

Kennedy was genuinely puzzled by his wife's outbursts. He did not understand how any woman would not be thrilled at the prospect of becoming First Lady and living in the White House.

'It's beyond me,' he said without amusement.

Jackie stayed in bed most of the time in Florida, writing letters and memos by hand on large blue-lined yellow note pads. 'I suppose I was trying to organize my life while I was there,' she said later. 'My office side – moving my furniture –'

She refused to join the rest of the clan for meals, preferring instead to receive her food in her room so she could avoid the swirling activity taking place in the Ambassador's house, which was becoming as congested as the N Street house in Georgetown.

'It was so crowded,' she complained, 'that I could be in the bathroom, in the tub, and then find that Pierre Salinger was holding a press conference in my bedroom!'

Rose Kennedy, the energetic matriarch, bustled about, taking the confusion in stride as she went about her daily schedule of early morning Mass, playing golf, and supervising the continual flow of people. Perturbed by her daughter-in-law's seclusion, she approached Mary Gallagher one day.

'Do you know if Jackie is getting out of bed today? You might remind her that we're having some important guests for lunch. It would be nice if she would join us.'

When Mrs Gallagher relayed the message, Jackie responded by mimicking her mother-in-law's sing-song speech: ' "You might remind her we're having important guests for lunch," ' Jackie repeated.

The luncheon guests arrived and departed without seeing Jackie, who remained in her room, insisting on her privacy so she could begin organizing her new life.

During this time alterations experts arrived from Bergdorf Goodman to fit the white silk crepe gown Jackie had designed for the Inaugural Ball. It was a complicated creation with a silver-threaded bodice under a sheer white chiffon over-blouse: deceptively simple but exquisitely detailed. Since she had no spectacular jewellery of her own to wear, Jackie desperately wanted to borrow a splendid diamond pin and pendant diamond earrings from Tiffany to complete the outfit, but when Kennedy found out his wife was negotiating a loan of the precious jewels he refused to allow her to do it. Having already made the arrangements, Jackie told her secretary to tell Tish Baldrige to go ahead anyway, saying if Tiffany would back up her story that she was borrowing the pin from her mother-in-law, she would wear it along with the earrings.

'Tell Tish that if it gets in the newspapers, I won't do any more business with Tiffany. If it doesn't, we'll buy all our State presents there.'

With that settled, Jackie turned her attention to her outfit for the Inaugural Gala being planned by Peter Lawford and Frank Sinatra for the night before the Inauguration.

Earlier, Oleg Cassini had written her a letter offering his services, saying that America's First Lady, like the Queen of England, should have her own designer. Because Kennedy insisted she wear only American fashions in the White House, Jackie decided to appoint the Hollywood costumist as the official White House designer, the first time in history a First Lady had made such a designation.

The Kennedy men, who enjoyed partying with jet-setters like Oleg and his brother Igor (who wrote the Cholly Knickerbocker column), knew that the designer, a notorious womanizer, was not homosexual. So they felt they would be safe from a sex scandal which could embarrass the administration.

The socialite designer, who was once married to movie star Gene Tierney, was not accepted on Seventh Avenue; but he created elegantly simple clothes which Jackie liked, and he always catered to her like a Continental courtier, which she found amusing. Although he was insulted when she decided to work with Bergdorf's on her Inaugural gown, Jackie felt confident that she could control Cassini with regard to the rest of her wardrobe, which was occupying much of her time in Palm Beach.

Jackie did not see the Inaugural Ball as a party but as a political pay-off for campaign aides eager to feed at the public trough. Still, since she was going to be thrust into the public spotlight of television, she was determined to look the role of a regal First Lady, which in her mind was fathoms beyond the tiered ruffles and rhinestone jewellery of Mamie Eisenhower.

Chapter Eight

Jack Kennedy yearned to return to Washington and the round of parties awaiting him as President-elect. Eager to celebrate his victory, he accepted with enthusiasm every invitation offered. Although he had no appreciation for classical music, he looked forward to attending the Inaugural Concert at Constitution Hall. Five balls were planned throughout the city, and he was determined to dance at each of them. The plans for the Inaugural parade in front of the White House delighted him, although he would have to sit four hours barely shielded from the freezing weather. Having enjoyed for years the company of movie stars, he was excited by the many Hollywood celebrities ready to perform for him at the Democratic fund-raising gala being staged by Frank Sinatra and Peter Lawford. He was proud that Robert Frost would recite a poem at his swearing-in and that Marian Anderson would sing 'The Star-Spangled Banner'. In all, he approached the celebration with a small boy's sense of wonder and excitement.

Jackie, meanwhile, dreaded it as an ordeal. She loathed the prospect of roaring crowds, sweaty handshakes, klieg lights. She refused to attend the pre-Inaugural reception for distinguished women at the National Gallery of Art, a chore that would have placed her in a receiving line to greet 4,500 guests. She refused to go to the reception honouring Vice-President and Mrs Johnson, whom she snidely referred to as 'Colonel Cornpone and his little porkshop'. Nor would she appear at the Young Democrats' dance or the Governors' reception. She also declined the invitation of Mr and Mrs George Wheeler to attend a private dinner party before the Inaugural Ball and refused to attend the dinner-dance given by Jean Kennedy Smith and her husband in Georgetown. So the new President had to go to most of these activities alone.

Kennedy left Palm Beach before Jackie because she was

adamant about not returning until she absolutely had to. She insisted that Pierre Salinger issue a statement to the press saying, 'On the advice of her doctors, Mrs Kennedy will restrict her participation to the main inaugural ceremonies and festivities.'

Ordinarily, it takes a woman four to six weeks to recuperate from a Casearean operation, which entails an incision in the abdomen and uterus to deliver the baby. Although Jackie already had had two months to rest since the birth of her child, she had been greatly weakened by the operation and understandably refused to exert herself.

As Kennedy boarded a plane for Washington, newsmen approached him and one said, 'We understand Mrs Kennedy is the best-dressed woman in the world.' Kennedy gave them an icy glare and snapped: 'If you'd like to talk about something serious, I'll be glad to talk with you.'

He had dreaded this question from the moment he found out that Jackie had been elected First Lady of Fashion and selected for the official 1960 Best-Dressed Women of the World list. Earlier, when Jackie learned in Palm Beach that she was on the international fashion roster, she was ecstatic. But she tried to appear uninterested because her husband was furious, shouting that her 'inordinate interest in clothes' and 'fashion binges' would ruin his new administration.

'I can just see it now,' he yelled. 'The New Frontier is going to be sabotaged by a bunch of goddamned French couturiers.'

Joe Kennedy was highly amused by the incident. 'All my life I've been spending thousands of dollars to dress the women in my family,' he said, 'and now I've got to deny it all.'

As upset as the President-elect was his mother, Rose, who stoutly managed to congratulate her daughter-in-law but felt very hurt that she herself had not made the best-dressed list. Jackie dismissed the honour in an effort to spare the matriarch's feelings.

'Here I am on the best-dressed list for the first time in my life and I've been pregnant the whole year,' she said. 'I am glad to help the fashion industry, but I think I am being taken advantage of by retailers. I don't want to be a fashion symbol.

I just want to be appropriately dressed. Clothes are a nuisance to me. A nuisance. Dressing is just something that has to be done.'

Jack Kennedy, who knew better, began worrying about his wife's secret obsession with expensive French designs. She tried to reassure him. 'Jack, I promise to buy only American clothes in the future – only from Oleg – and I will even resort to muu-muus if it will save you embarrassment.'

Later she told a reporter, 'I am determined that my husband's administration – this is a speech I find myself making in the middle of the night – won't be plagued by fashion stories.'

She immediately instructed Tish Baldrige to issue a statement saying, 'Mrs Kennedy realizes that the clothes she wears are of interest to the public, but she is distressed by the implications of extravagance, or over-emphasis, and of the misuse of her name by firms from whom she has not bought clothes. For the next four years, Mrs Kennedy's clothes will be by Oleg Cassini. They will be designed and made in America. She will buy what is necessary, without extravagance – and you will often see her photographed in the same outfit.'

As First Lady, Jackie was never photographed wearing the same outfit twice. Spending a huge sum each year on clothes, she could easily afford to wear something different every day.

Despite her pleas that the Presidency should not be exploited, Jackie was much like Nellie Taft in working out personal arrangements for herself. Mrs Taft, while First Lady, was allotted only $12,000 for transportation. So she bought White House cars at a cut rate in return for allowing manufacturers to advertise that they were privileged to supply the President.

Jackie was not above playing favourites with certain photographers like Richard Avedon and Mark Shaw. She allowed them to photograph her and her children in the family quarters, then distributed their pictures to national publications, while insisting that Pierre Salinger protect her privacy by keeping ordinary press photographers away from the premises at all times. Jackie juggled her hairdressers, too, summoning her favourite, Kenneth Battelle, from New York for special evening occasions and sending a White House limousine to pick him up, while permitting Jean-Louis of Georgetown to do her hair only during the day.

'When she was First Lady,' Jean-Louis recalled, 'I had to go to the White House three or four times a week to do her hair and was kept waiting so often that I finally made her do her own wash and I'd come over to do the set. But then she always got Kenneth to come down and do her for state dinners. We both went to her house during the inauguration, and I did her hair for the swearing-in and Kenneth did it for the balls. She was a bit impossible.'

Leaving her children in Florida with their private nurses, Jackie finally flew to Washington the day before the Inaugural Gala. Arriving alone, she went directly to her N Street house in Georgetown. It was brimming with maids, valets, secretaries, hairdressers, movers, an Irish masseuse, and a husband receiving a constant stream of visitors.

Since she had consented to attend the private dinner party being given by the Philip Grahams before the concert and Gala, her personal maid, Provi, was rushing about trying to organize her wardrobe, neatly laying out her clothes for each occasion, assembling her accessories with meticulous attention, and even ironing her nylons. The President-elect was sent over to Bill Walton's for the day to do his official business so Jackie could have the house and the hairdressers to herself.

'Kenneth and I flew down from Lily Dache in New York to do Jackie's hair during the Inauguration and it was a madhouse, I can tell you,' said Rosemary Sorrentino. 'It was snowing like crazy, traffic was jammed all over town, and police were all over the place.

'Even though I was a lifelong Republican I always liked Kennedy, ever since the first time I met him in Hyannis Port when I flew up to do Jackie's hair during the campaign. I still remember she introduced me as her hairdresser and said, "Jack, Rosemary also does Marilyn Monroe's hair and Joanne Woodward and Lauren Bacall, too." We were sitting at a table having lunch and he was talking to Ted Sorenson. He looked up and the first thing he said was, "Is Marilyn

Monroe really as temperamental as everyone says she is?" He was so curious about Marilyn. Then he asked me if I knew anything about the primaries and how important they were. I had to tell him I didn't know anything about politics, period, but I could tell him anything he wanted to know about permanents. And do you know that man actually said, "Well, tell me all about permanents then," and like an idiot, I told him.

'When we arrived in Washington two days before the inauguration, we went to their house in Georgetown and stayed upstairs most of the time to do Jackie's hair and help her get ready for the Gala and the swearing-in ceremonies and the Inaugural balls. The President hated to see her in rollers. He was just horrified when he walked in once and saw me teasing her hair all over her head. He took one look at her. "Oh, my God," he said, and walked out of the room as fast as he could. He was very out-going and energetic then, but Jackie was terribly withdrawn and didn't seem to be having too much fun.'

On Inaugural day Kennedy attended Mass at Holy Trinity Church with Walton, then returned home to rehearse his speech behind closed doors in the downstairs library. While Jackie ate breakfast, Provi packed the ball gown to take to the White House for the First Lady to wear that evening. Because she was instructed personally to deliver the clothes herself and lay them out in the Queen's Room, the personal maid was unable to attend the swearing-in ceremonies at the Capitol. Tish Baldrige was already over at the White House, trying to supervise the movers and get ready for the afternoon reception.

President Eisenhower had personally phoned the Kennedys the night before to ask them to stop by for coffee before proceeding to the Capitol. Kennedy, who always complained about his wife's tardiness, pleaded with her to be ready on time so they would not be late.

He began dressing early that morning but got frantic when he couldn't fasten his collar owing to the weight he had gained after the campaign. All the secretaries in the house were called in to rifle through his drawers to find a collar that would fit. Finally, in desperation, he dispatched his chauffeur,

Muggsy O'Leary, to get one from his father who was staying nearby.

When the black Cadillac limousine pulled up in front of the N Street house, the President-elect, dressed in his cutaway coat, light pearl waist jacket, grey striped trousers and over-sized collar, was ready to go, but his wife, soon to become the third youngest First Lady in history, was still putting on her make-up.

'For God's sake, Jackie, let's go,' he said. Pacing back and forth, twirling his black silk top hat, Kennedy fidgeted nervously, waiting for his wife to appear.

Minutes passed without a word from Jackie. Finally she walked downstairs, looking elegant in a beige wool coat with a sable collar and a matching sable muff. Wearing high-heeled boots and a beige pillbox hat, she would be the only woman on the President's platform not wrapped in mink.

'I just didn't want to wear a fur coat,' she said later. 'I don't know why, but perhaps because women huddling on the bleachers always looked like rows of fur-bearing animals.'

'Just as the limousine was ready to go,' Mrs Sorrentino recalls, 'the President-elect dashed back into the house to get something he forgot, and he saw Kenneth and me standing at the window. When he got back in the car, he looked up at us and waved. And that did it for Kenneth, who up to then wasn't too impressed with him because of everything his clients were saying about the way Kennedy played around with other women. But when he saw that the man who was on his way to be sworn in as President wasn't too big to wave to us – the hired help – he began liking him.'

When the limousine arrived at the White House, the atmosphere between the Kennedys and the Eisenhowers was painfully strained, although everyone tried to be cordial. Later, during the drive down Pennsylvania Avenue to the Capitol, President Eisenhower was sitting in his place of honour on the right side of the limousine, and his wife, observing him, chirped brightly, 'Doesn't Ike look like Paddy the Irishman in his top hat?' Kennedy seemed visibly dis-tressed by the comment and Jackie, hardly amused, did not say a word.

At seventy, Dwight David Eisenhower was the oldest man to have served as President. At noon on 20 January 1960, the youngest man ever elected to the office would succeed him. John Fitzgerald Kennedy was also the first Roman Catholic ever to serve in the White House and the first US President to be born in the twentieth century.

All of this was symbolic to Jackie, who felt that she was witnessing more than a change in administrations as she listened to her husband deliver the shortest Inaugural message in history.

'I had heard it in bits and pieces many times while he was working on it in Florida,' she said. 'There were piles of yellow paper covered with his notes all over our bedroom floor. That day, when I heard it as a whole for the first time, it was so pure and beautiful and soaring that I knew I was hearing something great. And now I know that it will go down in history as one of the most moving speeches ever uttered – with Pericles' Funeral Oration and the Gettysburg Address.'

Unlike other Presidents, Kennedy did not kiss his wife after the oath-taking ceremony. Instead he bounded exuberantly off the platform as if he had momentarily forgotten she was even there. In the rotunda of the Capitol, when they met for the first time as President and First Lady, she tried to show her affection but was unable to express herself.

'I was so proud of Jack,' she said. 'There was so much I wanted to say. But I could scarcely embrace him in front of all those people, so I remember I just put my hand on his cheek and said, "Jack, you were so wonderful!" And he was smiling in the most touching and most vulnerable way. He looked so happy.'

While the President and First Lady attended a luncheon in their honour inside the Capitol, their relatives headed for a sumptuous buffet at the Mayflower Hotel hosted by the President's father. The Kennedys, Bouviers, Lees and Auchinclosses, most of whom had never met each other, milled around for a few minutes getting introduced.

'Before long, as soon as everyone had helped himself to a first course and found a place at a table, the various families had separated completely,' said John Davis, a Bouvier relative. 'Rose and Joe and the other Kennedys were seated together at five or six tables to one side of the room. The buffet table became a no-man's-land between the two camps, into which occasional forays were made by both sides. It was only after helping oneself to a lobster claw, say, or another slice of duck à l'orange, that an occasional exchange was made between a Kennedy and a Bouvier. Once served, each would retire to his corner.'

The temperature seldom rose above freezing that afternoon as the bands, soldiers, and crêpe-paper floats paraded up Pennsylvania Avenue and passed in review before the President and his First Lady. The new Commander-in-Chief was determined to salute each passing unit, but after an hour his wife got bored watching the martial display and, pleading fatigue and cold, summoned her friend Godfrey McHugh, the newly appointed Air Force military aide, to escort her back to the White House.

Getting up, Jackie shook hands with Vice-President Johnson and his wife, patted her husband on the shoulder, and left as the President continued cheering the frozen majorettes prancing by, their smiling faces numbed by cold.

As Jackie crossed the marble foyer of the White House, the Chief Usher welcomed her and escorted her upstairs to the Queen's bedroom which she would occupy, across the hall from the Lincoln Room where Kennedy would sleep.

The reception for the families of President and Mrs Kennedy was the first official party of the day to be held in the White House. Scheduled to start as soon as the parade was over, it began much earlier because the Kennedys, Lees, Bouviers and Auchinclosses, chilled to the bone, left the grandstand to seek warmth inside the Executive Mansion.

There they found an elegant table laden with great silver tea services and coffee urns, plus an immense punch bowl filled with Russian caviar. Rose Kennedy and Janet Auchincloss, acting as hostesses, began making introductions as everyone awaited the arrival of the President and First Lady. Soon guests started exploring the cavernous mansion, peeking into the East Room, peering at the gilt columns and enormous chandeliers, touching the damask walls, and examining the French eighteenth-century furniture.

When one relative started to walk up the stairway to inspect the State Rooms, a Secret Service man said the second floor was out of bounds. 'Mrs Kennedy's resting up there,' he said.

'But I'm her cousin.'

'I don't care – she left instructions she was not to be disturbed.'

Embarrassed by her daughter's refusal to come down to greet her relatives, Janet Auchincloss felt that Jackie should at least make an appearance at her first party as First Lady. She went upstairs to talk to her. Minutes later she returned looking chagrined and started making feeble but polite excuses.

'She's up in the Queen's bedroom, trying to relax,' explained her mother. 'She's taken a pill. I don't know if she'll be down.'

An hour later, after the parade was over, the new President walked in to be greeted by a swarm of sisters, cousins and aunts, all flinging their arms around his neck, excitedly offering their congratulations. Striding around the room, he greeted everyone and then asked where Jackie was. Someone said she was upstairs resting. After a quick drink, Kennedy announced that he had to go upstairs himself to prepare for the Inaugural Balls. The reception broke up, with some Bouvier relatives complaining that Jackie could have come down for a few minutes just to say hello to her family, some of whom had travelled thousands of miles from Italy and Peru.

'Later, over dinner,' said John Davis, 'the Bouviers concluded it was probably easier for Jackie, who had always been shy with her relatives, to face the entire nation on TV than it was to confront her four families on that momentous day. To America she was the new First Lady. To the Bouviers, Lees, Auchinclosses and Kennedys she was just Jackie. To play both roles required impossible shifts of emotional gear.'

During the parade Jackie had sent a White House aide to fetch Dr Janet Travell, who was sitting beside the President in the reviewing stand. 'When it was time to get ready for dinner – I couldn't get out of bed,' said Jackie. 'I just didn't have one bit of strength left and felt absolutely panicked. What could I do? Somehow I managed to get in touch with Dr Travell.'

The physician, who had been treating Kennedy with cortisone injections for his Addison's disease, rushed to the First Lady's bedside and gave her a Dexedrine pill. The amphetamine in the 'pep' pill would provide enough artificial energy to get her through the rigours of the evening ahead. Later she came to rely heavily on these pills to get herself moving.

Meanwhile, Kennedy hurried to get dressed because he wanted to go to the dinner party the Wheelers were holding in honour of the campaign caravan, a group of friends who had chartered a plane during the campaign and canvassed various states, drumming up votes. Members of the cabinet were included at the party, along with caravan members, Ethel and Bobby, Joan and Ted, Eunice and Sarge, Jean and Steve Smith, Pat and Peter Lawford, Arthur Schlesinger, Jr, Jeff Chandler, Angie Dickinson, Paul Fay, James Michener, Byron White and Stan Musial.

'Jackie was invited,' said one guest, 'but we knew she wouldn't come. It was no big disappointment to anyone, nor any great surprise for that matter. In fact, I think Jack probably had more fun without her there because he could really relax and not worry about her having a good time. After all, it was a party for the people who had worked for him – not her.'

'A party of people who had helped during the political campaign would not be something that would amuse Jackie,' said one of her friends, 'and besides, she knew perfectly well that the hostess, and every other woman there for that matter, would flirt with Jack and that kind of thing naturally irritated her. She had to put up with so much of that stuff anyway, she would never knowingly put herself in the position of watching women fawn all over her husband while she was ignored. She declined that invitation for good reason.'

It was well after nine when the President returned to the White House to pick up his wife. Vice-President and Mrs Johnson had been there for about twenty minutes, waiting in the Red Room by themselves. When Jackie heard her husband arrive, she walked downstairs in her sheath of white chiffon, her borrowed diamonds, and a billowing floor-length white silk cape. As the doorman escorted her into the room, Kennedy looked up and stubbed out his cigar. 'Darling, I've never seen you look so lovely. Your dress is beautiful.'

Turning to the doorman, he said, 'Bring some wine. This calls for a celebration.' After a champagne toast, the Kennedys and the Johnsons made the rounds of inaugural balls, stopping first at the Mayflower Hotel where former President and Mrs Truman were among the guests. Truman had strongly opposed Kennedy during the primaries, publicly accusing him of buying the Presidency, but once the convention made its choice and Kennedy became the Democratic nominee, the former President fell into line. En route to a meeting with Truman after the convention, Kennedy said, 'I guess he will apologize for calling me an SOB and I will apologize for being one.' From that time on Kennedy strained himself to keep on good terms with the former President, and made a point of making his first appearance at the Inaugural Ball Truman was attending.

To the strains of 'Hail to the Chief', the President and First Lady entered the ballroom, where cheering crowds erupted with applause and then stared in fascination at the guests of honour, refusing to dance.

'I don't know a better way to spend an evening – you looking at us and we looking at you,' quipped Kennedy to the adoring mob.

Jackie smiled, and stood like a beautiful statue as the flash bulbs popped in all directions. From her expression it was apparent that she enjoyed the attention but hated the clamour. At one point the President, thoroughly enjoying himself, spotted his friend Red Fay, who was escorting Angie Dickinson because his wife was in Switzerland. Kennedy couldn't resist teasing Fay about his glamorous date.

'As you stand here confidently basking in the appreciative glow of Hollywood's beautiful film star, Angie Dickinson, the hum of the cameras recording every loving emotion, I estimate it will take less than twenty-four hours before the bride will be able to enjoy this same intimate moment in the Swiss papers.'

When they reached the second ball at the Statler-Hilton, the President left Jackie sitting with the Johnsons in the Presidential box while he dashed upstairs to take a look at the private party Frank Sinatra was hosting for the celebrities who had performed the night before.

'I want to thank Sinatra personally – and all those Californians – who put on that great show last night,' he said, slipping away from his wife and the Vice-President. 'I'll only be a few minutes.'

Kennedy couldn't resist a party crowded with the gaudy presence of Ethel Merman, Nat King Cole, Jimmy Durante, Gene Kelly, Fredric March, Tony Curtis and Janet Leigh. By the time he returned, Jackie was peeved and let him know with a chilling look. She complained bitterly that no one was dancing and the ball lacked dignity. 'Just a bunch of people milling around like mesmerized cattle,' she said. The exuberant President paid no attention to her and began hopping from one box to another, greeting friends and receiving congratulations. Jackie remained seated by herself in the Presidential box.

She had had more than enough festivities by the time they reached the third ball. 'I just crumpled,' she said later. 'All my strength was finally gone, so I went home and Jack went on with the others.'

By 2 am, when he had made an appearance at every ball, the President said goodnight to the Johnsons and directed his Presidential limousine to Joseph Alsop's house on Dumbarton Street in Georgetown, where a few people had gathered for a nightcap. One young woman in particular was waiting for him to arrive. After Kennedy had a few drinks and a late night snack, the two of them went upstairs by themselves.

The next day, when the newspaper columnist was asked about Kennedy's late-night visit, Alsop was the soul of discretion. 'Well, the President was hungry,' he replied, 'and so I fed him terrapin.'

Chapter Nine

'This administration is going to do more for sex than Eisenhower's did for golf,' quipped Ted Sorenson during the early days of the New Frontier. His flippant prophecy proved accurate. With the protection of the Secret Service, the assistance of worshipful aides and the intercession of brothers and sisters, the new President was able to continue his free-wheeling lifestyle, which included sleeping with countless women, several of whom were young secretaries working in the White House.

While the First Lady was away from Washington, the President frequently amused himself with nude swimming parties in the White House pool. These were followed by cozy lunches in the family quarters and a session of sexual adventures in the Presidential bed. Then he would return to work in the afternoon, refreshed and apparently satisfied, ready to repeat the same pattern in the evening. On these occasions Kennedy would banish the servants from the second floor, leaving instructions to the staff that he was expecting company and to leave dinner in the warming oven, which he would serve himself.

Ordinarily, White House secretaries were summoned by phone to join the President for a swim before lunch. Other women would be contacted by Evelyn Lincoln, picked up in White House cars, and quietly brought into the Executive Mansion by Dave Powers. He would escort them upstairs to the family quarters, where Kennedy would give them a private tour of the White House and then serve them frozen daiquiris. Sometimes there would be another man present during dinner, but he would leave when Kennedy and the women retired to the bedroom. The President did not sleep through the night with his lady guests, but always returned to the rock-hard mattress in his own room. If the woman spent the night in the Lincoln Room, Kennedy appeared the next morning with a breakfast tray. After a decent interval, Dave Powers would arrive and wait for the President to leave for the Oval Office before unobtrusively escorting the young woman from the White House.

There were many women who enjoyed these warm, intimate interludes with Jack Kennedy while he was President. One in particular, a beautiful blonde socialite, was later mysteriously murdered in a crime that has never been solved.

Mary Pinchot Meyer moved to Georgetown after her divorce and spent four days a week painting in her studio, just a few steps away from her sister and brother-in-law, Tony and Ben Bradlee. She lived around the corner from her close friends, the John F. Kennedys. She had known Kennedy since college and occasionally had taken long walks with Jackie along the towpath by the old Chesapeake and Ohio barge canal when they were neighbours. Later, when she divorced Cord Meyer, an official with the Central Intelligence Agency, she attended many White House parties with the Bradlees.

Mary Meyer was enthralled that her friends were living in the White House. One night at a dinner party hosted by Carey Fischer, she regaled the guests with anecdotes about the domestic life of the President and First Lady and how much trouble they were having getting diaper service at the Executive Mansion.

'She went on and on about it until I finally asked in desperation why she felt the Kennedys' dirty laundry would be of interest to any of us,' recalled one guest. 'She turned on me with a vengeance and said, "Of course it's interesting. After all, he's the President of the United States." A few days later she sent word to me that she was sorry. She said no one's dirty laundry is interesting – not even the President's. But she was so captivated by the man she thought everything about him was fascinating.'

Mary's romance with Kennedy began a year after he was in the White House. According to a diary she kept, he first asked her to go to bed with him in December 1961, but she refused because she was having an affair with the artist Kenneth Noland at the time. Kennedy persisted, and when she broke off with Noland she began seeing him regularly the following year, visiting the White House two or three times a week for the rest of his Presidency, always when Jackie was out of town.

Mary confided details of her affair to her close friend, James Truitt, who says that one evening when she and Kennedy went into his bedroom Mary presented him with a surprise. 'I have something special for you,' she said. She took out a snuff box containing six marijuana cigarettes. The President said, 'Let's try it.'

'Mary said at first JFK didn't seem to feel anything, but then he began to laugh and told her, "We're having a White House conference on narcotics here in two weeks," ' Truitt recalled. 'She said that after they smoked the second joint, Jack leaned back and closed his eyes. He lay there a long time, and Mary said she thought to herself, "We've killed the President."

'They smoked three of the joints before he told her, "No more. Suppose the Russians did something now." She said he also told her, "This isn't like cocaine. I'll get you some of that." She said Jack wanted to smoke pot again a month later but never got around to it.'

Mary told Truitt that she loved Kennedy but realized their liaison would be limited to brief encounters, even though, as she said, he felt no affection of a lasting kind for Jackie.

A few months after the President was killed, the forty-three-year-old artist was painting in her Georgetown studio and decided to go jogging on the towpath. Donning a hooded sweater and a sweatshirt, she headed for the spot where she had occasionally taken walks with Jacqueline Kennedy. Although it was in the middle of the day, there were only a few people near the wooded embankment by the Potomac River. A gas station attendant remembers hearing a woman's screams coming from the vicinity of the towpath, crying, 'Someone help. Someone help me.' Then there was a gunshot and a few minutes later a second shot.

Running to the stone wall above the towpath, the attendant saw a black man in a light jacket standing over the body of a white woman in a hooded sweater. The police arrived minutes later and found the most beautiful girl of Vassar's class of 1942 dead with a bullet through her head.

Later that night, James Angelton of the CIA and his wife went to Mary's house to take her to a poetry reading. When no one answered the bell, Angelton checked her answering service and learned that she had been murdered that afternoon. They went immediately to the Bradlees to help make the funeral arrangements.

Before James Truitt left for his assignment as Tokyo bureau chief for *Newsweek*, Mary had talked to him about the disposition of her diary in the event of her death. She asked him to preserve it and show it to her son, Quentin, when he reached the age of twenty-one. When Truitt received word of the towpath murder, he managed to convey information about the diary's existence to Angelton, who was then CIA chief of counter-intelligence and a cherished friend of Mary Meyer.

Angelton immediately went to her house in Georgetown and, with the Bradlees and a college roommate of Mary's, looked desperately but in vain for the diary that recorded her intimate evenings in the White House with the President of the United States. The diary later was found by Tony Bradlee locked in a steel box filled with hundreds of personal letters. Mrs Bradlee turned it over to Angelton, who claims he took it to CIA headquarters and destroyed it.

The only known suspect in the murder was the black man in the light jacket who was seen by the gas station attendant standing over Mary Meyer's body on the towpath. Brought to trial, he pleaded not guilty. The prosecutor, lacking an eyewitness to the crime, had only circumstantial evidence on which to base his case. After many hours of deliberation, the jury reached a verdict of not guilty. The acquittal left the murder of Mary Meyer officially unsolved, opening her mysterious death to whispers of conspiracy. The diary, a secret for years, was never introduced as evidence, and everyone who knew about the affair kept it quiet until James Truitt broke the silence by going public with the story.

While sharing his White House bed with Mrs Meyer, the President also was seeing Judith Campbell, a stunning beauty he met through Frank Sinatra during the Presidential campaign. The affair nearly backfired, because during the period

Miss Campbell was visiting Kennedy in the White House, she was also sleeping with a Mafia chieftain, reputedly the most powerful boss in the Chicago underworld. FBI Director J. Edgar Hoover, keeping a close surveillance on the gangster, finally met the President to warn him that his White House mistress had close ties to organized crime. Hoover did not have to specify the frightening implications. The President quickly stopped seeing Miss Campbell.

This story probably would be a secret to this day if the Mafia boss, Sam Giancana, hadn't been gunned down in a gangland slaying days before he was to testify before a Senate committee investigating foreign assassinations and Giancana's links to the CIA. During the investigation of his murder the name of Judith Campbell repeatedly surfaced as the one person who was central to all the key characters in the intrigue, and she was forced to go public with the story of her affair with Kennedy.

Like Mary Meyer, she also fell in love with the President. She, too, remembers Kennedy telling her that his marriage was not happy. Without ever criticizing Jackie, he indicated that their relationship was far from satisfactory. 'There will be some changes in my life if I don't get the nomination,' he told her.

Other women who knew Jack Kennedy intimately while he was a Senator and later as President dispute the possibility of divorce. 'He was always very much married,' said one woman. 'There was never any question of divorce on his part or mine. We merely had an affair that was fun for both of us. He didn't get all he wanted out of his marriage so he went elsewhere, but Jackie was always his wife. He just wanted to have a good time. Jack absolutely hated to be bored. He could have never have been satisfied with only one woman.'

Another woman was involved with Kennedy during the last four years of his life and spent many evenings with him listening to Johnny Mathis mood music. She says frankly that she was only one of many conquests.

'I use the word conquest because that's how Jack approached the relationship,' she recalls. 'He did not perceive women as human beings, or even as objects of affection. He had a real need to capture and dominate, and he was quite straightforward about it.

'When he called me the night before the Inauguration, I went to his house in Georgetown. The presence of the Secret Service agents standing guard didn't bother him in the least. He couldn't have cared less. Jackie was not there at the time, and the man who opened the door was obviously expecting me. I was shown upstairs to the bedroom. An hour later, while Jack was putting on his white tie and tails, I left. I guess I was there to service him before he went out for the evening. I was fascinated by him at the time, but our love-making was so disastrous that for years later I was convinced I was frigid. He was terrible in bed, which I assumed was my fault. It wasn't until I had a loving relationship with someone else that I realized how awful my affair with Jack had been.'

Women who knew JFK intimately say he was a greedy man determined only to satisfy himself, with little regard for his partner.

A reporter in Washington admits that during a White House formal dinner the President approached her and said, 'Let's slip off to my office for a minute. I have something off the record for you.' Thrilled, the journalist, dressed in her floor-length gown and long white gloves, followed Kennedy to the Oval Office, where she was immediately tumbled on the couch. Within a matter of seconds her dress was over her head and she was gasping for air. When she recovered from the sudden tumble and looked around, the President was sitting at his desk, clothes all in order, going over some papers. 'He wasn't exactly a hesitant lover,' she said later, laughing about the incident.

Throughout the Presidential campaign Kennedy's insatiable appetite ranged from secretaries and stewardesses to desk clerks, hat-check girls, elevator operators and hotel maids, in addition to brief encounters with the Hollywood starlets and socialites that Peter and Pat Lawford arranged for him.

'During the campaign the only time Jack and I really had together was when we both stayed with the Lawfords,' said Joan Lundberg Hitchcock, a San Francisco beauty whose relationship with Kennedy lasted three years. 'We'd always meet at Peter and Pat's in Santa Monica,' she said. 'Sometimes we'd spend the night together in a small motel in Malibu and Jack would check in under the name of John Thompson. I spent a great deal of time on the road with him during the campaign in various hotels, but after he got the nomination we had to be a little more discreet. However, our relationship was no big secret to anyone in California but after it became so obvious to everyone, Pat Lawford put her foot down. I just wasn't allowed in their house again. It had become too well known by then.'

As President, Jack Kennedy did most of his entertaining in the White House. After he was caught hopping a fence in Palm Beach to swim with Flo Pritchett Smith, he realized he couldn't be so blatant. Still, he was convinced that none of the Secret Service men, his pals or the servants would ever say anything and, even if they did, no one would ever print it.

'Who would dare challenge the President in such a way?' asked a former White House aide. 'Kennedy felt quite safe, but instead of going out as he did in the past, he would bring women to the White House. Naturally, he encouraged Jackie to travel any time she wanted to, so he could use the White House for his private parties.'

The French Ambassador to the United States, Herve Alphand, and his wife, Nicole, spent a great deal of time socializing with the Kennedys, but once they were in the White House the Ambassador worried about the President's indiscretions. 'He loves pleasure and women,' he said. 'His desires are difficult to satisfy without causing fear of a scandal and its use by his political adversaries. That could happen one day because he does not take sufficient precaution in this puritan country.'

There was an instance during his Senatorial campaign against Henry Cabot Lodge when Kennedy was confronted with a picture of himself lying naked with a beautiful woman in Palm Beach. Worried that the Republicans might use the photograph to their advantage, Kennedy's aide finally brought the picture to his attention, fully expecting him to deny it. Instead, Kennedy merely grinned when he saw the photo. 'Oh, yes,' he said. 'I remember her. She was terrific.'

The picture never surfaced during the campaign and Kennedy never worried about his sexual indiscretions hurting him politically. He knew that no newspaper would publish a nude picture of him because of the immediate retaliation which would come from Ambassador Kennedy. In fact, he joked with reporters about his adventures, saying, 'I'm never through with a girl until I've had her three ways.' As much as they might enjoy his frank comments, he knew they would never print them.

For a while he was totally careless, but he became a bit cautious after the Georgetown run-in with Pamela Turnure's landlady, who wanted to use her photographic evidence of his affair to discredit his Presidential candidacy. The Duchess d'Uzes remembers when he visited Paris one year without Jackie and attended a party where he was lolling on the couch kissing a gorgeous French woman. A photographer took several pictures of them together and the Duchess, the former Peggy Bedford Bancroft, put the snapshots in her scrapbook. Weeks later, when she went to look for them, they had mysteriously disappeared. She was convinced that Kennedy had somehow managed to destroy them for fear they might haunt him later.

In the White House Jack Kennedy no longer worried about such matters and cavorted openly in front of his Secret Service men and servants. Traphes Bryant, the White House kennel-keeper for twenty years, remembers that during the President's private parties his girlfriends ran around nude, plunging in and out of the swimming pool and streaking through the White House corridors. Recalling one night when he was on duty, Bryant said, 'just as the elevator door opened, a naked blonde office girl ran through the hall. Her breasts were swinging as she ran by. There was nothing to do but for me to get out fast and push the button for the basement.'

Bryant claims that Jackie once found a woman's undergarment tucked in a pillowcase in Jack's room. She delicately held it out for him to see, saying, 'Would you please shop around and see who these belong to? They're not my size'.

J. Bernard West, the White House usher, knew about Jack Kennedy's private parties, but he remains discreet on the subject. 'The President did a good amount of private entertaining while his wife and children were away,' he says, refusing to elaborate.

Being married to a man like Jack Kennedy naturally had a debilitating effect on his wife, who outwardly feigned ignorance about what was so obvious to many around her. Inwardly, she protected herself by staying away as much as possible. Removed from the situation, she did not have to cope with it. Sheer mobility allowed her to put as much distance as possible between herself and her husband much of the time. As First Lady she spent four days of every week at her house in the Virginia hunt country.

Refusing to diminish the dignity she felt went with the role of First Lady, Jackie went to great lengths to avoid any situation in which she would publicly have to tolerate the flirtations of other women with her husband. She always needed to be in control of her social situations, preferring to be a hostess rather than a guest. She dismissed the extravagant fund-raising party held at Madison Square Garden to celebrate the President's birthday one year as nothing more than a vulgar public display.

More than 200,000 Democrats stampeded the Garden that night, paying $1,000 a ticket to watch Harry Belafonte, Jimmy Durante, Maria Callas and Ella Fitzgerald perform. The main attraction of the evening was the appearance of America's leading sex symbol, then the biggest show business celebrity in the world. When Jackie found out that Peter Lawford was arranging for Marilyn Monroe to sing 'Happy Birthday' to the President, she refused to attend. Instead she went to Glen Ora with the children, where the President joined her later the next day.

Almost nothing could have kept him from going to Madison Square Garden that night. When Marilyn Monroe slithered on stage in a dress that Adlai Stevenson said 'looked like flesh with sequins sewed onto it,' Kennedy was in his element. Marilyn gyrated on stage, twisted, oozed, and undulated for the roaring crowd, and then hugging herself with delight, she began purring, 'Happy Birthday, Dear Mr President'. The high art of mass seduction sent orgasmic screams pulsating through the Garden as the mob began shouting and stomping. Minutes later a very pleased President hopped on stage and said, 'I can now retire from politics after having had "Happy Birthday" sung to me by such a sweet wholesome girl as Marilyn Monroe.'

A few months later the dazzling blonde died from an overdose of sleeping pills. But prior to her death she, too, shared President Kennedy's bed, becoming yet another conquest during his sweet reign in Camelot.

'There's no question about the fact that Jack had the most active libido of any man I've ever known,' said George Smathers, his closest friend in the Senate. 'He was really unbelievable – absolutely incredible in that regard, and he got more so the longer he was married. I remember one night he was making it with a famous movie star and, by God, if Jackie almost didn't catch him right in the act. I also remember the cruise she arranged for his forty-third birthday when he was President. He shanghaied me to occupy her so he could go downstairs. Then he disappeared with someone else's wife. Jackie came over to me and said, "Where's Jack?" I pointed in the opposite direction and said, "He's over there, I think," hoping like hell she wouldn't go downstairs. He came back about ten minutes later. It was like a rooster getting on top of a chicken real fast and then the poor little hen ruffles her feathers and wonders what the hell happened to her. Jack was something, almost like a roto-rooter.'

That birthday party on 29 May 1963, was carefully arranged by Jackie, who was five months pregnant at the time. To amuse her husband she planned an evening cruise down the Potomac River on the *Sequoia*, and sent out invitations which read 'Come in Yachting Clothes'. She invited Bobby and Ethel, George and Rosemary Smathers, the Shrivers, Teddy Kennedy, a Boston politician, Clem Norton, a woman introduced only as Enid, Bill Walton, Mary Meyer, Lem Billings, the Bradlees, Red and Anita Fay, Charlie and Martha Barlett, David Niven and his wife,

Hjordis, Jim Reed and Fifi Fell. A three-piece band played through the evening, and there were many toasts and much carousing. Red Fay did his bawdy rendition of 'Hooray for Hollywood', an act that always convulsed the Kennedys but left everyone else dumbfounded.

Worrying about the President's back pain, Jackie asked Dr Janet Travell if there was any kind of shot she could give him to take the pain away so he could get through the evening with as little discomfort as possible. The President's physician assured her that there was such an injection but cautioned that it would remove all feelings below the waist. Kennedy ruled it out. 'We can't have that, can we, Jacqueline?' he said.

The President enjoyed himself immensely that evening and ordered the skipper back out to sea every time he headed the yacht in to shore. 'This happened no less than four times,' recalled Ben Bradlee, who mentioned that Kennedy's original orders had been to dock early just in case he wasn't having a good time.

The evening was a disaster for Jackie – and not just because her husband was downstairs romping with another woman. She had spent days scouring art galleries to find him an exquisite gift and was delighted when she located a beautiful, rare, antique engraving. The present cost over $1,000, and Jackie had it carefully boxed and wrapped.

Everyone crowded around the President as he opened his presents. Guests remember he was like a child as he ripped into the gifts, scattering the wrappings and ribbons, to see what he had. His favourite present seemed to be a scrapbook from Ethel Kennedy, a parody of the White House tour through her own Hickory Hill madhouse filled with children and dogs and cats and turtles. 'We've got everything out there except for cows.' she quipped, 'and they'll probably be next.'

Then Jackie presented Kennedy with her work of art. By this time the guests had had a lot to drink. Clem Norton lurched forward and inadvertently put his foot through the middle of Jackie's rare engraving, demolishing it beyond repair. There was a moment of stunned silence as everyone waited to see how she would react. She tensed visibly as she saw the antique smashed, but she didn't say a word. 'She greeted its destruction with that veiled expression she assumed,' said Ben Bradlee, 'and when everyone commiserated with her over the disaster, she just said, "Oh, that's all right. I can get it fixed." '

'That's too bad, isn't it, Jackie?' said the President, shoving the engraving aside and moving on to the next present. Jackie, totally unemotional about the incident, ignored Clem Norton for the rest of the evening and refused to speak to him.

As the dancing began, Eunice Shriver sidled up to George Smathers and in full view of his wife began flirting outrageously. 'Oh, George,' she said, throwing her arms around him. 'Don't you wish you had married me? You might have been President some day. Papa would have fixed it all up for you for the rest of your life. You made a big mistake, didn't you, Georgie?'

The Florida Senator smiled, and graciously asked the President's sister if she would like to dance. Excusing himself from his wife, he tried to whirl Eunice out of earshot of Mrs Smathers, who unfortunately heard every word. Eunice couldn't have cared less. 'C'mon, George, tell me why you didn't marry me. You really missed your chance is all I can say.'

'I kept telling her I already had a beautiful, sweet wife, but Eunice wouldn't let up,' he said later.

'No one was off limits to Jack – not your wife, your mother, your sister,' said Smathers. 'If he wanted a woman, he'd take her. I have no doubt that he gave it a run with Lee, but I don't think it happened. Jack was driven in that regard more than any man I've ever known. Just in terms of the time he spent with a woman, though, he was a lousy lover. He went in more for quantity than quality. I don't know how the women ever tolerated it.'

George Smathers and Jack Kennedy cut a wide swath on Capitol Hill during their days in the House of Representatives and later in the Senate. Both were handsome and, like matinee idols, they attracted hordes of eager young women. They spent plenty of time together, travelling frequently, taking vacations and playing golf. When the junior Senator from Massachusetts was thinking of marrying Jacqueline Lee Bouvier, he sought the advice of his friend.

'Jack came to me and said, "Do you think I ought to marry her?" ' Smathers recalled. 'Like a fool I said, "No, I don't think you should." I told him he was making a big mistake. Then, don't you know, ole Jack gets into bed with Jackie and, just to prove his love, the idiot says, "I'm going to marry you even though my best friend told me not to." Naturally, she wheedled out of him exactly what I had said and then she hated me for the rest of her life. She threw that up to me for years, even in the White House. Every time I danced with her, she'd say, "I know you didn't want Jack to marry me. You didn't think I was good enough for him." I'd say, "Oh, now, Jackie, where did you ever get that crazy idea," and she'd zero in on me with one of those looks of hers and I'd know damn well where she'd got the idea. Jack admitted to me later that he'd told her, the dumb fool. He absolutely ruined me with her after that. I just thought the world of her but she really had a hard time warming up to me, and understandably so.'

George Smathers was travelling with Kennedy in the south of France when Jackie lost her baby after the Democratic National Convention in 1956. It was Smathers who persuaded Kennedy to return to his wife's bedside and accompanied him back to the States, but Jackie knew they were both coming back under duress and hated interrupting their vacation. 'She always referred to that time we were horsing around in France when she lost the baby,' admitted Smathers. 'Even after they were in the White House, she'd bring it up. We'd go to those parties where the President would start dancing with Jackie and then all of his friends would cut in.

'When I danced with her, she always said in that affected little whisper of hers, "I bet you and Jack wish you were over in Vendôme, France, right now, don't you?" She was always sticking it to me.

'Jackie earned my respect and affection, though, because God knows she put up with a lot from that guy. More than any woman could ever be expected to tolerate, I'd say, and she damn sure knew the score. Jackie was a smart girl, and you'd have had to be a real dumb girl not to have known what Jack was up to. He was quite obvious about his other women. He never flaunted them to her but she knew. I wanted to kick him sometimes, he was so awful. One time I caught him messing around in the Cabinet Room in the White House and asked him how in the hell he thought he was going to get away with that kind of thing. He was convinced Jackie would never find out, but the fact of the matter is that she probably knew just about everything that was going on. By God, she knew. I was always on the defensive with her because she was constantly giving me the needle. She knew about my trips with Jack, but I'd have to deny everything just so he wouldn't get caught.'

During their days in the Senate George Smathers frequently covered for his friend. He made excuses to Jackie for Kennedy's late nights, saying they were working together on the Hill when actually he was at home. As a bachelor Kennedy would do the same thing with his sister, Eunice, who shared a house with him in Georgetown at the time. Once he told her he was going to the Rose Bowl game with Smathers, not realizing that his friend was supposed to be in town that weekend. While Kennedy was off with another woman, Eunice saw Smathers and his wife at a party and asked him why he wasn't at the football game with Jack. 'I don't mind covering for him when he told me about it, but when he'd take off and leave me holding the bag, I'd get after him,' said Smathers.

'Jackie never particularly liked me because she felt I was a bad influence on her husband. He told her stories about me moving in circles maybe I shouldn't have been moving in at the time. He was always using me as a cover for himself and I knew about it, but I loved the guy so what could I do? Call him a liar? I was catching hell for his running around and God knows he was a far worse influence on me than I ever could have been on him. I had trouble protecting my own limited territory from the guy.

'We had a nice little place on the river when we were both Senators, and we'd go there sometimes with a couple of girls.

I remember once I went down with this pretty little thing and Jack was already there with someone. He went into another room to make a phone call, and a few minutes later Evelyn Lincoln called and said I was wanted back on the Hill. So I left and was driving towards Washington when it dawned on me that I couldn't be wanted back there because the Senate was in recess. I knew then that ole Jack had pulled a fast one on me. So I turned around and drove back and entered the place just like I'd left it. What do you suppose I found when I walked in? There was the old rascal chasing both of the girls around, having himself a fine old time. He liked that sort of thing, you know. He was something, let me tell you.'

Jack Kennedy's sexual curiosity frequently led him into orgies at the Carroll Arms Hotel across the street from the Senate Office Building. While his colleagues were on the floor voting on various pieces of legislation, Kennedy would amuse himself with a couple of girls. 'That kind of thing was probably his favourite pastime,' said Smathers, who can barely repress a smile when he thinks of his old friend. Even as President, Kennedy managed to have a few gleeful romps in the White House with two or three women at a time.

'And not all of his women were good-looking,' said Smathers. 'He had a couple of dogs working for him in the White House nicknamed Fiddle and Faddle whom he was always playing around with. I couldn't believe it when I saw them. And if Jackie knew about them, I'm sure she didn't believe it either, because those two girls were the ugliest things I'd ever seen. They were awful.'

Ted Sorenson was right. President Kennedy's administration did more for sex than Eisenhower's could have done for golf with a hundred putters and Ben Hogan as Secretary of State. The atmosphere in the Oval Office seeped down to the rest of the staff, and most of the men around the President had at least one secretary stashed away in the Executive Mansion for safe-keeping. Compared to his brothers, Bobby Kennedy was a monk, and he objected strongly to what was going on in his brother's White House. He never criticized the President, whom he adored and protected fiercely.

One night when Gore Vidal attended a White House party,

Bobby Kennedy became irate. Gore began dancing with Jackie, holding her close and gliding across the floor like a Continental suitor. The sight of the President's wife being held so intimately by a man who publicly espoused bisexuality enraged the strait-laced Attorney-General. He stormed onto the dance floor and pushed Gore away from Jackie, saying, 'Don't you ever dance with the First Lady like that again. You make me sick.'

'Oh, Bobby,' said Jackie. 'You're so sweet to protect me, even when I don't really need it.'

Rather than cause a scene, Vidal sauntered away, leaving Jackie in the protective clutches of her brother-in-law. Jackie remained loyal to her brother-in-law by never seeing Gore Vidal again. Later Vidal wrote a devastating piece on the Attorney-General which tarred him as a ruthless man. That article ended the friendship between the famous writer and the famous Kennedys.

When Gore Vidal was ten years old his mother, Nina Gore, the daughter of a Senator, divorced Eugene Vidal and married Hugh D. Auchincloss. The family moved to Merrywood, the Virginia estate overlooking the Potomac River. They lived there for six years. When the marriage broke up, Hugh Auchincloss married Janet Lee Bouvier and Gore moved out of the upstairs bedroom so Janet's daughters, Jackie and Lee, could move in. Although they shared the same step-father, they did not meet right away. At that time Jackie was more impressed with their tenuous relationship than Gore was.

They didn't really become friends until Jackie married. Gore Vidal was one of her husband's biggest supporters. In 1960 he ran unsuccessfully for a New York congressional seat, and his relationship with the Kennedys was so close that Bobby helped him campaign. Jackie enjoyed being around him because he was handsome, witty, sexy, brilliant, talented, successful, charming, and an entertaining gossip. Being able to dish the dirt was a criterion for friendship with the Kennedys. They relished relationships with persons who were on a first-name basis with famous people who could discourse about their peccadillos.

'Jack was the most wonderful gossip,' said Gore Vidal.

'Much better than Jackie, probably because he had greater resources. But he was a marvellous repository. We would have long rambles about girls in Hollywood. He knew everything. But his was a continuing search for attractive women. That always came first with Jack.'

A few days before Kennedy went to Dallas he made a Presidential trip without Jackie on Air Force One. He flew to Miami to talk to a group of Latin-American newspaper editors, and despite his heavy schedule he still managed to find time to indulge himself before returning to the White House. His travelling companion on the trip remembers the President's escapades well. 'Oh, God, did he have himself a good time on that trip,' he said. 'There were a lot of women available to him by that time, and all were willing to be quite accommodating.'

Women were always available to Jack Kennedy, and throughout his marriage he made himself available to them. But sex was merely a one-dimensional, emotionally uninvolved activity to him which did not interfere with his role of husband. 'I think Jack loved Jackie in his own way,' said George Smathers. 'Those incidental pieces of ass didn't mean anything to him or have anything to do with his relationship with his wife. In the beginning Jackie was quite enamoured of him. She learned later.'

Despite her husband's philandering, Jackie hung on to that marriage because first, last and always she wanted to be Jack Kennedy's wife. She desperately needed to be married, and when she chose a husband she selected the most eligible Catholic bachelor in the United States, and considered herself the luckiest girl in the world to get him. Perhaps she was lucky in some ways, but not as Jack Kennedy's wife. Even as a husband the President of the United States remained a bachelor.

Chapter Ten

'I think the White House should show the wonderful heritage that this country has. We had such a wonderful flowering in the late eighteenth century. And the restoration is so fascinating – every day you see a letter that has come in from the great-great-grandson of a President. It was such a surprise to come here and find so little that had association and memory. I'd feel terrible if I lived here for four years and hadn't done anything for the house,' said the First Lady publicly. Privately she complained bitterly. 'It looks like a house where nothing has taken place. There is no trace of the past.'

The minute Jacqueline Kennedy realized the White House would be hers she decided 'to throw out all the crap', as she referred to the Grand Rapids reproduction furniture. She resolved to banish 'Pullman car ashtrays', 'Mamie's ghastly pink', 'the seasick green curtains', and all the 'eyesore ornamentation'.

'If there's anything I can't stand, it's Victorian mirrors – they're hideous,' she said. 'Off to the dungeon with them.' Declaring the ground floor hall 'a dentist's office bomb shelter', and the East Room 'a roller-skating rink', she began a grandiose plan to restore the mansion with authentic eighteenth- and nineteenth-century antiques.

This would be her sole project, her one major endeavour, her greatest commitment – and she worked feverishly to achieve it. Her husband balked at the thought of her tearing through the historic mansion, pitching furniture, and re-arranging everything in sight. The public uproar over the South portico balcony that President Truman added to the White House was very much in Kennedy's mind. 'I was warned, begged and practically threatened not to do it,' Jackie said, forging ahead anyway. She finally persuaded the President and convinced Congress that the White House must be restored to stand as the very finest American home in the land.

Her New York decorator, Sister Parrish, was asked to revamp the private living quarters. 'Let's have lots of chintz and gay up this old dump,' Jackie ordered. She secretly wired Stephen Boudin, head of Jansen, the famous Paris decorating firm, asking that he sneak into Washington as fast as possible to help her. Hiring a Frenchman to redecorate America's official residence was highly impolitic and, though she tried, she could hardly keep it a secret for long. Soon the bubbly little Monsieur Boudin was spotted bouncing around the White House, shrieking orders in halting English to the Chief Usher. 'He's merely a consultant to my committee,' lied Jackie.

With her decorators from New York and Paris on hand, Jackie and her committee hired curators, recruited scholars, formulated legislation, solicited contributions, and galvanized fine arts experts across the country to assist her. She wheedled and cajoled private donors to part with their historic furniture, flattered manufacturers into making costly donations, and begged museums to lend her over 150 priceless paintings. Within a year she transformed the President's house into a national monument with antiques and heirlooms worth more than ten million dollars.

'When I first moved into the White House, I thought, I wish I could be married to Thomas Jefferson because he would know best what should be done to it,' Jackie said. 'But then I thought no, Presidents' wives have an obligation to contribute something, so this will be the thing I will work hardest at myself.'

Jackie relied heavily on the generosity of multi-millionaire committee members like Mrs C. Douglas Dillon, Mrs Paul Mellon, Mary Lasker, and Mrs Charles Wrightsman, who contributed huge sums of money to the restoration project, frequently underwriting the cost of an entire room which in some cases ran as high as $250,000. The President was enraged by the gigantic sums of money being spent and pleaded with Jackie to slow down. He hit the roof when he learned that the antique wallpaper she installed in the Diplomatic reception room cost $12,500. He was further enraged when word leaked to the press and stories began appearing about Jackie's 'opulent plans for restoration'.

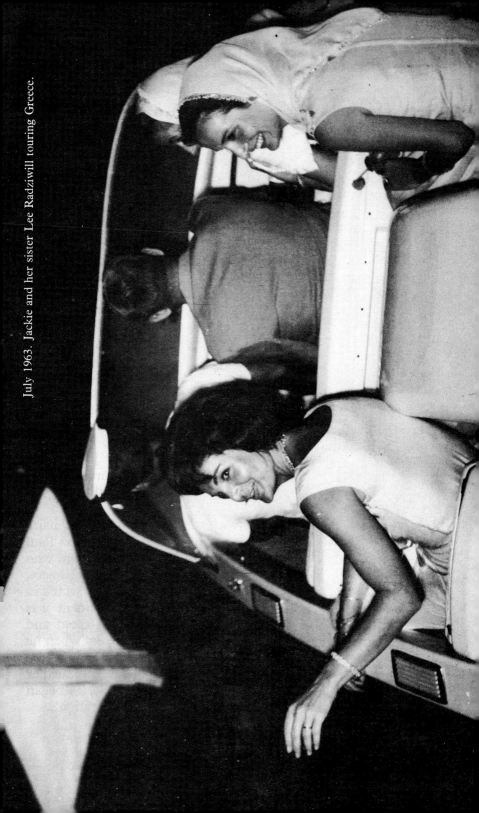

July 1963. Jackie and her sister Lee Radziwill touring Greece.

10 December 1967. Bobby Kennedy and Jackie at Democratic fund raiser at the Plaza Hotel, New York.

27 February 1969. Jackie and her dog leaving Chinese restaurant. Mrs I. M. Pei is sitting with her.

24 September 1969. Jackie and John Jr cycling in Central Park.

24 August 1970. Jackie with her niece on a shopping spree in Capri.

Jackie at a café in Capri.

7 November 1970. Jackie and Ted Kennedy at Logan Airport, Boston.

Jackie, Ethel and Joseph Kennedy at Cardinal Cushing's funeral, Boston

The nineteenth-century 'Scenic America' paper had been steamed off an historic house in Maryland and secretly transported to the White House, where it was gingerly applied strip by strip. Jackie managed to get the National Society of Interior Designers to underwrite the cost of the project, but when the President found out from the newspapers that new paper of exactly the same design was already available for a fraction of the cost, he was irate. Jackie tried to calm him down, saying the colours in the original wallpaper were much better. 'I don't give a damn,' he snapped. 'Twelve thousand, five hundred dollars is entirely too much money for wallpaper.' Years later, Lady Bird Johnson and Pat Nixon, on moving into the White House, were appalled by the dreary wallcovering which depicted what nineteenth-century Europeans imagined America to look like. But they lived with it. Rather than cause a public outcry, they left the wallpaper just as Jackie had installed it. When Betty Ford became First Lady, she said it was 'too depressing' and had it replaced.

Continuing her lavish restoration plans, Jackie swore her committee members to secrecy so there would be no more unfavourable publicity. Days later the *Washington Post* ran a story saying she planned to make the historic Blue Room white. 'The blue room won't be blue any more,' said the paper. The *Post* had photographs of Franco Scalamandre, the silkmaker, posed in his factory in front of the looms which were producing $60,000 worth of white-on-white silk he promised to donate for the transformation. Jackie immediately cancelled the silk and instructed Pam Turnure to call Scalamandre and tell him to take a full page ad in the newspaper to deny the story.

'How can I?' wailed the silkmaker. 'They have pictures showing the white fabric.'

Kennedy was incensed by the story. When he found out that *Newsweek* planned to run a picture of Scalamandre with the rolls of white silk, he called Ben Bradlee and insisted the photograph be killed. Bradlee obliged, and the picture never appeared in the magazine.

Scalamandre's public relations woman then fired off a strong letter to the President objecting to the public humiliation of her client. She said he had come to the United States to escape Mussolini's persecution and expected to find freedom in America. She never received a reply from the White House, and it was many months before Jackie consented to accept the Italian silkmaker's donation.

Continuing the restoration, she secretly ordered hand-woven $25,000 raw silk curtains from France, and directed her committee members to scour government warehouses and antique shops across the country to find exactly what she wanted. Soon the Red Room became cerise, the Green Room chartreuse, and the controversial Blue Room white. No corner of the White House was left untouched. Everything from little footstools and ottomans to settees and couches was sent out to be reupholstered with crushed silk and hand-painted brocade.

Jackie was a perfectionist – completely uncompromising. She ordered White House painters to re-do one room seven times until she got the exact shade of paint she wanted. The costly hand labour and time-consuming craftsmanship necessary to create the lavish blue and white fringe she demanded for her bedroom curtains cost over $50 a yard. She insisted that the wardrobe doors in her boudoir be adorned with realistic trompe l'oeil representations of the great moments in her life – the cover of JFK's prize-winning book *Profiles in Courage*, a photograph of Caroline, a model of a yacht. The painstaking ornamentation cost $800 and entailed fifteen days of work by one of Stephane Boudin's artists who was secretly hired to do the work.

After selecting $5,000 worth of chandeliers and a $35,000 eighteenth-century carpet, Jackie in a matter of weeks had nearly exhausted the entire yearly allowance for refurbishing the White House. Still, she was determined to finish her project no matter what it cost.

Complaining that there was no souvenir guidebook explaining the history of the White House for tourists, Jackie decided to publish one and sell it to people passing through on the public tours. The proceeds, she reasoned, would help finance the costly restoration. When the President objected that her idea sounded like profiteering, Jackie sent for the director of the National Gallery of Art, hoping to convince Kennedy that all historic houses had such booklets. Dispatching an impressive stable of experts to plead her cause, she outmanoeuvred anyone who opposed her – in this case even the President of the United States. Still, he fretted over her lavish plans, agonizing about the possible public outcry at the drastic changes she was making. He was convinced the taxpayers would never tolerate such extravagance.

Jackie reassured him. 'With Henry Francis duPont in charge of my committee, who would dare be critical?' she asked. 'Besides, he's a Republican.'

The octogenarian duPont was renowned as the country's leading expert on American furniture. As the benefactor of the Winterthur Museum, Jackie knew his credentials would impress the great-grandson of an Irish potato farmer who didn't know the difference between a cachepot and a credenza.

Determined to protect her privacy, Jackie contacted the Kennedy attorney, James McInerney, and instructed him to draw up legal affidavits for the White House employees. Giving the documents to the Chief Usher, she insisted that they be signed by all cooks, maids, butlers and secretaries, swearing never to write a word about the First Lady or their experiences in the Kennedy White House. Again, word leaked to the press and reporters wrote stories about 'JFK's Loyalty Oaths'. Headlines blazed across the country: 'WHITE HOUSE RULES SECRECY', 'JACKIE AND JFK MUZZLE MAIDS'. Editorials criticized 'the Kennedys' no kiss and tell policy', questioning the high-handed abuse of Presidential power.

Alarmed by the publicity, Kennedy tried to persuade his wife to withdraw the affidavits, but Jackie refused. He then turned to the Chief Usher.

'I want you to help me, Mr West,' he said. 'This pledge business is causing a lot of trouble. Would you take the blame for it?'

'I did ask the staff to sign the affidavits,' replied the usher.

'Good. Then we'll put out a statement saying it was your idea and you initiated it. It will look more official and less of a personal thing coming from you.'

While obsessed with her personal privacy, Jackie encouraged as much publicity as possible about her restoration project. She knew that press coverage increased public interest in the White House and stimulated more private gifts. So she willingly made appearances, posed for pictures, wrote letters and signed autographs. She was thrilled when Blair Clark, a vice-president of CBS-TV, contacted her about the possibility of a televised tour of the restored White House. He suggested a one-hour format, with the First Lady showing Charles Collingwood through the Executive Mansion.

'Oh, not Collingwood,' moaned Jackie. 'He's too square. Why don't *you* do it with me?'

Clark, then in charge of the news department, explained that he himself could not go on camera. But he assured her that he would oversee every detail of the production. When he mentioned that the network planned to donate $100,000 to her restoration project, Jackie quickly accepted Collingwood as the commentator.

The Kennedys vacated the White House one weekend so that CBS-TV could move in five tons of lighting equipment and cameras. Jackie spent Saturday and Sunday going over her notes for the broadcast so she would not have to read a script on camera. She appeared for the taping wearing a bright red two-piece suit, with a choker of pearls discreetly tucked into her neckline. This had become her fashion signature. With no idea of the complexity of such an operation, she only allotted three hours to complete the filming.

'I was the one who had to tell her it would take all day and we'd be lucky if it was only one day,' said Collingwood. 'She said she couldn't possibly give us that much time, because she had a dinner party to get ready for, but after I explained everything to her, she finally agreed to go through with it. We only had to do two retakes and one was my fault.'

More than 46 million Americans watched the Jackie Kennedy show, which was produced at a cost of $255,990. Refusing to use a script on camera, the First Lady strolled through the White House rooms, describing gifts and mentioning the names of private donors in a whispery little-girl voice that Norman Mailer said produced a small continuing shock in the country.

'... The voice was a quiet parody of the sort of voice one hears on the radio late at night, dropped softly into the ear by girls who sell soft mattresses, depilatories, or creams to brighten the skin,' Mailer wrote in *Esquire*.

'Do some of you remember the girl with the magnificent sweater who used to give the weather reports on television in a swarmy sing-song tone?' he asked. '... The girl who gave the weather report captured the voice of those pin-up magazines, dreamy, narcissistic, visions of sex on the moon. And Jackie Kennedy's voice, her public voice, might as well have been influenced by the weather girl. What madness it loosed in our public communications. And what self-ridicule that consciously or unconsciously, wittingly, willy-nilly, by the aid of speech teachers or all on her stubborn own, this was the manufactured voice Jackie Kennedy chose to arrive at. One had heard better ones at Christmastime in Macy's selling gadgets to the grim.'

'Television at its best,' wrote the *Chicago Daily News* of Jackie's tour. Norman Mailer disagreed, saying the First Lady moved like a wooden horse and sounded like an aspiring actress utterly without talent. 'Jackie Kennedy was more like a starlet who will never learn to act because the extraordinary livid unreality of her life away from the camera has so beclouded her brain and seduced her attention that she is incapable of the simplest and most essential demand, which is to live and breathe easily with the meaning of the words one speaks.' He concluded by lambasting the show as 'silly, ill-advised, pointless, empty, dull and obsequious to the most slavish tastes in American life'.

Kennedy was stung by Mailer's criticism and Jackie, savaged by the attack, redoubled her efforts to guard her privacy. When she hired Pamela Turnure to be her press secretary, she instructed her 'to just smile and look evasive', and added, 'My press relations will be minimum information given with maximum politeness.'

'I don't want some high-charging, tub-thumping fool with previous experience in charge,' said Jackie. She preferred to hire someone like herself, and in a way Pamela

Turnure was the obvious choice. She wore the same sleeveless dresses, triple-strand chokers and low-heel pumps as the First Lady. She sported the same bouffant brunette couiffure. She even copied Jackie's little rich-girl speaking manner. When asked to describe a tree, the twenty-three-year-old press secretary replied in a breathy whisper, 'Oh, it's an oh, so sort of a tree.'

Kennedy himself suggested Miss Turnure to his wife, saying she would be ideal to handle the kind of tasteful press relations Jackie wanted to establish. 'Of course he suggested her,' laughed George Smathers. 'That way she'd be right there in the White House close at hand when he wanted her.' But why would Jackie agree to hire a young woman who had had an intimate involvement with her husband? 'I think it was a smart move on Jackie's part,' replied Smathers. 'She figured, "I'm going to make this so obvious and easy for you that you are going to be bored." She knew what was going on.'

It is inconceivable that Jackie did not know about the neurotic landlady running around with her sign trying to capsize Kennedy's candidacy in 1960 with photographs of him visiting Miss Turnure's apartment. But, according to one friend, she never felt threatened by the young secretary. 'She just figured it was another one of Jack's flings, and she knew she could control Pam, that she would do exactly what Jackie wanted.'

Jackie's little tea party for the women of the White House press corps was an oh, so sort of a tea party, which hardly underscored her reputation as a scintillating hostess. Refusing to shake hands with 'the harpies', as she called reporters, she made Tish Baldrige receive the women. Jackie chose to show up later and spoke only to the few she could tolerate. To add further insult to the occasion, she served them soggy sandwiches and Kool-aid!

'God, I nearly died,' said one reporter. 'When the butler came around with a tray of drinks, I picked up what I thought was orange juice and nearly gagged when I swallowed this awful ersatz junk you mix up with water. It's something I wouldn't even let my kids drink or allow in the house, let alone serve to guests.'

The Kennedy motto 'Don't get mad – get even' became Jackie's own.

Unlike her husband, she never established a good working relationship with the reporters assigned to cover her. They, like her sister-in-law, soon were calling her 'the queen'.

'God, she should be living in Buckingham Palace instead of the White House,' sniped one. 'She treats us like peasants,' snapped another. 'Gives you a new appreciation of silent Bess Truman, doesn't it?' grated another.

Jackie continued to ignore them all with regal disdain. Then the President took to grabbing her and steering her towards the notebook-packing bunch, 'C'mon, Jackie,' he would say firmly. 'Let's go over and talk to the girls for a few minutes.'

As if greeting lepers, Jackie would smile sweetly, say hello and stand back, making her husband do all the talking. Kennedy was bemused. Once he confided to India's Prime Minister, 'My wife does not believe in a free press.' To the Shah of Iran he murmured, 'Jackie would like to incarcerate anyone who owns a typewriter.'

She could not keep reporters from covering White House state dinners, of course, but she once suggested stationing 'a couple of aides with bayonets near them'. In another memo to Pamela Turnure, she said the press could view the dining-room briefly before dinner – 'but it better be briefly' – and could watch the receiving line at official functions. 'But I wish we didn't have to have them come back after dinner – that is when they ask everyone questions and I don't think it is too dignified to have them around. It always makes me feel like some social-climbing hostess – Their notebooks bother me, but perhaps they should be allowed to keep them as, at least, you know they are press. But I think they should be made to wear big badges and be whisked out of there once we sit down to dinner.'

'I will send a copy of this memo to MacKilduff,' Jackie concluded. 'If we change the present arrangements he, or Pierre, should do it as it is not fair to you to pit you against the harpies. Also, they might take it better from a man.'

Still, the harpies were obliged to ferret out every possible tidbit of information. The public appetite for news about the glamorous First Lady was voracious. People clamoured to know everything about this fashionable young woman and her French clothes. Papers ran story after story on Jackie's pillbox hats, her bateau necklines, and her simple sleeveless dresses.

'Jackie is undisputed top femme in world,' headlined *Variety*. 'Her every seam is the subject of hypnotized attention,' claimed *Life* magazine. 'Jackie brings glamour to America,' said the *New York Daily News*.

In 1961 the country had never known a First Lady who was so young and beautiful. Accustomed to the sturdy black oxfords of Bess Truman and Mamie's folksy canasta games, people were mesmerized by Jacqueline Kennedy's couturier fashions and private fox-hunts. They were especially charmed by her children and devoured everything written about Caroline, who squealed merrily through the White House on her tricycle and tromped around in her mother's high heels. The little blonde youngster delighted readers with her outrageous comments. Her most famous remark came when a reporter asked her what her father was doing.

'He's not doing anything,' she said. 'He's just sitting up there with his shoes and socks off, doing nothing.'

Riding in an open convertible with his daughter, President Kennedy enjoyed watching her handle several photographers running towards the car. Imitating her mother, she raised her hand imperiously. 'No photographs, please,' she said.

When he introduced her to Sam Rayburn, the Speaker of the House of Representatives, Caroline stared at his bald head. 'Why haven't you got any hair?' she asked.

After showing the redecorated White House living quarters to Eleanor Roosevelt and Henry Morgenthau, the President offered them both a drink. Caroline, dancing at his heels, piped up. 'They've already had one, Daddy. See, there's their glasses.'

Understandably, President Kennedy's popularity soared. At one point the polls showed him standing higher in public esteem than the Democratic party as a whole. 'The difference is Caroline,' grumbled one Senator, 'and there's nothing we can do about it.'

One day in the Oval Office, Caroline picked up the phone. 'I want to speak to Grandpa,' she said. The White House operator immediately rang Joseph Kennedy in Palm Beach and Caroline chattered away. Then she turned to her father. 'Do you want to speak to Grandpa?'

'Caroline, what are you doing?' yelled the President. As he picked up the phone to speak to his father, Caroline grabbed another phone and told the White House operator to ring Mrs Charles Wrightsman.

'Now, I'm going to call Jayne,' she said.

Kennedy encouraged the friendly, photogenic little girl to talk to reporters at every opportunity. Photographers were allowed into his office specifically to take her picture. Jackie exploded. She loathed seeing her children used as publicity attractions for political ends Every time she saw them in a photograph which she had not authorized, she fired off a memo to Pierre Salinger, asking him what in God's name he was doing by allowing this kind of forbidden coverage. Salinger would meekly explain that the pictures were taken at the request of the President. 'I don't give a damn,' howled Jackie. 'He has no right to countermand my order regarding the children.'

When *Look* magazine wanted to do a photo essay on the President and his son, Salinger presented the idea to Jackie. She went into a tirade, saying it was too much of an invasion of the family's privacy. The President smiled when Salinger repeated her objections. 'Let's hold off on it for a while, then,' he said. 'We'll take another look at it the next time she leaves town.'

As soon as Jackie left for Italy to holiday with her sister, photographers were summoned to the Oval Office to take pictures of little John hiding in the cubby hole under the President's desk. When the First Lady returned, Salinger told her what had happened. Jackie screamed that he had no right to exploit her children.

'Just wait and see. You'll love the pictures,' said Salinger.

'You always say that,' snapped Jackie.

Privacy became such an obsession that she ordered high rhododendron bushes planted on the White House grounds to shield Caroline's playground from view. She instructed the Secret Service to confiscate film from photographers who took pictures without her permission.

Stories about the children's pets also sent her reeling. After reading one innocuous account of Charlie, the Kennedy's Welsh terrier, she stormed out to find the kennel-keeper. 'Don't you ever give another thing to those damn nosey reporters,' she yelled. 'I'm sick of their stories and I don't want you to ever tell any of those witches anything about me.'

The press, in turn, worked harder to get Kennedy stories. Features abounded about Caroline and John-John as well as their pet hamsters Marybell and Bluebell, Tom Kiteen, their yellow canary, Robin, their pony Macaroni, and Pushinka, the fluffy white puppy – a gift from Nikita Khrushchev. 'I'm so damn sick of reading about Macaroni I could scream,' said Jackie at one point, firing off another memo to Salinger.

When a photographer followed Jackie to Middleburg and took a picture of her being thrown off her horse, she immediately phoned the White House. She told her husband to bar the photographer from ever using the picture on grounds that it was an invasion of her privacy. Kennedy chortled. 'I'm sorry, Jackie,' he said, 'but when the First Lady falls on her ass, that's news.' The photographer sold his picture to *Life* magazine for $13,000.

Fortunately for Jackie, there were no photographers around the second time she fell. Her horse stepped in a gopher hole and threw her headfirst to the ground. She was knocked cold, swallowed her tongue, and turned purple before another rider galloped up to revive her. The First Lady dusted herself off, remounted and rejoined the hunt. 'Thank God, those damn photographers didn't get a picture of that,' she sighed.

Traumatized by the loss of her privacy, Jackie said, 'sometimes I think you become sort of a – there ought to be a nicer word than "freak" but I can't think of one.' She despised the title of First Lady and was livid when she saw messages addressing her as such. 'Please, Mr West,' she told the White House usher, 'the one thing I do not want to be called is First Lady. It sounds like a saddle horse. Would you notify the telephone operators and everyone else that I'm to be known simply as Mrs Kennedy and not as First Lady.'

She also abhorred seeing herself referred to as 'Jackie' in print. 'It is not dignified for the wife of the President to be addressed so familiarly,' she said. 'Why should I be called by a boy's name when I have such a beautiful name?' Firing off a memo to Pierre Salinger, she ordered that reporters be told they must refer to her publicly as Jacqueline Kennedy or Mrs John F. Kennedy – never Jackie. Photographers also received instructions. They were never to take a picture of the First Lady smoking. The President backed up this command because he did not like Jackie's chain-smoking habit and felt that pictures of her with a cigarette in her hand would be unseemly.

'He's such a bear about my smoking,' said Jackie, 'that I started encouraging him to have a cigar after dinner. That way he doesn't complain so much about my cigarettes.'

Hating the title, she was contemptuous of the traditional role of First Lady and refused to play the part. 'Why the hell should I traipse around to hospitals playing Lady Bountiful when I have so much to do here to make this house liveable?' she asked. 'I'll just send them some fruits and nuts and flowers.'

'She's not going to confine herself to the Easter Seal Child type of ceremony as First Lady,' explained Bill Walton.

As First Lady, Jackie refused to attend political events. 'Poor Jack,' she told one friend. 'He thinks if I don't go to those silly fund-raisers, he'll be impeached.' She shunned ceremonial duties and ignored anything she considered 'boring and a useless waste of my time'. That included voting.

Rather than accompany the President to Boston to vote in the November general election, Jackie stayed at Glen Ora while the White House issued a false statement saying she cast her ballot by absentee vote. 'Jack's not running, so why should I vote?' she asked a friend. 'I couldn't care less about who is elected to the House or Senate.'

Despite her husband's commitment to civil rights, Jackie refused to attend a luncheon of the National Council of Negro Women. She told Tish Baldrige, 'Just send them a little message and sign my name.' Then she escaped to her country retreat in Virginia to go fox-hunting. Later she made Tish represent her at the Congressional wives' prayer breakfast. 'I can't bear those silly women,' she said.

'Jackie crucified those dumb Senate wives and the stupid meetings they had to exchange recipes,' said a friend. 'Once she got to the White House she refused to have anything to do with them. God, how she mimicked them, making fun of their dowdiness and slobbering devotion to their husbands' political careers. She said that Lady Bird Johnson was such a pigeon she'd run down the street naked if Lyndon wanted her to. Jackie didn't know the first thing about the kitchen because she didn't know how to cook, so when she absolutely had to go to one of those meetings, she went to the chef to get her recipes.

'When the President absolutely insisted that Jackie make an official appearance, he was always sorry because she would arrive late and leave early,' said a Presidential aide. One day Kennedy insisted that Jackie entertain the wives of a group of newspaper editors convening in Washington. She invited the women to tea in the Blue Room, arrived at the function five minutes late, spent twenty minutes in the receiving line, and, with a smile and a wave, she vanished. Later she opened the Washington Flower Show, another traditional ritual assigned to First Ladies, and set a record by staying only fifteen minutes.

'Why scream at me?' snapped Jackie. 'You're the one who got caught eating meat on Friday.' She never let Kennedy forget the Friday his press secretary carelessly announced that the Catholic President had consumed a breakfast of orange juice, coffee, two poached eggs, toast and bacon. Salinger later tried to bail out, explaining to reporters that he had made a mistake. No bacon was served, he said, and the President did not eat meat on Friday. 'If they bought that story,' said Jackie later, 'they're dumber than I thought they were.'

The President strived hard to preserve his public image as a church-going man. 'Because Kennedy was a Catholic – and the first Catholic President in the White House – everybody was always wondering exactly how Catholic he was,' said Fishbait Miller, the Doorkeeper of the House of Representatives. 'Did he go to church? Or did Jackie make him go? Well, I dealt a lot with Secret Service men because of the many visits Presidents make to Capitol Hill, and though they seldom let anything slip that they shouldn't, one day I couldn't help overhearing two of them talk about what happened the Sunday before, when the Kennedys had gone to the Catholic church on Pennsylvania Avenue, only about eight blocks from the White House.

'As one Secret Service man was telling the other, the First Lady had said to the President, quite angrily, "Come on now, you son of a bitch. You got yourself into this and you know your public demands it. So get your damn tie and coat on and let's go." '

Democratic party leaders soon were calling for the First Lady to be as publicly visible as Eleanor Roosevelt. They wanted her to visit the handicapped, sponsor charity bazaars, and focus the prestige of her position on political affairs by accompanying her husband to fund-raisers. Jackie refused.

'The official side of my life takes me away from the children a good deal,' she said. 'If I were to add political duties, I would have practically no time with the children, and they are my first responsibility. My husband agrees with this. If he felt I should go on these trips, I would.'

Instead, she escaped to her rented country retreat in Virginia four days of every week, forcing the President to recruit his mother or one of his sisters to act as White House hostess.

'People told me ninety-nine things I had to do as First Lady,' Jackie told Nancy Tuckerman, 'and I haven't done one of them.'

Chapter Eleven

In the beginning Jackie was querulous about the White House. 'I felt like a moth banging on the windowpane when I first moved into this place,' she said. 'It was terrible. We couldn't even open the windows in the rooms because they hadn't been opened for years. When we tried the fireplaces, they smoked because they hadn't ever been used. Sometimes I wondered, how are we going to live as a family in this enormous place.'

'It must be wonderful, though, being the President's wife,' said a friend visiting the White House for the first time.

'So I'm his wife. So what?' snapped Jackie.

'But look at all the perquisites – the servants and maids and butlers. That must be fantastic.'

'Oh, yes,' she said. 'It's just like the French court. You ring a little bell and the serfs come running to slobber all over the King and Queen. Thank God that Jack is accustomed to this kind of life. Otherwise, it would be so corrupting to move in here and suddenly be surrounded by all this luxury.'

Baffled by all the servants, Jackie kept asking the Chief Usher if the seventy serfs had enough to do. 'I saw what it was like eating off trays with four butlers hovering around,' she said. 'Don't you think they could be better employed elsewhere?' Later she told a friend, 'It's all so embarrassing. Just ordering hamburgers for lunch is a major production.'

Jackie floundered as she tried to organize the details of her new life. 'Initially, she was overwhelmed by everything,' said Betty Spalding, 'and kind of lost. I remember once she was making various lists and trying to run everything and just couldn't seem to get coordinated. So Jack offered to help her by taking over the budget and handling the money and expenditures. He said he enjoyed that kind of responsibility and was more than willing to help her out in any way he could.'

The President called Tom Walsh in Ambassador Kennedy's New York office to set up a bookkeeping system for the personal budget. Mary Gallagher was assigned the duty of keeping the books. Struggling with the monthly records, Mrs Gallagher regularly submitted her financial statements to the President. Each time he saw the extravagant figures recorded for his wife's personal expenses, he exploded. Soon Mrs Gallagher began taking the long way around the White House to avoid meeting him. 'I just couldn't stand the reproachful look on his face,' she said.

He fumed over items such as 'Diette clock from Paris – $1,000' and 'Givenchy clothes – $4,000'. He criticized her spending $900 for riding accessories and $800 for a vacuum cleaner for her horses, but the toppling rage came when he spotted 'Department stores – $40,000'.

Storming out of his office with the statement, Kennedy roared over to the living quarters.

'What in the hell does this mean?' he bellowed.

'Oh, Jack, I don't remember,' whispered Jackie.

'What do you mean you don't remember?'

'Well, I can assure you it wasn't for furniture or a sable coat, or anything like that. Just little odds and ends we need around here. A few bathing suits – some clothes for the children and ...'

Kennedy was stupefied. Later, when he received Mrs Gallagher's statement of expenses for the year, he was enraged. Jackie's personal expenditures for the first twelve months in the White House, categorized as clothing, art, food and liquor, medical, jewellery, beauty salon and gifts, totalled $105,446.14.

'Do you realize I only make $100,000 a year as President?' Kennedy asked. 'If we didn't have a private income, we'd be bankrupt.'

That night at dinner he announced that he was calling in Carmine Bellino, an accounting expert and longtime family friend. Renowned for deciphering financial records of the Mafia, Bellino recently had been called by Bobby Kennedy to straighten out Ethel's finances. 'They were so tangled,' Bobby told the President, 'that Bellino had to move into the Hickory Hill house to find out who was stealing what.'

Jackie cringed. 'Maybe Carmine can save you from going off the deep end,' said her husband. 'At least he'll be able to tell me why it's costing us more to live here than it did in Georgetown, where we had to pay for everything. We should at least be breaking even here with all the services provided.'

Kennedy had cracked down on Jackie before. Ranting about her willful disregard for money, he accused her of being a spendthrift. Annoyed by his ravings, she called him a cheapskate. Other times she merely let him carry on. 'It's good for Jack to get it out of his system,' she told a friend.

In those days the bills were sent directly to New York and paid by the Ambassador's office. Occasionally Tom Walsh called Kennedy to question a large expenditure. 'That's when he would come home at night and start howling about money,' said Jackie.

Kennedy's vast income came from a million-dollar trust fund established by his father. His only concern was to live within that income without ever digging into his capital. When Tom Walsh pointed out certain areas where he might be going overboard, he said, 'Well, let me have the details on that and I'll find out why.' Inevitably, the reason was Jackie's spending.

'He thought he should remain within his income,' said Walsh. 'There is no doubt about that. All good husbands are that way.'

Kennedy had been giving his salary to charity ever since he entered Congress in 1947, and he continued the practice when he became President. When his wife learned that he was giving away his salary, she was annoyed. 'I could sure use that money myself, Jack,' she said.

Kennedy willingly dipped into his capital for the Presidential campaign, spending $13 million to finance his election. This aggravated Jackie, who felt that politics was a waste of money, especially when it curtailed her pleasures. 'I don't understand it,' she said. 'Jack will spend any amount of money to buy votes but he balks at investing $1,000 in a beautiful painting.'

When he complained about the money she spent on clothes, Jackie said she had to do it because he was in politics. 'I have to dress well, Jack, so I won't embarrass you. As a public figure, you'd be humiliated if I was photographed in some saggy old housedress. Everyone would say your wife is a slob and refuse to vote for you.' That argument fell on deaf ears.

'Kennedy's only complaint about Jackie in all the years I ever knew him was that she spent too much money,' said George Smathers. 'And I always laughed when he'd start bitching about it because if there was any guy who had no regard for money, it was Jack Kennedy. I'd travelled all over Europe with him for years and always got stuck with the bills. Finally, I had to work out a deal whereby I'd pick up all the checks and then bill him at the end. That worked out fine, and that's how we did our business from then on, because he never carried any cash.

'When Jack first arrived in the Senate his father hauled him over to my office and said, "George, I want you to do us both a big favour and explain to Jack here about money. He thinks it grows on trees and you find it laying around the street like gravel. I want you to tell him it's damn hard to make a buck these days and money needs to be kept track of. Jack doesn't know or understand why he should even keep records of his expenditures."

'I remembered that conversation every time I visited Jack in the White House and he'd begin screaming about Jackie. "That Jackie," he'd yell. "She's unbelievable. She absolutely does not appreciate the value of money. Thinks she can keep on spending it forever. God, she's driving me crazy – absolutely crazy, I tell you."

'I couldn't believe it, and I'd tell him so, but then he'd start hollering, "But, George, she's run through all the government funds and is starting to draw on my personal account. If the taxpayers ever found out what she's spending, they'd drive me out of office." I still laughed at him, and he never could convince me that Jackie was worse than he was about money.'

Jackie felt that her husband was unreasonably tight-fisted but, rather than harangue with him over money, she simply avoided discussions of it. Unless, of course, he brought up the subject himself. Even then she refused to tell him exactly what she spent.

'I remember two new, expensive rugs she put in the Georgetown house that she hid in her budget and paid a little bit on each month,' recalled Bill Walton. 'She didn't ever want him to know how much they cost, because they had been wild extravagances. He was crazy about them, of course. But there was that kind of little playback.'

That little playback in Georgetown escalated into guerrilla warfare in the White House. As President, Kennedy worried that Jackie's French fashions, French chef, and French decorator would ruin him. Publicity about an opulent life-style was the last thing he wanted, and he implored his wife to cut back. Jackie promised to economize.

Summoning the Chief Usher, she said, 'I want you to run this place just like you'd run it for the chintziest President who ever got elected. We don't have nearly as much money as you read in the papers. The bills for our personal enter-tainment have been astronomical, Mr West, and we've got to cut down drastically. Do you think we could buy our food where the White House buys its food?' The Usher made arrangements to transfer the Kennedys' personal grocery account from the expensive Georgetown market they had been using to the same wholesalers who serviced the Executive Mansion.

Jackie called Tom Walsh in New York to ask if there was any way she could get a tax deduction on Glen Ora by declaring it a farm. 'The four cows Lyndon gave us have already produced three cows and a bull,' she said, 'and if I sell them for beef, wouldn't that make it legitimate?'

Hanging up, she turned to her secretary: 'Mary, where do you think my heaviest expenses lie?'

'Clothing,' replied Mrs Gallagher.

'Oh, yes, Mary, and from now on if I ever order anything you think I really don't need, just slap my hand.'

Next she dictated a memo to Tish Baldrige: 'Food and liquor have been flowing through here as if it were the last days of the Roman Empire.' Admitting that she might have given the impression everyone could live off *pâté de foie gras* without ever thinking of the cost, Jackie said, 'Things have changed. We've just got to cut back.'

Minutes later she called Kenny O'Donnell, the President's appointments secretary. 'Carmine Bellino is after me, Kenny, and I need your help. Our liquor bills are sky-rocketing and Jack insists we do something about it. So would you please tell anyone who wants to give him a gift to make it booze.'

'I don't want the White House to get a reputation for serving Lucullan repasts,' said Jackie.

When criticized for using French to describe the menus, she backtracked. 'Change Oeufs Mollet à la Reine to Eggs Mollet,' she ordered. When *Newsweek* reported three French wines had been served at the President's lunch for newspaper editors, she called Ben Bradlee to complain. 'It was not three French wines,' she said. 'It was only one, and it was domestic – Almaden Cabernet Sauvignon.'

The economizing First Lady told the White House kitchen to stop sending food gifts to orphanages and begin using them for the Kennedys' private dinners. Provi was told to 'order something cheap' for Jackie's bubble bath. The mail room was instructed to stop giving away the gifts flowing in for Caroline and John-John. Instead, Jackie wanted them delivered to her so she and her sister could divvy them up for their children as Christmas presents.

'Everyone's falling in line,' she told the President a few nights later. 'We're all trying to economize, and I think you'll be quite surprised by the results.'

Privately, she groused about Kennedy's stinginess. Once, while lunching with friends at La Caravelle in New York, she said, 'The President seems more concerned these days with my budget than with the budget of the United States.'

But her compulsive buying continued. The storage closets on the third floor of the White House bulged to capacity with clothes that had never been worn. 'You should see the clothes Jackie has upstairs,' Lee Radziwill told a White House guest. 'They're unbelievable.' Not even Carmine, the scourge of mobsters, could stop her spending sprees. By the end of the second year Jackie's expenditures soared to $121,461.61.

Next to clothes, her biggest expense was renting Glen Ora. The owner had insisted that the Kennedys sign a lease stipulating that any changes they made would be removed when they left, restoring the house to its original condition. Jackie spent $10,000 redecorating when she moved in. Later she was forced to spend over $10,000 tearing off the wallpaper she had installed, repapering, replacing all the rugs and curtains she had ripped out, and recovering the 9,000 square yards of pasture she had converted into a golf course for the President.

'That was a total waste of money, Jackie,' stormed Kennedy.

'No, it wasn't,' she replied. 'Glen Ora is my salvation. I'd die if I didn't have some place to go to get away from the terrible pressures around here.'

The President was incensed, but Jackie felt the money was well spent. Glen Ora was her escape. 'This is an office building, not a home. It's almost a prison,' she wailed.

Jackie never expected that the day would come when she would hate to leave the White House and give up her royal privileges as First Lady. She felt she could not do anything, go anywhere, or say anything without public scrutiny. Refusing to accept the duties suddenly thrust on her as a public figure, she could hardly enjoy her new surroundings. While Kennedy was delighted to live in the White House as President and took pride in showing off the official residence to his friends, Jackie remained unawed. To her, the White House meant losing control of her life and becoming a target for public comment and political gossip. She was sickened that her entire existence was regulated by Presidential protocol. Her privacy shattered, she felt she had nothing to live for except 'a bunch of women's silly little tea parties'.

She knew she had no choice but to put up with the claustrophobic responsibilities, but she was too proud and too stuborn to surrender. Publicly she presented a regal appearance, controlled and smiling sweetly. Privately, she raged against her public role, despising the hypocrisy of it all, and yet still enjoying the adulation.

'At one moment she was misunderstood, frustrated and helpless,' said her friend Robin Douglas-Home. 'The next moment, without any warning, she was the royal, loyal First Lady to whom it was almost a duty to bow, to pay medieval obeisance. Then, again, without warning, she was deflating someone with devastating barbs for being such a spaniel to treat her as First Lady, and deriding the pomp of politics, the snobbery of a social climber. It was Pavlovian treatment.'

Jealous of her husband's overwhelming commitment to the Presidency, she withdrew, using her children as an excuse to avoid official duties.

'It isn't fair to children in the limelight to leave them to the care of others and then expect that they will turn out all right,' she said. 'They need their mother's affection and guidance and long periods of time alone with her. That is what gives them security in an often confusing new world.'

'You feel torn to pieces, pulled so many ways at once,' she said. 'That's why it was so hard for me. It is always hard in a new house. Everything and everyone is so new.'

The newness of her unwanted public role tormented her at first, making the White House a living hell. 'In the beginning it was quite an adjustment for her,' said her sister-in-law, Jean Smith. 'I think the fact that she went to Europe and created a bigger stir almost than the President was a surprise. I think that's when she really began enjoying it all. Up to that point she was just his wife, which was no big deal to her. Afterwards, she realized she had great influence on people.'

It was not until that trip to Europe in 1961 that the Kennedy family began to realize they had underestimated the public impact of Jackie. She was aware of the incompatibility between herself and her sisters-in-law. She knew, too, though they never said so, that they thought she would never measure up to the role of First Lady. Having been made to feel so inadequate for so many years, Jackie took a secret delight in upstaging her mother-in-law in Paris and overshadowing Eunice Shriver, who was also on the trip.

The Presidential state visit to France launched Jackie Kennedy as First Lady. Conquering Paris, she became an international sensation. Overnight, the President's pillbox-hatted wife emerged as a stellar attraction in her own right. Throughout France the French-speaking Jacqueline was hailed as 'Ravissante! Charmante! Belle!' 'LE MAGNIFIQUE', headlined French newspapers. 'Jack et Jackie: Triumphe "bon enfant" à Paris.'

Jacqueline Bouvier Kennedy was French herself. She had lived in Paris as an obscure student during her junior year in college, studying at the Sorbonne. Returning to France as First Lady signalled a romantic retreat to her roots. Parisians went wild. Lining the streets, they waited hours for her arrival. Seeing the official motorcade pull into view, they waved their flags, screaming, 'Jacquiii! Jacquiii! Jacquiii!' Along the route policemen mounted on black horses saluted. Trumpeters blared loudly and bowed. Along the Place de la Concorde crowds shrieked, 'Vive l'Amérique! Vive la France! Vive Jac-quiii!'

The Mayor of Paris gave her a $4,000 diamond watch and said her visit was the most heralded event since Queen Elizabeth paraded through the city.

'Queen Elizabeth, hell,' muttered Dave Powers to the President. 'They couldn't get this kind of turnout with the Second Coming.'

Kennedy was forced to agree. In fact, he was overwhelmed by the extraordinary impression his wife was making. Greeting reporters at a press conference, he said, 'I do not think it altogether inappropriate to introduce myself to this audience. I am the man who accompanied Jacqueline Kennedy to Paris, and I have enjoyed it.'

Jackie even charmed the messianic French President. 'Ah, the gracious Mrs Kennedy,' murmured Charles de Gaulle. Completely captivated, the downy old bird removed his glasses in her presence. He straightened proudly as she whispered how much she enjoyed reading his memoirs in French, and how she wished international translations were available so the entire world could benefit from his genius.

'God, she's really laying it on, isn't she?' observed Kennedy to an aide.

Jackie delighted de Gaulle with the story of her visit to

Malmaison, the home of Josephine Bonaparte. He winked as she told him about André Malraux, who described Josephine as 'a real camel', and expressed surprise that Napoleon cared so deeply for her. He laughed aloud when she said Josephine had been extremely jealous of Napoleon. 'She was quite right, too, and I don't blame her a bit,' whispered Jackie, batting her eyes. She chatted on about Louis XVI, the Duc d'Angoullême, and the dynastic complexities of the Bourbons. During lunch at the Elysée Palace, the French leader turned to President Kennedy. 'Your wife knows more French history than any French woman,' he said. Later Kennedy said it was as if Madame de Gaulle had sat next to him talking about Henry Clay.

In deference to America's oldest ally, the First Lady appeared at the Palace of Versailles the next night wearing a white silk gown created for her by Frenchman, Hubert de Givenchy. She had secretly ordered the dress especially for the state dinner. Parisian hairdresser Alexandre spent hours cutting, thinning, and twirling her hair into an elegant chignon bedecked with diamonds. He toned down her Palm Beach tan with light make-up. He taught her personal maid how to fit her long white leather gloves without wrinkling. The effect was spectacular. 'Apotheosis at Versailles,' screamed *France-Soir*. 'The First Lady is bursting with youth and beauty,' wrote *Le Figaro*. 'She is a wow!' teletyped United Press International.

Later General de Gaulle discussed Jackie with his Minister of Culture, André Malraux. 'She is unique for the wife of an American President, Sir,' replied Malraux.

'Yes, she's unique,' said de Gaulle. 'I can see her in about ten years on the yacht of a Greek petrol millionaire!'

France was bedazzled by Jacqueline Kennedy. She, in turn, was captivated by Gallic splendour. Walking into Louis XIV's lavishly decorated château, Jackie gasped at the elegance surrounding her. Gazing around the Hall of Mirrors, she sighed, 'I thought I was in heaven. Never could I imagine anything like this.' Following a six-course dinner served on gold-plated Sèvres porcelain dating from 1850, the de Gaulles escorted their guests into the exquisite theatre of the palace, where they sat in the royal box. Beneath antique chandeliers dripping with crystals they watched a ballet performance accompanied by an orchestra uniformed in eighteenth-century costumes, wigs, and buckled shoes. 'Such magnificence,' murmured Jackie. 'Such magnificence.' Even her husband was moved by the grandeur of the occasion.

'We've just got to do something different at the White House,' he said. 'I don't know just what, but we've got to think of something.'

From that point on the glory of France became the American First Lady's standard of excellence. She was determined that all state visitors would leave the White House as impressed as she had been with the Palace of Versailles. Soon her tables glistened with vermeil baskets and gold flatware dating back to the days of James Monroe. She tossed out the tattered linens of the White House and ordered pale pink silk sheets appliqued with satin sprays of lilies of the valley. She replaced the stodgy potted palms with elegant topiary trees reminiscent of the Tuileries Gardens. She brightened the mansion with fresh Flemish bouquets and French porcelain ashtrays. To the consternation of the Women's Christian Temperance Union, she served liquor at all social functions. For state dinners she insisted on French wine.

Inspired by the cultural salons of Marie Antoinette, Jackie began inviting the nation's finest artists and musicians to perform at the White House. She dazzled President Ferik Ibrahim Abboud of Sudan with a performance by the American Shakespeare Festival of Stratford, Connecticut. She summoned Metropolitan Opera stars Roberta Peters and Jerome Hines to sing for President Manuel Prado of Peru. She delighted Harry Truman with a piano recital by Eugene List and asked mezzo-soprano Grace Bumbry to sing at the dinner in honour of the Vice-President, the Speaker of the House, and the Chief Justice of the Supreme Court.

When she brought Pablo Casals out of exile to perform at the state dinner in honour of Puerto Rican Governor Luis Munoz and his wife, she achieved her greatest cultural success. The eighty-four-year-old cellist had refused to perform in any country which supported Generalissimo Francisco Franco's Spain, but he made an exception for Jackie. When he appeared in Washington he anointed the White House as a palace of culture.

'The Casals concert was much more than a mere evening of music,' wrote the *New York Times*. 'It was an indication that the White House is rising to its responsibilities and – in one respect, at least – coming of age.'

Exhilarated by her trip to France, Jackie was determined to stage the most dramatic state dinner in history. She dreamed of capturing the radiance of Versailles at a site which would romantically match the Sun King's palace. Naturally, the White House would never do. 'I want a more historic setting,' she said, 'some place that is steeped in American heritage.' Finally, she selected Mount Vernon, home of the first President. Fantasizing an evening of unforgettable elegance, she decided to honour President Mohammed Ayub Khan of Pakistan with a candlelight dinner on the lawn of George Washington's plantation overlooking the Potomac River.

'Oh, God,' moaned one secretary upon hearing the First Lady's plans. 'She might just as well have chosen the Eiffel Tower for all the work this one will entail.'

Cruising down the Potomac to view the site, Jackie called out to the White House usher. 'I suppose you're going to jump off the White House roof tomorrow?'

'No,' replied Mr West, 'not until the day after the dinner.'

'It was so complicated,' said Anne Lincoln, 'and we worked like dogs. Nothing like it had been done before.'

Staggering logistics faced the White House social staff, which had to translate Jackie's dream evening into reality. 'All I had to do was draw up the battle plan, implement it, rehearse it, and pray every day in all seriousness that it would not rain,' said Tish Baldrige. Saddled with the entire responsibility, the social secretary flew into action, ordering fleets of government yachts to ferry more than one hundred guests down the river from Washington to Mount Vernon. She commandeered Army trucks to transport all the White House china, silver, and gold ballroom chairs Jackie wanted on hand. She called the National Park Service to set up portable kitchens for René Verdon's gourmet dinner, ordered a bandstand built for the National Symphony Orchestra, and managed to rig a tent pavilion strung with garlands of greenery.

The director of the historic shrine watched in wonder. 'If he had but known what this little project would entail, he would probably have hoisted the Veto flag – and not the Welcome flag – on the Mount Vernon lawns,' remarked Miss Baldrige.

Enchanted by the entertainment at Versailles with the French orchestra dressed in eighteenth-century costumes, Jackie ordered the Colonial Color Guard and the Fife and Drum Corps of the Third Infantry to perform their intricate drill before dinner. 'Let's have the full regalia of a military pageant,' she said, insisting that the Corps be dressed in Colonial uniforms, including powdered wigs, tri-cornered hats, knee breeches, and red coats. 'Perhaps they could carry handmade copies of the eighteenth-century drums used in George Washington's army, too.'

She wanted a contingent of Marines standing at parade attention in full dress uniform to line both sides of the winding road leading from the Mount Vernon dock to the mansion. 'And let's have an evening serenade by the Air Force "Strolling Strings",' she said. She ordered mint juleps, in silver-frosted cups, served on the broad lawn overlooking the river.

The stately white-pillard mansion of Mount Vernon hardly touched the luxury of Versailles, but Jackie was determined to come as close as she could to recreating the effect. She told Tish Baldrige to 'beg, borrow and steal everything we need for the evening'. Miss Baldrige asked Tiffany & Co to donate the decorations, borrowed chairs and vermeil cachepots from Mrs Paul Mellon, prevailed upon John Vanderherschen, Inc of Philadelphia to provide the marquee tent, called Lester Lanin to contribute a string trio, and asked the National Symphony Orchestra to donate its services and pay for building its stand.

After firing off a series of memos on the dinner, Jackie flew to Hyannis Port to relax in the sun, leaving her frustrated staff in Washington to sweat out the details of her majestic fantasy. She returned the day of the dinner with a glorious tan.

Wearing a full-length ruffled sheath of white lace on white organza, nipped in at the waist with chartreuse silk, the First Lady made her dramatic entrance. If there was ever a moment to match Marie Antoinette in the Hall of Mirrors at Versailles, she captured it as she posed in front of the tall white pillars of Mount Vernon flanked by Marines in full dress uniform.

President Kennedy toasted his guest of honour: 'George Washington once said, "I would rather be at Mount Vernon with a friend or two about me than be attended at the seat of government by the officers of state and the representatives of every power in Europe." '

President Ayub Khan was impressed, the guests enthralled, and Jackie ecstatic. Her state dinner broke all precedents, going down in White House history as the most magnificent party ever staged for a visiting head of state. The next day the First Lady flew to Hyannis Port for the summer, not to return to Washington until October.

'I've just got to relax,' she told her husband. 'This party took every ounce of energy I had.'

Chapter Twelve

'The way we spend our evenings,' mused the First Lady, her eyes widening with enthusiasm. 'Let's see. Last night we had dinner alone, talking about Ed Gullion, the Ambassador to the Congo, and what a wonderful man he is ... and how he was put in the deep freeze for eight years ... and Jack said that Africa's the greatest challenge for a brilliant man these days. He was saying, "That's the place." The night before we had the Roosevelts and the British Ambassador to dinner, and once again it was fascinating to hear those three men talk. And the women listen, and break in with something occasionally, and it serves a purpose to those three men ... And after the Casals concert the Leonard Bernsteins were here and we had them for dinner, and that was fascinating ... I don't know, I feel much more ... so sort of ... I know so much more about it now. Think of this time we're living through. Both of us young, with health and two wonderful children ... and to live through all this.'

After more than a year as First Lady, Jacqueline Kennedy finally began warming to her role. She enjoyed her access to world leaders, to diplomats, to celebrities. 'People are always asking what Adenauer and Macmillan are like,' she said. 'Two of the most interesting people were President Abboud of Sudan and President Keikkonen of Finland ... You get to know them well, even though you only have three days.'

Later she told her husband, 'I just hope once before we get out of the White House I have an interview, because someone's going to ask me who's the greatest statesman that I've ever met. And it isn't going to be de Gaulle or Nehru or Macmillan or anyone. It's going to be Lleras Camargo of Colombia.'

Another of Jackie's favourites was the French Minister of Culture, André Malraux – an intellectual, statesman, art historian, and novelist who participated in the Chinese Revolution, the Spanish Civil War, and fought with the Resistance during World War II. 'He's a true Renaissance man,' said Jackie, explaining that Malraux as a French army officer had been wounded, was captured and escaped, and then became active in the French underground, where he was captured again, escaped again, and finished the war as an officer in Alsace.

Before his White House arrival, she carefully examined the guest list that had been prepared for dinner. Noticing that five Nobel Prize winners were included, she thoughtfully struck their names. 'It might make André feel bad,' she said, 'because, after all, he deserves a Nobel Prize but has never won one.' Later she told a friend how fascinated she was by the Frenchman. 'Listening to him makes me feel as though I'm on a raft. It's very exciting and exhilarating but so very dangerous. I have to hang on for dear life because I really don't understand everything he says.'

To the President's dismay, Jackie amused Malraux with entertaining gossip about the foreign heads of state she had met. 'Whenever a wife says anything in this town, everyone assumes that she is saying what her husband really thinks,' said Kennedy the next day. 'Imagine how I felt last night when I thought I heard Jackie telling Malraux that Adenauer was "un peu gaga"!'

The President heard his wife correctly. She lambasted the German Chancellor as 'a little nutty', and went on to say how much she despised Queen Fredericka of Greece and how pompous the Shah of Iran was. Then, a propos of nothing, she asked the French Minister, 'Have you ever seen your wife throw up?' Malraux was entranced. Years later he dedicated his book, '*Anti-Memoirs*', to Jackie.

The White House opened a world of privilege and pleasure to Jackie. As the President's wife she became a figure of international importance, cultivated by kings and princes and emperors around the world. When she received a $100,000 diamond, emerald and ruby necklace from the President of Pakistan, Kennedy teased her. 'You'll admit now there are a few plusses to being First Lady, won't you, Jackie,' he said, admiring the exquisite jewels.

When Prince Hassan of Libya presented him more than $50,000 worth of gifts for the First Lady, the President said, 'My wife will be delighted with these.' Actually, Jackie was unimpressed by the silver boudoir set and cigarette box that accompanied several gold bracelets and pins. Still, Hassan's gifts topped the gold filigree bowls and ivory elephant tusks from minor dignitaries. But they could not touch the black and white monkey fur rug given by the Prime Minister of the Somali Republic, the vicuna poncho from Argentina, the nineteenth-century carved figurines from Governor and Mrs Munoz Marin of Puerto Rico, and the mother-of-pearl nativity scene from King Hussein of Jordan.

Pleased with the leopard skin from the Nigerian Economic Mission, she was ecstatic about the full-length leopard fur coat presented by Haile Selassie, the Emperor of Ethiopia. Greeting the diminutive ruler with open arms, the First Lady walked him outside into the garden to model the luxurious coat worth over $75,000. Seeing the President, she exclaimed, 'Oh, Jack, look what he brought me. Can you believe it? He brought it to me. Just for me.'

'I had wondered why you were wearing a fur coat in the garden,' replied the President, adding his thanks for the magnificent gift.

'Oh, I'm just overcome,' said Jackie, whispering in French to the Emperor.

King Moulay Hassan of Morocco endeared himself forever to Jackie by presenting her a white silk caftan and huge gold belt encrusted with hundreds of tiny jewels. 'I wrote him a five-page letter in French to thank him for his gorgeous gifts,' she said. 'And I'll always love Ayub for giving me Sadar,' she said of the Pakistani President who gave her a gelding horse. 'No one is going to ride him but me.' One of her favourite gifts, in addition to the diamond wrist watch she received from the Mayor of Paris, was an 18-carat gold minaudière from President de Gaulle. The gold mesh evening bag from Van Cleef & Arpels was valued at $4,000.

The luxurious gifts being lavished on his wife placed the President in a delicate position. During the campaign he ranted against office-holders accepting substantial gifts for themselves or their families, saying, 'I want my appointees, like Caesar's wife, to be above reproach.' He promised that 'all gifts which cannot appropriately be refused, such as gifts from public organizations or foreign governments to the President of the United States, shall immediately be assigned to the Smithsonian Institution or other federal agencies for historic, scientific, or welfare uses. The President must set an example.'

Having made the point during the campaign, Kennedy as President refused to release to the press a complete list of gifts from foreign heads of state, especially the jewels, furs, rare paintings, and oriental rugs presented to his wife. Later, in 1966, Congress passed a law stipulating that First Families could not keep anything valued over $100.

'They always displayed the gifts in the private dining-room,' recalled one regular White House guest, 'and I'll never forget the night after the Prime Minister of the Somali Republic visited. Jackie hauled us in to see his gift, which was a lamp fashioned from a rhinoceros tusk mounted with an ostrich egg that lit up. "Look at this ghastly thing," she said. "I'm afraid to turn the damn thing on for fear it will have babies or something. Some of the crap they give us would not be fit for an Italian wedding!" She complained about spending so much time trying to dream up reciprocal gifts. She designed some wonderful paper weights made of gorgeous minerals and stones which looked like precious jewels. She gave her sketches to the jeweller David Webb to execute, and they were quite magnificent. She called the jeweller Cellini because of the wonders he produced, but she said one more gift of a rhinoceros tusk and she was going to start giving visiting heads of state Caroline's gloppy old finger paintings.'

Having never owned more than a few bits and pieces of gold jewellery, Jackie secretly borrowed diamonds from Tiffany's to wear to the Inaugural Ball, and again as First Lady secured loans for state occasions. 'I heard the President teasing his wife about having to borrow the best from all the nation's leading jewellers in order to stack up to Iranian royalty,' said Tish Baldrige, reporting that everyone around the White House began wondering how the First Lady would dress for the dinner honouring the Shah of Iran and his wife.

Jackie knew the young Empress would arrive flashing immense diamonds and royal emeralds the size of eggs. She dreaded standing next to the jewel-laden queen. Having fallen in love with an antique diamond eighteenth-century sunburst clip, she decided to buy it to wear in her hair for the occasion. To pay for the $6,140 gem, she sold some of her jewellery, including the huge aquamarine given to her by the Brazilian government, the diamond clips Ambassador Kennedy gave her as a wedding present, and the gold laurel leaf pin she received from Greece. She did not tell her husband she was trading in state gifts to make the purchase; she knew he would refuse to let her do it.

The night the Iranian monarch arrived at the White House, President Kennedy eyed the Shabanou emblazoned with jewels. He glanced at his wife with the one diamond spray embedded in her hair. 'She's topped you,' he grinned. 'She's really topped you.'

Watching the wives of dignitaries arrive sporting the world's finest jewels made Jackie feel inadequate. Soon the word seeped into diplomatic circles that gems of any sort would be an appropriate state gift for the First Lady, and jewels began flowing into the White House from most of the sixty-six heads of state who visited the Kennedys.

King Hassan of Morocco arrived with a magnificent gold sword encrusted with fifty diamonds. Jackie quickly decided to have the diamonds removed for herself and glass gems substituted. She told her secretary to make the arrangements.

'Jackie asked me to call New York and have Tom Walsh come to the White House in strictest confidence,' said Mrs Gallagher, explaining that the First Lady wanted him to take the sword to a discreet jeweller and watch the man take out the stones. 'Then Walsh was to keep the jewels for Jackie.' Tom Walsh flew to Washington to handle the transaction, but once he examined the sword he decided the Saudi Arabian diamonds would be too difficult to remove and told Jackie the cost would be prohibitive.

'Sometimes I get furious with myself thinking about all the

energy I wasted worrying about what life would be like in the White House,' said Jackie. 'We had such a wonderful home in Georgetown. You'd come in at night and find the fire going, and people talking, and you didn't stay up late. And my fears were that we wouldn't have this any more in the White House. But that's been the most wonderful side of it. You can talk when he comes home at night. It's better than during the campaign – you don't just dump your bags and go off again. And that's been wonderful for the children. Sometimes they even have lunch with Jack – if you'd told me that would happen, I'd never have believed it.

'But I should have realized, because, after all, the one thing that happens to a President is that his ties with the outside world are cut. And the people you really have are each other. I should think that if people weren't happily married the White House would really finish it.'

Yet Jack Kennedy, as President, was hardly isolated. With the help of close friends and top aides, he lived like the playboy of the western world within the confines of the Executive Mansion. 'For Jack, the White House was a playpen,' said George Smathers. For Jackie, it was a haven of sorts. For the first time in her marriage she saw her husband on a regular basis. Never before had she enjoyed the uninterrupted pleasure of his company. 'We actually have days when we have breakfast, lunch and dinner together,' she exclaimed. 'I can't believe it.' Later she remembered strolling through the south grounds of the White House thinking, 'Let me stay as happy as this forever.'

Still Kennedy needed the intimacy of various women. He also thrived on the diversion of certain pals like LeMoyne Billings, his roommate from Choate, who visited the White House every weekend. 'He just moved into his room there without anybody even knowing he was coming,' said the Chief Usher, who always informed the First Lady of his arrival.

'Oh, Mr West,' said Jackie. 'He's been a house guest of mine every weekend since I've been married.'

For years she had to contend with Jack Kennedy's overbearing sisters as well as share her house with his political entourage. 'They were always underfoot,' she said. 'I couldn't even have breakfast alone without stumbling into someone sitting around the kitchen table in the morning smoking cigars.' In those days she never knew if her husband was going to be home for dinner at night, or arrive with ten unexpected guests. (Once she had walked into his Senate office unexpectedly to visit him, only to learn that he was out of town. Understandably embarrassed, she never stopped by again.)

The long separations she endured while he travelled were painful and strained their relationship. But in the White House that all seemed behind her. She felt she could put those seven hated years of politics in the past and forget the emotional upheaval. 'Now that Jack's in the White House, maybe he can finally relax and start enjoying us as a family,' she said.

Kennedy refused to be domesticated. 'When I start to ask him silly little insignificant questions about whether Caroline should appear at some reception, or whether I should wear a short or long dress,' Jackie said, 'he just snaps his fingers and says, "That's your province." And I say, "Yes, but you're the great decision-maker. Why should everyone but me get the benefit of your decisions?" '

Kennedy did take an interest in his wife's clothes, insisting that she never wear brown or flowered patterns, which he did not like. She also avoided turquoise, feeling that the colour made her look sallow. Modelling everything for him beforehand, she once displayed a collection sent to the White House by Oleg Cassini. 'Jackie,' said the President, 'You've got to send those dresses back. They make you look like a gypsy.' So back they went.

Respecting her husband's requests that she support the millinery industry as First Lady, Jackie began wearing hats. On occasion Kennedy winced when he saw some of her headgear, and insisted that she change. One day when Kenneth flew down from New York to do Jackie's hair, the President walked into the room. Seeing the sophisticated coiffure he had created for the First Lady, the President gulped. 'My God,' he said to the hairdresser. 'What are you trying to do –

ruin my political career?' Kenneth spent a half hour re-combing Jackie's hair before the President was satisfied.

Never an affectionate husband, Jack Kennedy remained as aloof in private as he was in public. 'It wasn't until he had Caroline that he was able to show affection of any kind,' said Betty Spalding. 'Jack loved teasing her and playing games and rough-housing with John-John.' Jackie, too, lavished affection on her children, ignoring their tantrums and allow-ing them to run about as they wished. With her children she was loving and warm, but, being so psychologically taut, she could never break through her deep reserve to reach her husband.

'They both so rarely show any emotion, except by laughter,' said Ben Bradlee. 'They are the most remote and independent people we know most of the time ... They are not normally demonstrative people, period.'

'Jackie communicated her affection towards Jack in the only way she knew how,' said a friend. 'She created a home for him in the White House and amused him with little dinner parties for close friends.'

'I want my husband to be able to leave the office, even for a few hours,' Jackie told the Chief Usher. 'I want to surround him with bright people who can hold his interest and divert his mind from what's going on over there!'

During the Bay of Pigs crisis in April 1961 – Kennedy's biggest blunder as President – Jackie desperately tried to dis-tract him from the disastrous military invasion of Cuba. Hoping for a pleasant evening with no one discussing the abortive attempt to overthrow Fidel Castro, she invited Paul and Anita Fay and Bobby and Ethel Kennedy to a small dinner party. During the main course the men drifted into a discussion of the catastrophe in which 1,200 anti-Castro exiles aided by the Central Intelligence Agency had tried to invade Cuba's beachhead. Jackie tried to keep the conversa-tion light, but the Attorney-General and the Under-Secretary of the Navy kept asking the President questions about the eighty-seven men who lost their lives and the imprisoned survivors who were being held for ransom.

'I'll never again accept the recommendations of the Joint

Chiefs of Staff without first challenging them,' vowed Kennedy, complaining bitterly about the faulty information he was given.

The President grew more serious and intense as the evening wore on, and soon everyone fell into a hush. After dinner Jackie chided Paul Fay: 'You know, I had hoped we were going to have a pleasant dinner instead of having Jack go through another one of those sessions on the Bay of Pigs.'

Jackie demonstrated the same kind of concern for her seventy-three-year-old father-in-law, who suffered a stroke the first year the Kennedys were in the White House and remained paralysed the rest of his life. Although the old man was confined to a wheelchair and unable to speak, except for unintelligible grunts, she insisted that he be included in private White House dinner parties for the President. Barely able to feed himself, he drooled out of the crooked side of his mouth, but Jackie quickly wiped his face each time while carrying on a steady conversation. She teased him affectionately and talked fondly about many things. She especially enjoyed reminding him how he had worked on his son to marry her.

'The private parties the Kennedys gave at the White House were fascinating,' recalls one guest. 'I remember once they wanted to fix up Godfrey McHugh, JFK's Air Force aide, with the daughter of one of Nicole Alphand's friends. Nicole and her husband, Hervé, the French Ambassador, were great pals of the Kennedys, and that night they had a small dinner party and we all spoke French and discussed the difference between French and American women. Jack said French women were sexier because they knew how to flirt. Jackie agreed and said American women were just too blunt and completely without charm. She was always talking about sex in that way. I still remember the President saying, "I can't think of one fascinating woman in Washington." I thought it was an obtuse comment to make in front of his wife, but Jack was like that. When I asked him why French women were so exciting, he said, "Well, it's sort of an attitude they have that says to a man ... Wouldn't it be kind of nice to do it? American women don't really like men. They're too antiseptic." '

During the Russian missile crisis in October 1962, Jackie agonized with her husband. The night the President appeared on television to inform the country of the Soviet build-up taking place in Cuba, she held a small black-tie dinner party for him at the White House, trying once again for diversion. As the nation teetered on the edge of war with the Soviet Union, the First Lady led her guests to the piano. People fidgeted nervously as Jackie tried to dispel the unspoken feeling that this was hardly the appropriate time or place for gay singing. 'She tried desperately to jolly the party along so that, first and foremost, the President could enjoy a brief respite from the crisis,' said one uncomfortable guest.

'When all the other guests had gone except for her sister, Mrs Kennedy sat down, exhausted, by the piano, seeking reassurance that in spite of everything the President had enjoyed himself at least a little,' commented Robin Douglas-Home.

'It was naive and infantile for a grown woman as smart as Jackie, but it was rather sweet the way she conceived her wifely role,' said a friend. 'She felt her duty was to amuse her husband and to distract him at all times, rather than ever broach a subject seriously and discuss his problems.'

Jackie admitted as much herself. 'We never talked of serious things,' she said. 'I guess because Jack has always told me the one thing a busy man doesn't want to talk about at the end of the day is whether the Geneva Convention will be successful or what settlement could be made in Kashmir or anything like that. He didn't tell me those things. He wanted me as a wife, and seldom brought home his working problems – except once in a while the serious ones.'

Kennedy, who never accepted women as equals, tended to treat his wife as a child. Occasionally he was irritated by her silliness. Once, while he was waiting to be photographed, Jackie grabbed a floral wreath and hung it around his neck like a prize-winning horse. According to the photographer present, the President snapped at his wife, saying, 'Damn it, Jackie, take this thing off me, and don't act so stupid. I can't be photographed this way, for Christ's sake.' Jackie merely made funny faces at him.

'Jack thoroughly enjoyed being President, and unlike Jackie, who had such a hard time adjusting, never once got bored in the White House,' recalled a friend. 'When she finished the restoration project and started getting restless, he babied her a little bit, encouraging her to take that trip to India and Pakistan with her sister.'

Her sister, Lee, then living in London with her second husband, Stanislas Radziwill, became Jackie's closest friend and companion in the White House. They talked regularly on the trans-Atlantic phone, and Lee frequently visited Jackie in Washington and accompanied her on vacations and trips abroad.

'The relationship between the two sisters became very close because their husbands got on so well together,' explained a friend. 'Kennedy always described Stas to me as "the genuine article", by which he meant bona fide royalty. "A real Polish prince," he'd say. Stas was a self-made millionaire, which was something else Kennedy respected. He admired people who made vast amounts of money on their own. Besides being rich, Stas was also charming, generous, and good-hearted. Being a sexually cynical man, he had a great rapport with the President. Kennedy liked to be around him. He could be himself about women because Stas understood. He was the same kind of guy.'

Jackie was equally fond of her brother-in-law. In many ways Stanislas Radziwill reminded her of her father. While the Polish nobleman was not as handsome as Black Jack Bouvier, he had the same Continental charm and droll sense of humour. 'He says the most outrageous things,' exclaimed Jackie. 'I just love it when he's so naughty!'

One of the most elaborate parties she gave as First Lady was a private dinner dance honouring the Radziwills. Not trusting the White House kitchens with Poulet à l'Estragon, she ordered *haute cuisine* from Washington's finest French caterers and spent hours poring over the guest list. She invited planeloads of New York socialites down for the occasion and placed Lee near her favourite Cabinet member, Robert McNamara, the Secretary of Defence. Jackie insisted Lester Lanin's orchestra play non-stop until dawn. 'Tell them I don't want any breaks,' she said. 'They can figure out how to do it without breaking their union rules.'

President Kennedy had promised his in-laws a royal welcome when they arrived in Washington. Disappointed that they couldn't attend his swearing-in ceremonies, he called them twice in London during the Inauguration to say how much he missed them. He was especially grateful to his brother-in-law for drumming up Polish-American support in his Presidential campaign. American Poles recognized him as a prince and a man of power. Having fled Poland at the beginning of the war, he had worked for the underground throughout Europe and then settled in London, where he became a British citizen and had to renounce his title. Although publicly deprived of his rank, he insisted on his royal prerogatives, and his young wife, assuming the role of a princess, demanded hers as well. When asked how she preferred to be addressed, Lee replied, 'Oh, Princess Lee Radziwill will do just fine. I was born Caroline Lee Bouvier but I've always been called Lee – and I hate it.'

When President Kennedy and the First Lady visited the Radziwills in London, they received a royal invitation to dine at Buckingham Palace. The court circular later listed the Radziwills as Prince and Princess, although the Queen had never granted them a royal licence to use their foreign titles in England. 'It was a matter of courtesy at the time and under those circumstances to call them what they normally call themselves,' explained a palace spokesman. 'The Kennedys, like so many democratic Americans, are thrilled to have a princess in the family, and so the Queen graciously decided to let them enjoy the thrill for that one evening.'

In London Stanislas Radziwill founded a real estate business and construction firm which boomed during the post-war years, making him one of the richest men in England. In addition to a large Georgian mansion in London near Buckingham Palace, he owned a twelve-room Fifth Avenue apartment in New York, a Queen Anne country estate on forty-nine acres of park near Henley-on-Thames, complete with stables and a mammoth swimming pool, and a villa in Greece.

When Lee divorced Michael Canfield to marry him in 1959, the marriage was not recognized by the Church, and it bothered the Catholic Radziwill that his wife was technically considered an adulteress living in a state of sin. The marriage to Lee was Radziwill's third. His first marriage was annulled by the Vatican and his second was a civil ceremony that ended in divorce and was never recognized by the Church. Knowing how much a sanctified marriage meant to him, Lee applied for a decree of nullity from the Sacred Congregation of the Holy Office. They ignored her case for months. Finally she talked to her brother-in-law, who assured her that he would take care of everything once he was elected President. Kennedy personally discussed the matter with the Apostolic Delegate living in Washington, and arranged for lawyers to plead her case in Rome. Lee appealed to the Rota, Rome's final court of appeal. Asking for a ruling that her first marriage be annulled because of an essential flaw in the marital contract, she testified that Michael Canfield had been impotent and unable to have children. In the eyes of the Church, this was sufficient reason to invalidate the marriage.

When Jackie and Lee decided to visit India and Pakistan, President Kennedy suggested they stop off first in Rome for a private audience with the Pope. 'You two better start practising your curtsies so you can show His Holiness what fine Catholic girls you are,' he teased. Despite his joking, Kennedy believed that a visit from the First Lady would help Lee, and politically it was important to him that his sister-in-law's marriage be recognized by the Church. So he arranged for Jackie to talk privately during that visit with Cardinal Cicognani, the Vatican Secretary of State.

The controversial annulment, which cost over $50,000, was officially granted in 1964. Later Lee explained why she went to all the trouble. 'It was important to Stas and his father, for one thing,' she said. 'And because of the children. Besides, all the grounds for annulment were there and perfectly valid. I saw no reason why I could not be given one or at least try to be given one.'

Sharing the world spotlight with her famous sister pained Lee as much as it pleased her. While she enjoyed the adulation heaped on her as the First Lady's glamorous young sister, she was forced to assume a secondary role. 'Actually, the roles should have been reversed,' said a friend. 'Jackie would have been happier married to someone like Stas and living a quiet life of luxury with her children, while Lee would have given anything to be out front in the public spotlight as First Lady. It was so obvious on the trip to India and Pakistan. Lee was shunted back with all the camel drivers while Jackie was treated like royalty. Naturally it bothered her, but she was always very correct. Jackie could not have made the trip without Lee. She needed her there as her mainstay and moral support.'

As it was, Jackie cancelled that trip three times before summoning the courage to go. 'I was almost sick before we left, thinking I just couldn't do it,' she said. 'Jack is always so proud of me when I do something like this, but I can't stand being out in front. I know it sounds trite, but what I really want is to be behind him and to be a good wife and mother.'

'Jack was so nice to let me come,' said the wife-child. 'He says I'm young and ought to do things like this that I want to.'

Wearing her $75,000 leopard skin coat, the First Lady embarked on her trip with an entourage that included her sister, her hairdresser, her personal maid, a press secretary, her favourite Secret Service man, Clint Hill, twenty-four security guards, and sixty-four pieces of luggage. Travelling 16,000 miles in twenty days, the Bouvier sisters stopped in Rome for their private audience with Pope John XXIII. They viewed the Taj Mahal by moonlight, visited the Pink City of Jaipur, gazed at the Shalimar Gardens of Lahore. They rode elephants in India and camels in Pakistan. They watched a duel between a cobra and a mongoose. They cheered the Maharaja's polo team. They sailed down the Holy Ganges River past Hindu pilgrims and water buffalo bathing in the mud.

Yet everywhere they went the Princess trailed the First Lady. She watched servants wearing crimson and gold uniforms hold a white silk parasol over Jackie's head to shield her from the sun. She saw bread flown in from Beirut just because Jackie liked cream-cheese sandwiches for lunch. As a contingent of Secret Service men ran interference for the First Lady, Lee stood awed by the photographers following her sister. Questioned by reporters, Lee whispered: 'I shrink from talking about myself because I believe that a person should have accomplished something on her own before she starts giving interviews. Why should anyone care what I do when there are so many more interesting people in the world? I haven't done anything at all.' She watched Jackie lay a wreath of white roses on Gandhi's grave. She waved from the rear of every motorcade while Jackie sat up front in the lead car flowered with rose petals.

'Lee was just marvellous,' said Jackie after the trip. 'It must have been trying sometimes. Though we'd often ride together, sometimes I'd go ahead with the most interesting person, and Lee would follow along five cars behind and, by the time I got there, I couldn't even find her. I was so proud of her – and we would always have such fun laughing about little things when the day was over. Nothing could ever come between us.'

Clothes were paramount to Jackie. Lee appeared regularly on the world's best-dressed list and was considered by many to be much more fashionable than her sister. But she never felt that she measured up to Jackie. 'It's funny, isn't it,' she told a friend. 'All the compliments in the world can be said to you all the time. But if you didn't hear them as a child – or even thought you didn't hear them – then you just never believe it.' While in Washington to accompany Jackie to the Capitol to hear the President's State of the Union message, she spent hours in the Queen's Room getting ready. As she walked out, a secretary complimented her on how pretty she looked. 'Oh, I don't feel it at all,' she said. 'Jackie's the one, in her mink coat. Oh, well ... no one's ever going to notice me anyway.'

Occasionally the chic little princess pulled rank and demanded to be noticed. When asked to pose for a *McCall's* magazine story, she went to Paris to select her clothes from the new fashion collections and stirred a controversy by demanding entrance into the house of Hubert de Givenchy. She was turned away on the grounds that she was technically a member of the working press and reporters were not allowed inside until the formal showings. 'Mr Givenchy is just trying to get himself some publicity,' sniped Lee. 'But it really doesn't make any difference anyway. I haven't been buying his clothes for months. I've been wearing Yves Saint Laurent.' The feud made the papers, and Lee promptly called the White House to apologize for causing a ruckus.

Growing up as outsiders in the snobbish Auchincloss family, 'the two little given-ups', as they called themselves, clung to each other for emotional security. 'We've had many bonds in common – mainly our father,' said Lee. 'Our parents were divorced quite early, and he never remarried. We were everything to him. He was a lonely man later on – we spent part of every summer and vacation with him – and we shared a strong responsibility. He was very handsome and always thought of wonderful things to do. In spite of time and extraordinary happenings, all those childhood memories are a great bond.'

That divorce caused Jackie to become embittered towards her mother. Lee shared her animosity, although she was always the maternal favourite. 'Their mother began to bloom towards them only after Jackie was First Lady and Lee a princess,' said Paul Mathias, a close friend. 'They accepted her late attentions to them and they have behaved very correctly towards her ever since – very, very, very correctly. Deep in their hearts they feel bitter but the world does not know it. They are loyal to Mrs Auchincloss – but they don't overdo. Jackie and Lee conceal their feelings. Their mother can't.'

Enjoying her prerogatives as the First Lady's mother, Janet Auchincloss frequently visited the White House to see her daughter and grandchildren. 'Every time she comes, she starts carping at me about how to dress and what to wear,' complained Jackie to her sister. 'I know,' said Lee. 'Just say "Yes mummy, yes mummy, yes mummy." '

At times Mrs Auchincloss tried sending her messages through Jackie's secretary. 'She once asked if I would approach Jackie about her manner of dress,' recalled Mary Gallagher. 'That happened several days after she and Jackie had gone to an embassy tea. Mrs Auchincloss was rather distressed over the short dress that her daughter had worn. She said that when Jackie bent over for something, you could see her garters on the tops of her hose. "Could you just mention to her that you think she should start wearing her dresses a little longer?" Much as I would have loved to oblige Mrs Auchincloss, I never could muster enough courage to tell Jackie.'

As children, Jackie and Lee always banded together against their mother in support of their father. 'They considered me an ogre because I didn't spoil them like he did,' said Mrs Auchincloss. 'I was the one who had to raise them properly and teach them manners and instruct them on how to behave. He didn't.'

'One of the biggest fights Jackie and Lee ever had was over their mother,' recalled a friend. 'Lee had taken Jackie's side against Mrs Auchincloss and they were virtually not speaking for weeks. Then Lee discovered that Jackie had secretly made up with her mother without ever telling Lee, and that made her furious. So she and Jackie had the boxing gloves on for a while.'

Despite their quarrels, 'Pekes' and 'Jacks', as they nicknamed each other, maintained a strong relationship. 'I'm convinced that Jackie is only happy with one other woman, and that is Lee,' said Robin Douglas-Home.

Kennedy, too, enjoyed his jet-set sister-in-law, and frequently pointed her out to his friends, saying, 'Look at her. Isn't she something?' To Jackie's exasperation, Lee returned this affection without reservation. Their sibling rivalry as children plagued them as adults, and the devotion to their father was later transferred to their husbands. Both sisters loved the same type of man. First it was Black Jack Bouvier. Then Jack Kennedy and Stanislas Radziwill. Later, it would be a Greek shipbuilder by the name of Aristotle Socrates Onassis.

Chapter Thirteen

The First Lady was expecting her third child in the fall and was determined to keep her pregnancy a secret until April, when the White House would make an official announcement.

'I don't know how I'm going to keep this a secret until then,' she told the President. 'I have an uncanny ability to sense when someone is pregnant, and I just know someone like me is going to find out about it.'

'Not if you don't get fat,' he replied.

'After the baby comes I'm just going to sit back and enjoy myself for the next few years.'

A prodigious writer of candid notes and letters, Jackie continued running the White House with memos penned in her spidery schoolgirl script punctuated by breathlessness. 'Sometimes I get so mad,' she admitted, 'I have to dictate – that's when I'm in a white heat.' One day she targeted her rage at Vaughn Meader, who achieved brief fame with remarkable imitations of the Kennedys. His record, 'The First Family', parodied Kennedy's Boston twang and Jackie's debutante whisper and sold millions. Somewhat flattered, the President was amused by parts of the skit. He especially liked Meader's imitation of him getting into bed: 'Good night, Jackie, Good night, Bobby, Good night, Ethel, Good night, Teddy, Good night, Caroline, Good night, John-John.' Jackie didn't consider it funny.

Jackie's memos were treated like Presidential directives, and her aides snapped into action whenever one appeared. As First Lady she surrounded herself with women who grew up in her same social milieu and were conversant with French antiques, designer clothes, and gourmet chefs. All were schoolmates at Miss Porter's School in Farmington, Connecticut, or had known her at Vassar, and each – except Letitia Baldrige – catered to her whims.

In the beginning Jackie relied heavily on her high-charging

social secretary to handle everything pertaining to official social life at the White House. Tish selected the elaborate French menus, planned entertainment for every state dinner, and functioned as a booking agent in arranging performances of musicians, poets, actors, and dancers. She glamorized state dinners, making an invitation to the White House the biggest status symbol in Washington. She supervised the publicity for each occasion and executed every painstaking detail of decor. 'The power house behind the glittering evenings at the White House was the First Lady's social secretary, Letitia Baldrige,' said the Chief Usher.

Tish also advanced every trip Jacqueline Kennedy took, sometimes spending weeks abroad to arrange the accommodations, meetings, tours, and motorcades. Brimming with ideas for creating the image Jackie wanted as First Lady, Tish suggested she host a White House dinner for Nobel Prize winners and sponsor musical concerts for the children of the diplomatic corps. She also pushed the President's wife to make public appearances on occasion. 'You just have to do this,' she would say, handing Jackie an 'URGENT' folder filled with detailed instructions. Complaining to the Chief Usher, Jackie said, 'Mr West, I don't *have* to do anything!' The Chief Usher agreed.

Jackie began to complain privately about 'Tish's increased high-handedness', but publicly she acknowledged the superb contributions of her longtime friend. Returning from her extravagant trip to India and Pakistan, she told a reporter, 'Do you know Tish went ahead and checked every detail in every place we went? When we got there everything was always perfect – the right presents for everyone and nothing mixed up. If she ever leaves the White House, I'm going too!'

'The minute I read that in the *Saturday Evening Post* I knew Tish's days were numbered,' laughed a friend. 'Jackie is so erratic, offering love and affection one day and then, without provocation, withdrawing it the next. Unfortunately, Tish learned the hard way.'

Friction grew as the energetic social secretary pushed the First Lady into more official duties, more morning coffees, more afternoon teas. Then Jackie learned that Tish had been systematically destroying her personal memos. That's when she complained to the President, insisting that he think of a diplomatic way to get rid of her so she could hire Nancy Tuckerman as social secretary. Miss Tuckerman had been Jackie's best friend at Miss Porter's School.

'Tucky would be perfect for me, and now that I have everything so well organized around here, she could do the job blindfolded,' said Jackie. 'Tish is just too overbearing, and with a new baby coming you can hardly expect me to carry on as I have been as First Lady, doing all those things Tish just insists I do!'

Having rammed heads with Miss Baldrige on occasion, the President understood. At the first official party held in the White House, which happened to be on a Sunday, Tish served hard liquor – a forbidden practice during the Eisenhower administration. Newspapers noted the breach of precedent with roaring headlines: 'LIQUOR ON SUNDAY AT THE WHITE HOUSE DRAWS CRITICISM', and 'NEVER ON SUNDAY AT JFK'S HOUSE SAYS BAPTIST CONGRESSMAN'.

Kennedy wanted to fire her on the spot. 'I had no right to make that decision myself without consulting him,' Tish said later. 'He was mad – and rightfully so.'

Further contretemps involving the social secretary finally persuaded him secretly to negotiate a consultant job for her at the Merchandise Mart in Chicago, working for Ambassador Kennedy. Tish was delicately informed of her new position and, without much choice, she accepted. When it was decided that she would leave the White House in May, Jackie felt relieved. But she continued to steam about the junking of her memos.

Cautioning her press secretary to save everything, Jackie said, 'This close to the Presidency, all our tiny things are history – if only to be burned by me later. I would not have mentioned it if the President and I had not been so rocked by the happy little holocaust that has been going on for two years.'

Usually Jackie confined her irreverence to memos. Only occasionally did she slip in public. Her appraisal of the Daughters of the American Revolution as 'a group of old and lonely women' made front-page headlines. The President blanched when he saw them: 'FIRST LADY BLASTS DAR: BUNCH OF OLD BAGS' ... 'JACKIE DUMPS ON THE DAR'.

'Jesus Christ,' he groaned. 'I'm going to have to muzzle the First Lady.'

'I'm afraid your wife calls 'em as she sees 'em,' laughed their friend, Bill Walton.

Jackie delighted friends with her sense of humour. 'That was her one redeeming feature,' said one. Tony Bradlee convulsed with laughter remembering the day the First Lady took her turn as supervising mother in Caroline's nursery school on the third floor of the White House. 'She had been appalled that she had to help the little boys go to the bathroom, and especially appalled by one little boy in particular. Jackie said afterwards, "He had virtually no pecker at all." '

René Carpenter, the beautiful wife of astronaut Scott Carpenter, became a favourite of the Kennedys and spent delightful afternoons with her children visiting in the White House. She remembers Jackie's concern about John, Jr. 'She commented once about the nanny, Maud Shaw, hovering around John-John so much. "I'm so afraid he's going to grow up and be a fruit," she said. She cared a lot about her children and thought the ever-pregnant Ethel was awful the way she had babies all the time.

' "She's just like a rabbit the way she drops those kids and I think it's terrible," said Jackie.'

Jackie took special delight in Caroline's play school. While preparing for the state visit of the Shah of Iran and his young bride, she promised the children she would bring the Iranian queen upstairs to see them.

'She hired a dance teacher to come in and teach the little girls how to curtsy and the boys how to bow,' recalls one mother, 'and the youngsters practised all week long. Jackie suggested they all draw a picture for the Shabanou to take back to her child, and she lined up the class to bow and curtsy to the Empress while presenting her with a flower in one hand and their drawings in the other.

'The kids were in a high state of excitement at the prospect of meeting a real live queen, but when Jackie appeared with the Shah's wife, who was dressed in regular street clothes rather than flowing robes, they forgot their curtsies and bows and just stared. "You're not really a queen," they yelled. "Where's your crown?" Jackie tried to explain how royalty dressed in the twentieth century, but the kids were unimpressed. They thought the Shabanou, whom they kept calling the Shah Bunny, was a fake.'

Jackie struggled with the problems of raising her children the right way and frequently seemed perplexed. When Ambassador Kennedy was paralysed by his stroke and could only utter a few meaningless sounds in a raspy, guttural voice, Caroline was frightened. She could not understand the noises coming from her grandfather or why he had to be wheeled around. Rather than deal with the harsh reality, Jackie told her that he was in a wheelchair because he was not feeling well and his voice sounded strange because he had laryngitis. The next day Caroline told her classmates, 'My grandfather is sick and has a sore throat.'

As she awaited the birth of her third child, Jackie devoted more and more time to Caroline and John-John. Often, while taking them on picnics and to the amusement park, she wore a wig to disguise herself so they would not be pestered by the press. During the winter she brought an old-fashioned horse-drawn carriage to the White House to give the children a sleigh ride, then was enraged to see photographers standing by. She continually raged at them, insisting that she couldn't raise her children normally with the press looking on. On Halloween she donned a mask and secretly took her children trick-or-treating in Georgetown. Once, when she saw a reporter taking a picture of Caroline, she begged the woman not to publish it. The reporter agreed, and Jackie responded with a grateful note: 'I appreciated your asking about using the picture of Caroline in the costume class – then not using it when I said I hoped you wouldn't. That is just an incredibly decent gesture ... I know that newspapers need to print different – or rather unusual pictures – and there is the conflict of trying to raise one's children fairly normally – So when you – who are torn both ways – respect a little girl's chance to have a happy day with the other children who fortunately treat her as just another four year old (that is almost the only public place where she isn't singled out and fawned over) – it is amazing and consoling ...'

During her pregnancy Jackie cancelled all official engagements and insisted that photographers be forbidden from snapping her in maternity clothes. 'It's just not dignified,' she said. 'Besides, it's an invasion of my privacy.'

After the White House announced the impending birth of her baby, the first time in sixty-three years a child would be born to a President in office, wires of good wishes poured in. Kennedy, with a wry smile, remarked, 'Now Jackie will have an excuse to get out of things.' The First Lady was swamped with letters of congratulations, including one from Roswell Gilpatric, then Kennedy's Under-Secretary of Defence. She wrote back:

'It was so thoughtful of you to write me about the baby. It is such a happy thing and thank you so much for taking the time – And now that I don't have to go to all those ladies' lunches I hope I can come and see you and Madelin some lunch in May or June.'

Madelin, then Gilpatric's third wife, despised the flirtatious First Lady. She felt that her fifty-seven-year-old husband gave the President's wife more attention than was necessary. Consequently, Jackie, who made no secret of her fondness for Gilpatric, never received a luncheon invitation from his wife.

Instead, she invited him to lunch with her alone and spend the day at Camp David while the President was on the West Coast checking military installations. Jackie was in her seventh month of pregnancy, and Gilpatric, having resigned his position, was preparing to return to New York to practise law. The First Lady enjoyed the time spent with the courtly Under-Secretary. A few days later she wrote a long letter thanking him. When that tender missive became public, assumptions arose that Jackie was doing to President Kennedy what Guinevere did to King Arthur. Gilpatric was cast as Sir Launcelot.

'I loved my day in Maryland so much,' she wrote. 'It made me happy for one whole week – It is only Thursday today –

But I know the spell will carry over until tomorrow – and I will go back to Camp David – and see those West Virginia motel shacks with their bomb shelters churning underneath – as great white columned houses –

'We had some people to dinner last night who had been to another farewell party for you at Anderson House. I always push unpleasant things out of my head on the theory that if you don't think about them they won't happen – but I guess your departure – which I would never really let myself realize until tonight – is true –

'I feel sorry for whoever succeeds you – (for them) – and I will never really like them – no matter who they turn out to be – and neither will anyone else – They will always live in your shadow – and no one else will be able to have force and kindness at the same time –

'But I feel much sorrier for us – In this strange city where everyone comes and goes so quickly you get rather used to its fickle transiency – So when anyone's departure leaves a real void – you should be really proud of that – although you are the last person who would care about such a thing.

'I know you will find some peace at last – But I also know that the change of pace will be an awful readjustment. I wish you so well through all of that – Please know Dear Ros that I will wish you well always – Thank you – Jackie.'

Kennedy never understood his wife's attraction to the slight, balding Gilpatric, or to Robert McNamara. He liked both men and found them exceedingly intelligent but did not think either particularly handsome. 'I think it's that father image of yours,' he teased her. He discussed the subject at dinner one night with another couple, after Jackie said again that she thought Roswell Gilpatric was one of the most attractive men in Washington. 'Men just can't understand his sex appeal,' she said. Seeing the two men's quizzical expression, she started laughing. 'Look at them. They look just like dogs that have had a plate of food grabbed from under their noses.' Later she said, 'I think men over sixty are often more attractive than younger men. For instance, General Maxwell Taylor was marvellous and lean while classmates of Jack's let themselves go and looked awful.

General Taylor's over sixty and plays tennis and is lean.'

Jackie spent a secluded summer in Hyannis Port, relaxing with her children, while the President made state visits to England and Germany and a sentimental journey to Ireland. Jackie remained in constant contact with the White House, arranging her fall social schedule and ordering new clothes from Oleg Cassini.

She spent hours updating her family scrapbooks and, being compulsively organized, she selected her White House Christmas cards, plus all the gifts she and the President intended to give. She informed Evelyn Lincoln and Tom Walsh that what she wanted from her husband was a chinchilla bedspread costing $4,000. 'I know it's too expensive for words but maybe it could be a joint gift from everyone,' she suggested. 'If not, I'll just settle for rabbit or white fur.'

The morning of 7 August she took her children riding in Osterville, a few miles from Hyannis Port. Returning home, she began feeling labour pains and summoned her obstetrician, John Walsh, who was on holiday nearby. He called for a helicopter and alerted the military hospital at Otis Air Force Base that Mrs Kennedy was arriving immediately. The baby was ahead of schedule.

'Dr Walsh, you've just got to get me to the hospital on time,' Jackie pleaded. 'I don't want anything to happen to this baby. Please hurry! This baby mustn't be born dead.'

As Jackie was helped into an open convertible, the President's physician appeared at the front door. 'Mrs Kennedy, would you like me to call the President?' inquired Dr Janet Travell.

'No,' shouted Jackie from the car. 'Don't call him.'

As soon as the car was out of sight Dr Travell went to the Secret Service trailer and called the White House, informing the President that his wife was on her way to the military hospital beyond Cape Cod Canal.

At 12:52 pm, an hour after Jackie went in for Caesarean surgery, the hospital announced that Mrs John F. Kennedy had given birth to a baby boy weighing four pounds and ten and a half ounces. The child, born five and a half weeks prematurely, was immediately baptized Patrick Bouvier

Kennedy in honour of his paternal grandfather and Black Jack Bouvier.

The President arrived and was informed that his wife was recovering nicely but the baby had a serious respiratory problem involving a hyaline membrane. He immediately conferred with the doctors, who recommended that the infant be taken to special facilities at the Children's Hospital in Boston for treatment of the idiopathic respiratory distress syndrome which is common in premature babies. After a few minutes with Jackie, he conferred again with the doctors. Later that afternoon he proudly wheeled his new son in his isolette into Mrs Kennedy's suite and placed the baby in her arms. That night he accompanied the infant in an ambulance to Boston, where he visited the hospital four times during the next day to check on his condition. That night he slept on a vacant cot near Patrick. The baby, unable to bear the strain on his weak heart, slipped into a coma and died the next day.

The President was desolate. 'He put up quite a fight,' he said in a trembling voice. 'He was a beautiful baby.' Then the bereaved father began to cry. 'It was an agonizing moment for a man never known to have had an emotional outburst,' said Cardinal Cushing.

Flying back to Otis, the President broke the news to his wife and then collapsed in her arms in tears. 'Oh, Jack, oh, Jack,' she sobbed. 'There's only one thing I could not bear now – if I ever lost you.'

'I know, I know,' he murmured.

'That was the only time I ever saw him cry,' she told a friend later. 'He was inconsolable. As shocking as it was for me, it was worse for him. Jack nearly collapsed over it. Although he never said so, I know he wanted another boy – John was his real kin spirit.'

Later in the day the President brought Caroline to the hospital to see her mother. Arriving in tennis shoes, her blonde hair in a ponytail, the five-year-old clutched a bouquet of black-eyed susans she had picked in the garden. Jackie smothered her firstborn with kisses and begged her husband to bring John in that evening.

Helicopters arrived later, bringing Janet and Hughdie

Auchincloss and their young children, Janet and Jamie, to join the rest of the Kennedys. Lee Radziwill interrupted her vacation in Greece to fly to Massachusetts to be with her sister. Together they all flew to Boston to attend the funeral Mass celebrated by Cardinal Cushing, who appeared in white robes rather than requiem black.

Jackie spent that morning alone in her hospital room. Although she did not attend the funeral of her baby, she insisted that his coffin, like her father's years before, be covered with flowers. After the Mass of the Angels, the President carried the tiny casket in his arms and placed inside it the St Christopher medal he had received from Jackie as a wedding present on the day they were married. The child was buried in Holyrood Cemetery in Brookline, a few miles from where the President was born. Kennedy touched the baby's coffin as it was lowered into the gravesite. 'Goodbye,' he whispered, again unable to hold back his tears. 'It's awfully lonely down there.'

'My dear Jack, let's go, let's go,' said Cardinal Cushing. 'Nothing more can be done.'

Barely composed, the President flew back to the Cape to comfort his wife. Jackie remained in bed for seven days and then relaxed for the rest of the summer at Hyannis Port. As she left the hospital, she thanked the nurses. 'You've been so wonderful to me that I'm coming back here next year to have another baby. So you better be ready for me.'

For the first time in his public career, the President, standing by his wife's side, lovingly took her hand and led her to the car.

Chapter Fourteen

'It's so hard for Jackie,' said the President. 'She wanted so to have another child. Then, after all the difficulties she has in bearing a child, to lose him is doubly hard. It has been so much fun with Buttons and John-John. It would have been nice to have another son.'

Fearful of the depression his wife was sinking into, Kennedy made a special effort to join her every weekend on the Cape after the death of Patrick. Still, there was always time for other women. On 24 September he made a cross-country trip to honour the cause of conservation and took Mary Meyer with him to Milford, Pennsylvanis. Ostensibly, the Presidential trip to Milford was to accept on behalf of the US Government a mansion and some land from Mary's first cousin, who was the son of the late Governor. 'That in itself was probably not enough to command the President's presence,' admitted Ben Bradlee, Mrs Meyer's brother-in-law. Mrs Meyer, who had been secretly visiting the President in the White House while Jackie was on the Cape, teased him about the reception her arch-Republican mother would provide. Kennedy could not resist the opportunity of visiting Ruth Pinchot, his mistress's mother, and posing for a few photographs.

A few days before, he had celebrated his tenth wedding anniversary with Jackie at Hammersmith Farm in Newport, Rhode Island. There Jackie gave her husband a gold St Christopher medal, soldered on a money clip, to replace the one he had put in the baby's coffin. She also presented him a red leather, gold-tooled scrapbook featuring the White House rose garden.

The first spring he was in the White House the President asked Bunny Mellon, an expert horticulturist, to redesign the scraggly patch with flowers that would be in bloom throughout the year just outside his office window. 'It was absolutely atrocious before Bunny took over,' said Jackie. 'Now it's magnificent ... The beauty of it seems to affect even hard-bitten reporters who come there just to watch what is going on.'

On each page of the scrapbook were before and after pictures of the garden taken every day during its renovation, plus a copy of the President's schedule for that day and a quotation on gardening written by Jackie in long-hand.

Kennedy handed his wife a letter from J. J. Klejman, the New York antiquities dealer, listing his entire inventory with a description and the price of everything. Nothing on the list cost less than $1,000, and Kennedy told her she could choose anything on the list she wanted as an anniversary present. Pondering the Degas drawings, Fragonard etchings, pre-Christian statues and Etruscan objets d'art, Jackie finally selected a simple bracelet in the form of a coiled serpent.

During this time she received a phone call from her sister, who had spent the summer vacationing with Aristotle Onassis in Greece. Lee had returned to Athens after Patrick's funeral, and over dinner one night she told the shipping magnate how despondent Jackie was about the baby's death. Listening sympathetically, Onassis suggested a cruise on his luxurious yacht to cheer up the First Lady. When he offered to put the *Christina* at her disposal, Lee immediately jumped up to call her sister.

'Tell Jack that Stas and I will chaperone you,' she said. 'Oh, Jackie, it will be such fun. You can't imagine how terrific Ari's yacht is, and he says we can go anywhere you want. It will do you so much good to get away for a while.'

Kennedy agreed to let his wife accept the invitation, although he worried about the publicity that might result from accepting the Greek's hospitality. 'It's so dicey,' he told a friend, referring to Onassis's publicized liaison with the famous opera star, Maria Callas. 'But what bothers me more is that goddamned indictment.'

During the Eisenhower administration Aristotle Onassis had been slapped with criminal charges of conspiring to defraud the US Government by using surplus American ships without paying taxes. He eventually paid a whopping

184

$7 million fine rather than face a court trial in the United States.

A further complication for the President was the intimate relationship developing between the shipping magnate and his sister-in-law, who was spending most of her time on his yacht and flying with him to London and New York. 'Lee wanted to marry Onassis at that time, but he was not hell-bent on marrying her,' recalled Betty Spalding, who had several conversations with the Kennedys on the subject. 'And Jackie did not want Lee to leave Stas and marry Onassis either. That was really the point of her trip to Greece. Not just to recuperate, but to talk some sense into Lee.'

Bobby Kennedy was equally apoplectic about the situation. Frightened by the political ramifications of having his sister-in-law, who was secretly negotiating an annulment with Vatican officials, suddenly dump her second husband to marry Onassis, the Attorney-General cornered Jackie one evening and said, 'Just tell Lee to cool it, will you.' Jackie reassured him she would do exactly that.

The President meanwhile called his Under-Secretary of Commerce, Franklin Delano Roosevelt, Jr, and insisted that he and his wife, Sue, accompany Jackie on the cruise. 'Your presence will add a little respectability to the whole thing,' the President said. 'People won't talk so much if you and Sue are there.' So the Roosevelts agreed to go.

A few days later Pamela Turnure announced to the press that Jackie was planning a private visit to Greece for two weeks in October and would spend part of her vacation at the villa of Markos Nomikos, whom she had visited as First Lady in 1961. 'Her itinerary will also include a few days on a cruise,' added Miss Turnure, who reluctantly admitted the cruise would be on a yacht owned by Aristotle Onassis.

Asked if the golden Greek would be on board with the First Lady, Miss Turnure replied, 'Not to my knowledge.' She said that Prince Radziwill had secured the yacht from Onassis, and that he and his wife and the Franklin Roosevelts would accompany Jackie.

Actually Onassis, aware of the political embarrassment his

presence might cause, offered to stay in Athens to avoid any scandal, but Jackie insisted that he be aboard the *Christina* to accompany her. 'I could not accept his generous hospitality and then not let him come along,' she said afterwards. 'It would have been too cruel. I just couldn't have done that.'

Onassis stocked the yacht with rare vintage wines, eight varieties of caviar, and fresh fruits flown in from Paris. He summoned a crew of sixty, plus two hairdressers, a Swedish masseuse, and a small orchestra for dancing in the evening. These amenities cost him over $40,000. In addition to the Radziwills and Roosevelts, the guests included Onassis; his sister Artemis and her husband, a Greek playwright; the dress designer Princess Irene Galitzine and her husband, and Accardi Gurney, a charming, hand-kissing bachelor who was a good friend of Lee.

'Poor Franklin didn't want to go along at all,' said Jackie. 'He said he was working on a new image and a trip like this wouldn't do him any good, but I persuaded Jack to call him and ask him to go with me. I really wanted Franklin as a chaperone.'

The trip was no joy-ride for Roosevelt. 'Jackie teased him unmercifully and was quite mean to him at times,' recalled one guest. 'When Franklin appeared in a pair of red shorts and a sweater, she taunted him in a most derisive way. "Oh, God, Franklin," she said, "you look like John-John in those shorts. Why do you wear those awful things?" It wasn't stylish then for men to wear shorts, and Jackie, who is ever so style-conscious, thought Franklin was quite tacky. She acted as if he was an embarrassment to her. She also rode him hard about a brown suit of his which she hated. She told him he looked like a carpet-bagger in the old rag.'

Like schoolgirls, Jackie and Lee plotted silly tricks to play on the beleaguered Under-Secretary. One guest remembers an evening when hallucinogenic drugs were discussed. 'Someone said that nutmeg taken in great quantities would produce the same effect as LSD. So the next day Jackie and Lee, who always acted very silly when they got together, thought it would be humorous to drug Franklin and watch him hallucinate. They persuaded Ari's chef to load his soup with nutmeg, and the poor man nearly gagged when he tasted it. His wife looked quite perplexed about the whole thing. In fact, all of us thought it was too silly for words and not at all funny, but then we were unaccustomed to the silly pranks that Jackie and Lee thought were so amusing. They were really strange, those two. So childish and silly. Throughout the cruise they kept saying things like, "Oh, let's call Jack and tell him we're stranded in Istanbul and can't get back." That kind of thing.'

Jackie's childish antics threw the Secret Service men into a frenzy. 'She used to love to drive that poor Clint Hill crazy,' recalled one friend. 'He was her favourite Secret Service man and she always arranged for him to be in charge of her detail when she went out of town. Once in New York when she went night-clubbing with Chuck Spalding and the Roosevelts, Clint was sitting in the front seat with the driver, who asked "Where to?" Jackie piped up, whispering, "Oh, let's go to Harlem." Clint's blood practically congealed when he heard what she said. She always suggested going to some disreputable place just to terrify him. Once she saw his horrified reaction, she would giggle and say, "Oh, Mr Hill. Don't be afraid. I'll try to be a good little girl." '

Other times Jackie wasn't so playful. Once she instructed Hill to confiscate the film of a photographer she saw taking pictures of her from behind a chain link fence. 'Give me that film!' Hill yelled at the photographer. 'Jackie's giving me hell. She's just giving me hell!' Finally airport police intervened and hauled the photographer off to a security room to check his credentials, giving the First Lady time to flee. Only after the White House was called and Pierre Salinger intervened was the man released and his film returned. By then Jackie was gone.

On the trip to Greece Jackie reassured Clint Hill. 'You can relax on this one,' she said. 'There won't be any press so we'll have a good time.'

She was greeted in Athens by Chrysanthemis Papacotis, a twelve-year-old girl who had a special reason for liking the First Lady. During Jackie's first trip to Greece in 1961 she had heard that the child, as a result of a heart ailment, was not expected to live beyond her fifteenth birthday. Jackie asked the American Embassy in Athens to investigate the case, saying that if an operation could save her the child should be sent to the United States. Jackie promised to take care of all expenses.

Days later the Embassy had the youngster flown to a hospital in Athens for examination. It then informed the Walter Reed Hospital in Washington that she needed specialized surgery for the blockage surrounding her heart. US Army surgeons performed the operation, and after two months at Walter Reed the child visited the First Lady in the White House. Jackie arranged for Chrysanthemis to fly on the Kennedys' private plane to New York, where she toured the zoo and the Statue of Liberty. She stayed in the Kennedys' suite at the Carlyle Hotel and visited the United Nations as the personal guest of Ambassador Adlai Stevenson. The First Lady also arranged for her to fly home to Greece with a stop-over in Paris for a few days of sightseeing.

'Jackie's kindness probably saved that little girl's life,' said a friend, 'and although it was an easy gesture for her to make, it surprised all of us that she actually did it. In retrospect, it was the finest thing she ever did as First Lady.'

Newspapers throughout Greece lauded Jackie for her generosity. When she returned in the fall of 1963, it was no surprise that adoring crowds turned out to greet her. Chrysanthemis gave her a gardenia corsage as she stepped off the plane. Then, hugging her sister Lee, Jackie departed in a limousine for the Nomikos villa on the coast of Cavouri, fourteen miles south-west of Athens.

The *Christina* set sail a few days later, weighed down with buckets of red mullet packed in ice, canned hams, crates of grapes, black figs, pears, peaches and pomegranates. Before leaving, Onassis told reporters that the first stop would be Delphi. 'Then we'll go where Mrs Kennedy wants to go. She's in charge here. She's the captain.'

In Istanbul Jackie was cheered by hordes of enthusiastic Turks as she walked ashore to see the famous Blue Mosque. 'Come back,' they yelled as she departed. 'Come back.'

'I will return when my husband is no longer President,' she promised.

The cruise continued on the Ionian Sea, heading for Onassis's dream island of Skorpios, which he had purchased six months before for $110,000. Shaped like a scorpion, the uninhabitable hillside acreage was covered with magnificent olive trees. 'It's simply lovely, Ari,' murmured Jackie. 'Simply lovely.'

'This is nothing,' said the Greek, waving his hand grandly. 'Wait until you see what I am planning to build at the top of the hill. I am going to build a copy of the Cretan Palace of Knossos up there and it will have 180 rooms.

'By the way,' he asked facetiously, 'how many rooms do you have in the White House?'

'Oh, not nearly as many as you will have in your palace,' laughed Jackie. 'But I have grown very attached to the place … you see, I've done a lot of redecorating and I feel a lot of me is there now. Can you understand how I feel?'

'Of course, of course,' replied her gracious host. 'I have heard a great deal about your efforts to restore the White House and I am impressed. Perhaps you will advise me on decorating Knossos when it is finished.'

Basking in the bright Aegean sun, Jackie told everyone how wonderful it was not to be enslaved by a daily schedule.

'That's the beauty of it,' said Franklin Roosevelt, Jr. 'We make up our minds where we want to go as we go along.'

Throughout the cruise the First Lady never mentioned the death of her infant son, Patrick. 'She said she got tired walking and once she stumbled into a hole at the site of the Oracle of Delphi, but she never once discussed the baby,' said a guest. 'Onassis was a wonderful host, very considerate and dynamic, but I can assure you there was nothing between him and Jackie on the cruise. In fact, she kept telling him how wonderful it was to feel so relaxed and said over and over again, "I just wish Jack could be here with us." '

Jackie longed to share the experience with her husband. The President called twice during the cruise, but each time the connection was poor. She could barely hear him tell her about signing the nuclear test ban treaty. She began writing him ten-page letters every night.

'I miss you very much – which is nice though it is also a bit sad,' she wrote. 'I know that I always exaggerate – but – I feel sorry for everyone else who is married – I realize here so much that I am having something you can never have – the absence of tension – I wish so much that I could give you that – so I give you every day while I think of you everything I have to give.'

The last night of the cruise, Onassis, as was his custom, planned an elegant dinner party and presented all the women luxurious gifts. Lee Radziwill received three jewelled bracelets. Sue Roosevelt got an 18-carat gold minaudière rimmed with diamonds from Van Cleef & Arpels.

Mrs Roosevelt opened her present and found a dazzling French evening bag. 'Oh, Sue,' Jackie exclaimed. 'It's just like the one President de Gaulle gave me – only mine doesn't have all those diamonds.'

Guests went slack-jawed when Onassis gave the First Lady her gifts, the most extraordinary being a diamond and ruby necklace that could be converted into two bracelets. 'Oh, God,' moaned Lee Radziwill. 'It's so stunning I can't believe it.' Later the princess wrote to the President: 'Ari has showered Jackie with so many presents I can't stand it. All I've got is three dinky little bracelets that Caroline wouldn't even wear to her own birthday party.'

The President grimaced when he picked up newspapers and read about Jackie's cruise. The news stories told of 'the brilliantly lighted luxury yacht' being 'gay with guests, good food and drink and lavish shipboard dinners'. Kennedy worried about a public outcry arising over the First Lady's luxurious vacation, but he never tried to cut short the trip.

'Every two or three days Jackie and I would call him from the *Christina* to tell him what we were doing,' recalled Franklin Roosevelt, Jr. 'He never once mentioned the criticism and he certainly did not order Jackie to return early. I read stories later that claimed he had called her and said to come home, but that's simply not true.'

Kennedy once asked his wife which country she would

visit if she had a choice of Italy, Ireland, or Morocco. 'I know you want to go to Ireland more than anything in the world,' she said, 'but I would go to Morocco.' The day after the Onassis cruise she flew directly to Marrakesh to stay in the Casbah residence of the King's cousin.

The First Lady arrived with her sister during the celebration honouring the fortieth day of life of the monarch's firstborn son, Prince Mohammed. 'You know,' she giggled, 'Hassan used to be such a playboy, almost as bad as the Shah of Iran. But now that he's King, he's become quite serious. Jack says he's overcompensating.'

King Hassan called the First Lady soon after her arrival to invite her to a Fantasia – an exhibition of Berber horsemanship – being held on the palace grounds. When she admired a spirited white stallion, the old ruler immediately sent a page to the field to order the owner to dismount and present his steed to his royal guest. So ordered, so done.

The King also flew in a hairdresser for Jackie from Casablanca, 140 miles away, and at her request he barred newsmen from taking any pictures of her. Then the Arab ruler decreed that anything Jackie admired was to be presented to her as a gift. Strolling through the Marrakesh bazaar, she admired a good many things. As she was leaving, three station wagons crammed full of presents, not including the white stallion, were readied for the White House. Jackie said she wanted the horse sent to Greece for her sister and brother-in-law to use at their villa.

The President was waiting at the airport in Washington with Caroline and John-John to meet her plane the night she returned – something he didn't ordinarily do. A crowd of admirers broke into applause when she stepped off the plane, smiling and looking happy in the bright glare of the searchlights. 'Oh, Jack,' she whispered, 'I'm so happy to be home.' Kennedy, uncomfortable with any display of affection, accepted a quick, clumsy hug in the limousine before speeding off to the White House.

A few nights later Jackie told friends about her cruise and talked about her host. 'Onassis is no more conscious of his wealth than Rock Hudson is of his good looks. It just comes natural to them – even though Rock was born with his blessings, while Ari had to work like a galley slave to get his.' At dinner with the Bradlees, Jackie said she felt remorseful about all the publicity stirred by the cruise. 'Jackie's guilt feelings might work to my advantage,' the President told his guests. Turning to his wife, he said, 'Maybe now you'll come with me to Texas next month.'

'Sure I will,' she replied.

The First Lady invited Robin Douglas-Home to spend the afternoon with her a few days later at the country home she had built in Atoka, Virginia, near Rattlesnake Mountain. 'She was immensely more relaxed, more outwardly composed and happy than at any time in our previous meetings,' he said. 'There was a new composure. Gone was much of the bewilderment, the repressed frustration, the acidity, and – yes – even the bitchiness that had run through her conversations of the previous year. To put it rather cruelly, I suppose one could summarize it by saying she had clearly grown up a lot in that year; a batch of her pet illusions had been shed; she was learning to accept that her ideals were just not all one hundred per cent attainable one hundred per cent of the time. Some of the arrogance had gone; there was a new humility in its place. The moods were less shifting, the wit less biting, the flares of aggression dimmed and deeper.'

Over dinner that evening the President's wife poured out her heart to her friend, telling him about the unexpected and touching way her husband had reacted to the death of little Patrick three months before. 'The birth, and then the death of that child unquestionably seems to have acted as a kind of catalyst in the relationship between Jacqueline Kennedy and her husband,' recalled the Englishman. 'His reaction to the child's death, as recounted by her ... her own reactions to his ... This tragedy brought them closer together than ever before, to a new plateau of understanding, respect, and affection. The way she touched the rocking chair in the sitting room ... the way she described his fresh awareness of how lucky he was to have the two children she had borne him successfully, how much he valued their presence, watched their growing up with fascination, groped for their love and approval and acceptance, treasured their moments of intimacy together. Paradoxically, Patrick's death had brought new life to their marriage and had also strengthened their self-sufficiency as a family. She had never been happier.'

Although Jackie despised politics, she agreed to accompany her husband to Texas that month. Although she made thirteen trips abroad as First Lady, she had refused to travel in the United States, never venturing west of her riding stables in Virginia. This would be her first political trip as the President's wife and her first public outing since the death of her child.

The President had to visit Texas to do something about the factionalism splitting its Democratic party. The conservative governor, John Connally, and the liberal Senator, Ralph Yarborough, were tearing each other to shreds, and if they weren't reconciled soon the Presidential ticket in 1964 wouldn't stand a chance in the state. Even with Lyndon Johnson as Vice-President, Kennedy barely carried Texas in 1960, winning by only 46,233 votes. He needed the Lone Star State solidly behind him in the 1964 election, so he felt he had no choice but to make the trip.

Adlai Stevenson had visited Texas in October for a United Nations Day ceremony and was spat on and booed by angry crowds. Kennedy aides were cautioned by Secret Service agents who worried about possible demonstrations against the President, and several close friends advised him not to make the trip to Dallas, a John Birch–Dixiecrat–Republican stronghold. The President's decision to integrate the University of Mississippi by sending US marshals in to accompany James Meredith had not been well received in that part of the country. Segregationists despised him for the federal intervention. But Kennedy was determined to make the trip. 'Nobody had to force the President to go to Texas,' said Kenny O'Donnell, 'least of all Lyndon Johnson. He could not have been held back from going to Texas.'

A few days before his scheduled departure, the President flew to Miami with Senator George Smathers to address a group of Latin American newspaper editors. Returning on

Air Force One, he said, 'I've got to go to Texas in a couple of days and I hate like hell to make the trip and get into a pissing match with Lyndon and Ralph Yarborough, but I guess I've got to go. Jackie's going with me.'

'Hey, that's terrific,' said Smathers.

'Yeah, it's about time, isn't it, that she started making some of these damn trips. I'm pleased that she'll be along.'

The White House had announced early in the month that the First Lady would accompany her husband on 21 and 22 November on the two-day swing through the south-west, including fund-raising speeches in San Antonio, Houston, Fort Worth, and Dallas. The Kennedys planned to spend the following weekend at the LBJ Ranch outside Austin, and Jackie promised to accompany the President on his rounds of receptions, breakfasts, luncheons, and dinners. 'She will help in every way she can, consistent with other obligations and continuing good health,' stated the White House spokesman.

Jackie told her friends that, while she dreaded the trip, she was determined to go. 'Jack knows I hate that sort of thing,' she said. 'But all he said to me was, "I'd love you to come with me, but only if you really want to come. You would be a great help to me. But if you don't want to, I will quite understand." So now I'm quite firm in my decision to go to Texas even though I know I'll hate every minute of it. But if he wants me there, then that's all that matters. It's a tiny sacrifice on my part for something he feels is very important to him.'

Chapter Fifteen

President Kennedy wanted this trip to be enjoyable for his wife. He instructed his Air Force aide, Godfrey McHugh, to call the Weather Bureau and get the temperature in Texas so he could tell Jackie what clothes to pack. He wanted her looking her best, especially in Dallas.

'There's going to be all those rich Republican broads at that luncheon wearing mink coats and diamond bracelets,' he said, 'and you've got to look as marvellous as any of them. Be simple – show those damn Texans what good taste really is.'

'If it's so important that I look all right in Dallas, why do I have to be blown around in a motorcade first?' asked Jackie.

Putting up the bubble top on the Presidential limousine was out of the question. Kennedy wanted to be exposed. Barring rain, they had to be out in the open where people would see them.

The first stop was San Antonio, where the President was to dedicate an Air Force school for aerospace medicine, and then on to Houston, where Jackie would deliver a brief speech in Spanish to the League of United Latin-American Citizens. Not nearly as fluent in Spanish as she was in French, she insisted that a Spanish teacher accompany her on the trip and be aboard Air Force One to coach her for the speech.

McHugh reported that the weather would be cool, so the President told his wife to pack autumn clothes.

Trying to decide what to wear, Jackie tramped in and out of his room modelling various outfits. Finally she selected two dresses in beige and white, two suits in blue and yellow, and for Dallas a shocking-pink Chanel suit trimmed with navy blue silk, and a matching pink pillbox hat.

Mary Gallagher was in charge of her wardrobe for this

trip and watched carefully as Provi packed a huge cosmetics case, plus extra pairs of white kid gloves.

Before breakfast on Thursday, 21 November, the President of the United States dressed alone in his bedroom. He put on his back brace, slipped into the clothes his valet had selected, and laced his shoes, the left one of which had a quarter-inch medical lift inserted. He adjusted the PT-boat clip on his tie and grabbed the spectacles that he refused to wear in public, or be photographed in. He pocketed his wallet containing the St Christopher medal money clip he had received from Jackie as an anniversary present.

In another room a hairdresser fussed over Jackie's bouffant, as Caroline slipped in before school to say goodbye to her father. The President intended to take his young son, who loved helicopters, with him to the airport before saying goodbye.

Still fretting about the weather, Kennedy asked his secretary to check the report one more time to make sure. A few minutes later Mrs Lincoln tiptoed in to tell him the bad news. There was a new forecast from Texas saying that the next two days would be unseasonably hot. 'Jesus,' moaned the President, picking up the phone to call his wife's maid. 'Pack some cool dresses.'

'Too late, Meester President,' replied Provi in her broken English. 'Muggsy peeked them up at nine o'clock. They already in the chopper.'

Kennedy hung up and called Godfrey McHugh to chew him out for the faulty weather report. He fumed about it all morning.

Meanwhile, the forty reporters assigned to cover the trip had assembled with the thirteen Texas Congressmen who were accompanying the President. The Secret Service men had prepared the elaborate security precautions which always went into effect whenever the President left Washington. Referring to the Commander-in-Chief as Lancer, who was married to Lace, they prepared to depart from the White House, which was referred to as Castle, leaving behind Lyric and Lark, the fitting code names for Caroline and John-John.

Everyone was ready to go – except for Jackie, who was habitually late.

'See if she's ready yet,' the President ordered one of his aides.

Five minutes later the First Lady appeared in a two-piece white wool boucle dress. Noticing her winter outfit, the President glared at Godfrey McHugh.

Already behind schedule, Air Force One departed Andrews Air Force Base at 11:05. On board, Jackie went directly to her private compartment while the President mingled with some of the Congressmen on board. The First Lady planned to wear a mink hat in San Antonio, but minutes before landing she summoned her secretary and asked about the weather, wondering if perhaps the fur hat might be too warm. Finally she decided that another hat would be more suitable, so she asked Mrs Gallagher to remove the grip-comb and transfer it for her. Then the President knocked on her door.

'Yes, Jack, what is it?' she asked.

'Oh, Jackie, just thought I'd check to see if you were all right.'

'Yes, Jack, I'm just fine. Now will you just go 'way?'

When the stars and stripes of the Presidential plane glided into the San Antonio airstrip, the assembled mob roared with excitement. Jackie emerged first, smiling brightly, and received a huge bouquet of yellow roses with a card reading: 'Respect and gratitude for your contributions to the cultural advancement of our country and to the image of the American Woman which you have carried abroad.' She smiled as she saw some of the placards and hand-lettered signs being waved in her direction: 'JACKIE COME WATER-SKI IN TEXAS', 'WELCOME JFK', 'BIENVENIDO MR AND MRS PRESIDENT'.

Delirious crowds of waving and shouting people greeted the Presidential motorcade, dousing the limousine with a blizzard of confetti. Accustomed to the jumpers and screamers who followed him everywhere, Kennedy smiled broadly and waved as hordes of women screamed in frenzy. Clutching her yellow roses, Jackie waved too. But, unaccustomed to so much tumult, she was stiff and tentative at first.

The crowd in Houston was even more enthusiastic. When the President asked Dave Powers about the turnout, he replied with a smile, 'Well, Mr President, your crowd here today was about the same as last year's, but a hundred thousand more people came out to cheer for Jackie.'

'You see,' exclaimed Kennedy to his wife. 'You do make a difference.'

Later Jackie blurted out how much she disliked Governor Connally.

'Why do you say that?' asked the President.

'I can't stand him. He's just one of those men – oh, I don't know. I just can't bear him sitting there saying all those great things about himself. And he seems to be needling you all day.'

'You mustn't say you dislike him, Jackie. If you say it, you'll begin to think it, and it will prejudice how you act towards him the next day. He's been cozying up to a lot of these Texas businessmen who weren't for him before. What he was really saying in the car was that he's going to run ahead of me in Texas. Well, that's all right. Let him. But for heaven's sake, don't get a thing on him, because that's what I came down here to heal. I'm trying to start by getting two people in the same car. If they start hating, nobody will ride with anybody.'

Jackie was irritated by the friction between Senator Yarborough and Vice-President Johnson, each refusing to ride with the other. She resented her husband's having to spend so much time arbitrating between them. She was exasperated by Governor Connally, disgusted by the gawking crowds, and worn out by the continual smiling and waving she had to do all day. By the time she reached the hotel in Fort Worth she was snapping at her husband, complaining that Mary Gallagher was never where she was supposed to be to help her get ready. The President immediately had the First Lady's secretary paged in the Texas Hotel and lashed into her for her tardiness.

'Mary,' he said, 'Jackie's in the bedroom waiting for you. She's upset over your delay in getting here. You'll just have to make arrangements to get to the hotels before we arrive.

Speak to Muggsy about riding in the luggage car. It takes a different route from the motorcade and reaches the hotel first.'

Dressed in blue and white striped pyjamas, the President was lying down on the bed in his room when his wife entered. The hotel's luggage crew had removed the double mattress and replaced it with a single sleeping board for his bad back. The other half of the bed was bare springs, so Jackie had to return to her own room that night to sleep by herself. She and her husband embraced, but both were so exhausted from their strenuous day that the embrace was, as she said later, 'like a couple of bookends'.

Jackie turned out the light and said good night as she walked out of the room.

'Don't bother getting up with me,' called her husband. 'I've got to speak in that square downstairs before breakfast, so you stay in bed. Just be at the breakfast at nine-fifteen.'

In drizzling rain the crowds in Fort Worth began gathering outside the Kennedys' hotel at 5 am. Jackie complained later that she had a rotten night's sleep, but Kennedy, awakened by his shuffling valet, was delighted with the turnout awaiting him. Rushing into his wife's room to get a better look at the mob cramming the parking lot downstairs, he said, 'God, look at the crowd. Just look! Isn't that terrific?'

A Secret Service man standing outside the door confided later that the First Lady was enraged by the people milling around, yelling up at her window, pleading with her to come and wave to them. Despite the President's request, she refused to go to the window and continued complaining that Texans weren't refined.

The President walked out to speak to the group, calling back to his wife, 'I'll meet you here later, Jackie. Try to be ready.'

After eating breakfast in her room, the First Lady went into the bathroom and then came out to ask her secretary for her make-up. Mrs Gallagher, chastised once by the President, was now being overly efficient and had already packed the cosmetics. She quickly unpacked the make-up bag and Jackie examined herself in the mirror.

'One day in a campaign can age a person thirty years,' she sighed, detecting a new little wrinkle around her eyes.

Standing outside in the misty rain, the President pointed to the eighth floor windows of his suite. 'Mrs Kennedy is organizing herself,' he said. 'It takes her a little longer but, of course, she looks better than us when she does it.' The crowd laughed loudly. Then the President went inside to address the 2,000 Texans waiting in the hotel ballroom for the Chamber of Commerce breakfast.

Jackie was still upstairs getting ready, trying to decide whether to wear short white kid gloves or long ones. Finally she selected the short ones, and held up her wrists so Mary Gallagher could button them. Downstairs her husband stalled for time as he waited for her to arrive.

'Two years ago I introduced myself in Paris by saying that I was the man who accompanied Mrs Kennedy to Paris. I am getting somewhat the same sensation as I travel around Texas. Why is it nobody wonders what Lyndon and I will be wearing?'

The opening formalities dragged on as the choir sang 'The Eyes of Texas Are Upon You'. The President kept glancing toward the kitchen from where his wife was supposed to make her entrance. Twenty minutes passed before Jacqueline Kennedy finally appeared in her pink Chanel suit and pillbox hat. Pandemonium broke loose as she entered, momentarily blinded by the klieg lights and blinking chandeliers. The crowd stomped its approval, standing on chairs to applaud her.

An hour later they were aboard Air Force One heading for Dallas. Glancing at the morning newspaper, Kennedy read an ugly black-bordered advertisement lambasting his administration. For months the *Dallas News* had been fulminating against the President, branding him 'fifty times a fool' for signing the nuclear test ban treaty, which his wife considered his greatest accomplishment in the White House. Reading each word of the diatribe against him, he handed the paper to Jackie, saying, 'Oh, God, we're really heading into nut country today. You know, last night would have been a hell of a night to assassinate a President. I mean it. There was the rain, and the night, and we were all getting jostled. Suppose a man had a pistol in a briefcase,' he said, pointing to the wall and jerking his thumb twice as if pulling a trigger. 'Then he could have dropped the gun and the briefcase and melted away in the crowd.'

Jackie did not pay much attention to what he was saying. She was worrying about the forty-five-minute motorcade ahead of her and how her hair would look after riding in an open car for that long. 'Oh, I want the bubble top,' she said.

The bubble top, a heavy plastic covering put over a convertible, was neither bullet-proof nor bullet-resistant, as many people assumed. It was merely used as protection in case of rain or snow. 'Jackie loved it because it kept her hair from getting windblown,' said Kenny O'Donnell. 'The President, of course, disliked it on a political appearance because it shielded him from the people.'

As Air Force One touched down at Love Field outside Dallas, cheers went up from the boisterous crowd assembled at the airport. But amid the applause there was evidence of hostility. A Confederate flag was held high above the crowd. A few distressing placards read: 'CAN THE CLAN', 'HELP KENNEDY STAMP OUT DEMOCRACY', 'MR PRESIDENT, BECAUSE OF YOUR SOCIALIST TENDENCIES AND BECAUSE OF YOUR SURRENDER TO COMMUNISM I HOLD YOU IN COMPLETE CONTEMPT'.

Vice-President and Mrs Johnson were waiting at the bottom of the ramp to welcome the Kennedys for the fourth time in less than twenty-four hours. Jackie laughed as Lyndon shrugged comically at the absurdity of yet another staged receiving line. Although she mimicked Johnson's heavy twang behind his back, she was rather amused by the man her husband referred to as a riverboat gambler. 'He's so picturesque,' she once told a friend. 'Whatever her outward loyalty to Lyndon Johnson as her husband's Vice-President, Johnson to her and her husband had always been a bit of a private joke,' said Robin Douglas-Home.

Accepting a bouquet of red roses from the Mayor's wife, the First Lady watched her husband go to the fence to start shaking hands. 'There he goes,' she said as he plunged into the crowd.

A big blue Lincoln Continental convertible with flags flying on the fenders rolled up, and the doors were held open for the Kennedys and the Connallys. Motorcycle police led the way with the Governor and his wife, Nellie, sitting on the jump seats in front of the President and his wife, who were in the rear seat with the red roses between them.

The sun beat down as the motorcade began winding slowly towards the Trade Mart where the President was scheduled to make his luncheon speech. Flushed by the heat, Jackie began to wilt in her wool suit. The bright sun made her squint and she put on her dark glasses. The President told her to take them off, explaining quickly that people had come to see her and the glasses masked her face. She complied, but kept sneaking them on when he wasn't looking.

The President stopped the motorcade twice along the route to greet a group of children carrying a sign that read: 'MR PRESIDENT. PLEASE STOP AND SHAKE OUR HANDS'. Then later he stopped for a group of nuns. He always made a beeline for the clergy. Jackie later remembered that during the weekend of their tenth anniversary he noticed some nuns in a crowd of people watching him play golf. He had his car stopped then to say hello to them and nearly convulsed her when he said, 'Jackie here always wanted to be a nun. She went to a convent school and really planned to take orders.'

At Live Oak Street the noise was deafening. People were standing twelve deep on the sidewalk waiting for the President and First Lady to pass. 'You sure can't say Dallas doesn't love you, Mr President,' said Nellie Connally. Kennedy smiled with pleasure. 'No, you can't,' he said. 'No, you can't.'

Zigging off Main Street onto Houston, the limousine continued inching along its route. The crowds along the way screamed so loud that Jackie could barely hear anything. She was getting parched riding in the blazing sun. Then Mrs Connally pointed to the underpass ahead and said, 'We're almost through. It's just beyond that.' Thank God, thought Jackie. How pleasant that cool tunnel will be.

Suddenly there was a sharp, shattering crack, then two more explosions. 'My God, I'm hit,' said the President, holding his throat. Governor Connally shrieked, 'They're going to kill us both.' As if reaching for the top of his head, which was no longer there, the President's hand faltered.

Smelling gunpowder, Senator Yarborough jumped up in the Vice-Presidential car. 'My God,' he yelled. 'They've shot the President.'

'Oh, no, that can't be,' gasped Lady Bird Johnson.

Hearing all the noise, Jacqueline Kennedy turned towards her husband and noticed a quizzical expression on his face. Then he slumped towards her and she saw the blood pouring from his head. 'My God, what are they doing?' she shouted. 'My God, they've killed Jack. They've killed my husband. Jack! Jack!'

Cradling his gaping head in her lap, Jackie sobbed: 'He's dead – They've killed him – Oh, Jack, oh, Jack, I love you.'

'We've got a hit!' yelled the driver. Within seconds he accelerated the car into a mad race for Parkland Memorial Hospital six miles away. Frantic and dazed, Jackie started to flee. Abandoning her husband to the back seat, she began scrambling head-first towards the boot of the car to get away. Within moments her Secret Service man reached the moving limousine in a gallop. He threw himself onto the back of the President's car, climbed up the boot, and grasped Jackie's hand, pushing her back into the seat.

As the car sped towards the hospital, Jackie embraced her husband in her arms, refusing to let anyone see him. Hospital aides were waiting with stretchers for the bullet-torn body of the President of the United States and the Texas Governor, who was still conscious but badly wounded. Clutching her husband, Jackie refused to let go of his body.

'Please, Mrs Kennedy,' begged Clint Hill. 'We must get the President to a doctor.'

'I'm not going to let him go, Mr Hill,' she moaned.

'We've got to take him in, Mrs Kennedy.'

'No, Mr Hill. You know he's dead. Let me alone.'

Suddenly the Secret Service man realized what was

paralysing Jackie. He immediately ripped off his suit coat and laid it in her lap so she could cover the President's head. The sight of his spilling brains and tissues was too unbearable for others to see.

Caked with blood, Jackie stumbled into the hospital, never letting go of the coat covering her husband's head while he was wheeled into the trauma room in the emergency surgery section.

Gripped by grief and terror and disbelief, Kennedy aides swarmed into the hospital with the Vice-President and Mrs Johnson and their dazed entourage. Panic-stricken Secret Service men dashed about, not knowing whether their Commander-in-Chief was dead, wondering if they should transfer their allegiance to the Texan. Mary Gallagher fingered her rosary beads and Dave Powers, thinking he was having a heart attack, asked a priest to hear his confession. Reporters sprang for telephones. Strangers began invading the hospital corridors, drawn by macabre curiosity. Finally a priest was summoned, as in vain the doctors began giving John F. Kennedy blood transfusions.

Jackie sat motionless outside the trauma room, smoking cigarettes. When she heard someone say 'resuscitation', she began hoping for a minute that he might actually be alive. Was there a chance that he could live? Oh, my God, she thought, I'd just do everything for him the rest of my life.

'I'm going in there,' she told a nurse. 'I want to be with him when he dies.'

Watching her husband receive the last rites of his church, Jackie dropped on the floor in a pool of his blood to kneel by his side. 'Eternal rest grant unto him, O Lord,' murmured the priest, blessing the President's forehead with oil. 'Let perpetual light shine upon him,' responded his wife.

A bronze casket was ordered, and when it arrived the doctors tried to make Jackie leave the room. 'Do you think seeing the coffin can upset me, doctor?' she asked. 'I've just seen my husband die, shot in my arms. His blood is all over me. How can I see anything worse than I've seen?'

The doctor stepped aside and allowed her to stay. In front of Kenny O'Donnell and Dave Powers, she slipped her wedding ring off her left hand and moved to her husband's body to lift his lifeless hand. She dipped her hand in a jar of Vaseline and began massaging his finger so she could shove the ring on. Then she kissed him on the lips and said goodbye.

In the corridor outside she turned to Kenny O'Donnell. 'The ring,' she said. 'Did I do the right thing?'

Undone to the point of collapse, O'Donnell reassured her: 'You leave it right where it is.' Later he would get the ring back for her, but right now all he could think about was taking the President's body back to Washington as soon as possible. The Dallas medical examiner kept insisting that the body remain in Parkland for an autopsy according to state law. O'Donnell was adamant that Jackie be spared this excruciating ordeal. Shoving the doctors out of his way, he began pushing the casket towards the door, aided by Larry O'Brien, Dave Powers, and Kennedy's Secret Service agents. They lifted the bronze coffin into a waiting hearse and ordered the driver to speed to Love Field, frantically wondering if the Dallas police would apprehend them at gunpoint to reclaim the body before they reached the plane.

On board Air Force One, Jackie wondered if she should change her blood-stained clothes. Finally, she decided not to. 'No,' she whispered fiercely, 'Let them see what they've done.' She did comb her hair and wash her face. When O'Donnell asked her if she wanted to watch Lyndon Johnson take the oath of office, she said, 'I think I ought to. In the light of history, it will be better if I was there.'

Refusing to sit with the Johnsons after the swearing-in, Jackie returned to the back of the plane. There, surrounded by Kenny O'Donnell, Larry O'Brien, and Dave Powers, she sat next to her husband's casket, never once moving from her vigil.

Members of Kennedy's staff began stumbling back to the rear compartment to offer stammered condolences, to drink Scotch whisky, to cry and share their pain. During that long flight to Washington Jackie was flanked by her husband's Irish Mafia. She sat entranced, listening to their warm, sentimental reminiscences, begging them to tell her more about her husband, relishing their political recollections which had never been part of her life with John F. Kennedy.

'How I envied you being in Ireland with him,' she said. 'He said it was the most enjoyable experience of his whole life. I must have those Irish cadets at his funeral. And he loved the Black Watch pipers. They must be at the funeral, too.'

As the funeral began taking shape in her mind, Jackie vowed that she would make up to her husband in death what she did not give him in life. 'What if I hadn't been there,' she said over and over. 'I'm so glad I was there.' Her final farewell to him would be a royal state occasion, giving the nation an opportunity to mourn its slain leader. She wondered how Abraham Lincoln had been buried and decided she would follow the historical precedent of that day. She remembered once asking her husband the first year they were in the White House where they would be buried. He had told her, 'Hyannis, I guess. We'll all be there.' She recalled what she had said: 'Well, I don't think you should be buried in Hyannis. I think you should be buried in Arlington. You just belong to all the country.'

History made Jack what he was, she thought, and now he is part of history.

Chapter Sixteen

Shattered by the news of Kennedy's death, the country sank into a pervasive depression. Sadness mixed with hysteria. Businesses closed and schools dispersed. People began their death watch in front of their television sets. They absorbed every detail of the President's life and death as it flashed in replays across the screen. Constricted by sadness, most remained transfixed in front of the electronic eye for the entire weekend. Television became a national tranquillizer, serving as the people's only connection to the unspeakable event that would affect them for the rest of their lives.

They watched the terrible sight of John Fitzgerald Kennedy, the 35th President of the United States, being carried off Air Force One by his friends. They recoiled as they saw his beautiful young widow, an empty husk of a woman in blood-spattered clothes, emerge on the arm of the Attorney-General.

'Oh, Bobby – I just can't believe Jack has gone,' Jackie whispered to her brother-in-law as they accompanied the body to Bethesda Naval Hospital.

'I don't want any undertakers,' she said, still focusing on the funeral. 'I want everything done by the Navy.' Then she began telling Robert Kennedy in graphic, unrelenting detail everything that happened to his beloved brother in Dallas. 'That was unbearable for Bobby,' said a friend later, 'absolutely unbearable, but he felt he had no choice but to listen, and listen he did.'

The Auchinclosses were waiting at the hospital for Jackie along with Nancy Tuckerman, Jean Kennedy Smith, and the Bradlees. Eunice Shriver arrived later, as did Charlie and Martha Bartlett. There Robert Kennedy learned that Lee Harvey Oswald was being held in custody in Dallas as his brother's assassin. Beckoning Jackie aside, he said, 'They think they've found the man who did it. They say he's a Communist.'

Jackie turned to her mother. 'He didn't even have the satisfaction of being killed for civil rights. It's – it had to be some silly little Communist,' she said. 'It even robs his death of any meaning.'

From that day forward, controversy clouded the assassination of President Kennedy. Millions of dollars were spent investigating his death, but his widow never cared whether it was an international conspiracy that felled him or the bullet of one deranged man. He was gone and he would never return. That was all that mattered to her the rest of her life. She would testify before the Warren Commission, but she would never pay any attention to the subsequent hearings, the trials, the books, and the voluminous reports questioning whether Lee Harvey Oswald acted alone.

'Jackie, are you going to tell the children, or do you want me to, or do you want Miss Shaw?' asked Janet Auchincloss.

'Well … John can wait. But Caroline should be told before she learns from her friends.'

The British nanny who had had to tell Caroline about the death of her baby brother three months before was forced now to tell the youngster that her father would never again clap his hands to call for her. Maud Shaw couldn't bear to ruin her day, so she waited until Caroline was going to bed that night. Then, putting her arms around the child, she said, 'I can't help crying, Caroline, because I have some very sad news to tell you. Your father has gone to look after Patrick. Patrick was so lonely in heaven. He didn't know anybody there. Now he has the best friend anyone could have.'

John-John learned of his father's death later. When Maud Shaw explained that he had gone to heaven, the three-year-old asked curiously, 'Did he take his big plane with him?' 'Yes, John, he probably did.' 'I wonder when he's coming back,' said the uncomprehending child.

Dazed and unbelieving, Jackie began again to unburden herself, pouring out the awful events in Dallas to her friends. 'I can remember now only the strangely graceful arc she described with her right arm as she told us that part of the President's head had been blown away by one bullet,' said Ben Bradlee. 'She moved in a trance to talk to each of us there and to new friends as they arrived, ignoring the advice of friends and doctors to get some sleep and to change out of her bloody clothes. Those were some kind of dreadful badge of the disaster she had been through, and no one could persuade her to remove them.'

She told the story again and again over the next few days and weeks and months, purging herself of the catastrophe. To Robin Douglas-Home she recounted her husband's bravery. 'Governor Connally was squealing like a stuck pig. Jack never made a sound.' To Betty Spalding she told of trying to hold her husband's brains inside his head. 'I was in a state of shock. I don't remember ever trying to get away and climb out of the car.' To the White House usher she said, 'To think that I very nearly didn't go. Oh, Mr West, what if I'd been here – out riding in Virginia or somewhere – Thank God I went with him!' To Dave Powers she said, 'Do you know what we should have in the Kennedy library? A pool – so Dave can give exhibitions of how he swam with the President.'

Remembering that evening at the Bethesda hospital, she said later, 'I was sort of keyed up in a strange way.' And it was that excess of energy which enabled her to carry the awesome dignity. 'Somehow we've got to get through the next few days,' she told her secretaries. 'Be strong for two or three days, then we'll all collapse.'

That night Robert Kennedy took charge of everything, calling for a catafalque, cannon, the military, and requesting a representative from the Special Forces, the guerrilla-trained troops in green berets whom President Kennedy had sent to the jungles of Vietnam. At the White House, Sargent Shriver and Bill Walton began draping the East Room in black for the White House memorial service. Already the funeral was taking shape. The dead President's body would lie in state in the great frescoed rotunda of the Capitol on Sunday and be buried on Monday after a funeral Mass.

Early that evening the new President spoke to a brokenhearted nation. 'This is a sad time for all people,' said Lyndon Johnson. 'We have suffered a loss that cannot be weighed. I know the world shares the sorrow that Mrs Kennedy and her family bear. I will do my best. That's all I can do. I ask for your help – and God's.'

Jackie was determined to spend the night at Bethesda if need be. 'I'm not leaving here 'til Jack goes, but I won't cry till it's all over,' she said, refusing all sedatives and chain-smoking one cigarette after another. She turned on the television and watched the replay of the swearing-in, of her arrival at Andrews Air Force Base, of Americans praying in the streets, gathering to pay homage to the fallen President. She begged everyone to stay with her, pleading with her parents to spend the night at the White House. 'Will you sleep in Jack's room?' she asked her mother. 'I'd like it if you slept in Jack's bed.' She insisted that Larry O'Brien, Kenny O'Donnell, and Pierre Salinger stay there with her, too, and Jean Kennedy Smith, Bobby, and Eunice Shriver.

'It's almost as though she doesn't want the day to end,' reflected Martha Bartlett.

'She can't bear to be alone,' said Janet Auchincloss.

Close to dawn Jackie was driven back to the White House, where she accompanied her husband's coffin up the steps of the North Portico. Then she went upstairs and finally shed her stained clothes. As she was bathing, her personal maid packed the blood-spattered garments in a box and hid them. Later Janet Auchincloss took the box to her Georgetown home. She put it in the attic next to the box containing Jackie's wedding dress, where it still remains, untouched and unseen by anyone.

That morning Jackie accepted a full gram of amytal from Dr John Walsh and drifted off to sleep.

When her sister and brother-in-law arrived from London, Stas Radziwill was struck by the regal atmosphere pervading the White House. 'It's just like Versailles when the King died,' he said. He would repeat that observation later when Jackie, imbued by the glory of France, insisted that an eternal flame be installed over her husband's grave, like the flame flickering over the Tomb of the Unknown Soldier under the Arc de Triomphe in Paris. Robert Kennedy was stunned by this theatrical gesture. 'I could understand a memorial, but she wanted a goddamned eternal flame,' he muttered to the Secretary of Defence.

As the White House movers began crating Kennedy's office furniture, President Lyndon Johnson was operating out of the Executive Office Building next door, determined to let John F. Kennedy's widow have the White House as long as she wanted it. She stayed for eleven days.

Jackie glanced over the guest list for her husband's funeral as State Department aides made trans-Atlantic phone calls, summoning heads of state to Washington to walk with the cortège from the White House to the Pontifical Requiem Mass at St Matthew's Cathedral and then to the final military rites at Arlington Cemetery. Le Gran Charles was the prize catch. At first the French President insisted on remaining in Paris. His foreign policy differences with Kennedy had been bitter and, being a proud man, he didn't want to appear hypocritical. When he changed his mind and decided to attend the funeral, his acceptance paved the way for others, unleashing a flood of acceptances from kings and queens and emperors around the world. Following the example of the legendary de Gaulle, ninety-two nations sent delegations to Washington for the funeral. Without de Gaulle's presence, the funeral of President Kennedy might not have been so internationally spectacular.

When Jackie learned that President de Gaulle would be arriving at the White House, she ordered the curator to remove all the Cézannes from the walls of the Yellow Oval Room and hang Bennet and Cartwright prints. 'I'm going to be receiving President de Gaulle in this room,' she said, 'and I want him to be aware of the heritage of the United States. These prints are scenes from our own history.' Yet, when she selected a painting for the Kennedy family to leave in the White House in memory of the late President, Jackie chose a dreamy painting of water lilies by the French landscape artist Claude Monet. The choice illustrates the complex, inconsistent reasoning of this woman who was determined to represent America to the President of France but chose to leave a French memorial in honour of her American husband who served as the President of the United States.

The Gaelic buoyancy that John Fitzgerald Kennedy represented to the country began to manifest itself in the White House during the tragic days of his funeral. 'It was like an Irish wake,' said one close family friend. 'There was a euphoria inside the mansion during that weekend, a false gaiety and frivolity that kept us going. Everyone, including Jackie, who refused to be alone during that time, was buoyed up, feeling spritely and gay. I still remember when Aristotle Onassis arrived, we all piled into a sports car and raced to Arlington, and later we all laughed and sang and carried on with great hilarity back at the White House.'

Bobby Kennedy badgered the Greek ship-owner endlessly about his yacht and his wealth. During dinner the Attorney-General presented Onassis with a formal document stipulating that he give half his wealth to the poor in Latin America. Responding to the tease, Onassis signed the document in Greek and everyone laughed.

'I can still remember everyone singing "Heart of My Heart", and Teddy Kennedy getting very drunk and doing his marvellous Irish imitations, and Dave Powers telling outrageously funny stories of the days Jack first ran for office in Boston,' said another friend. 'There were no tears, and no grim solemnity or sad mourning inside the White House during those days. Just a lot of smart-aleck bantering among all the Kennedys, who loved to needle everyone and bombard their conversations with sarcasm and tart remarks and loud, boisterous humour. It was really quite unreal, considering why we were all there.'

The horseplay began shortly after Ethel Kennedy arrived wearing one of her numerous wigs. Some prankster snatched the dynel curls off her head and began passing the mop around until it was finally plopped on the bald pate of Robert McNamara, the Secretary of Defence. He looked like a bespectacled grandma, which amused everyone.

Upstairs in the Presidential suite, obsessed with ceremonial details, Jackie made endless lists of everything she had to do. She dispatched memos around the White House.

She wanted Bunny Mellon to arrange the flowers on the President's grave. She ordered a black veil to cover her face for the funeral. She designed a black-bordered Mass card saying, 'Dear God – Please take care of your servant John Fitzgerald Kennedy. Please take him straight to heaven.' She ordered black-bordered sympathy cards. She selected from the President's personal belongings certain things to give to his aides and friends and family as treasured mementos. These she presented with personal letters. She wrote thank-you notes to everyone on the White House staff, and sent a note of condolence to Marie Tippit, the widow of the policeman shot by Oswald in Dallas. Although Jackie, preoccupied with her own grief at the time, refused to speak to Mrs Tippit on the phone, she later sent her a photograph of herself with the President which she personally inscribed. 'There is another bond we share. We must remind our children all the time what brave men their fathers were,' she wrote. She insisted that Luigi Vena, the tenor soloist at her wedding, sing the Ave Maria at her husband's funeral. She also stipulated that everyone walk with her from the White House to the Cathedral in solemn procession. Then she began thinking of moving out of the White House and worried about where she would go. John Kenneth Galbraith reassured her, saying that he had already made arrangements for her to move into the Georgetown mansion of Averell Harriman until she decided what she would do with her life.

In her darkened bedroom she wrote a final impassioned letter to her husband, filling page after page with her love and remorse. She sealed the envelope, and went to the nursery with her blue stationery. There she told her daughter, 'You must write a letter to Daddy now, and tell him how much you love him.' Caroline took a ball-point pen and began printing in block letters: 'Dear Daddy: We are all going to miss you. Daddy I love you very much. Caroline.' John-John, too young to write, marked Caroline's letter with an X. Then Jackie took the letters and a piece of the President's scrimshaw, a pair of his gold cufflinks which she had given him, along with two sapphire bracelets offered by Lee Radziwill, and placed them all in his coffin. Robert Kennedy added his gold PT-boat tie clasp and watched as Jackie cut a lock of hair from the slain President's head.

The country sat mesmerized in front of television sets, watching the regal First Lady leave the White House with her two young children to visit the flag-draped coffin of her husband lying in state under the Capitol dome. There they heard the eulogy of the Montana Senator, Mike Mansfield, who kept repeating in five trembling refrains, '… and so she took a ring from her finger and placed it in his hands … and so she took a ring from her finger and placed it in his hands, and kissed him and closed the lid of a coffin …'

The sight of Jacqueline Kennedy approaching that bier, clutching the white-gloved hand of her little blonde daughter, sent tremors through the nation. 'We're going to go say goodbye to Daddy and we're going to kiss him goodbye, and tell Daddy how much we love him and how much we'll always miss him,' she whispered to Caroline. As they rose to approach the coffin together, they struck a chord deep in hearts across the nation. Blinded by tears, the country ached for this widow and cried with shame. In their agony the people elevated her like a beloved icon. She became a national folk heroine. Her legend began the hour she appeared in front of the White House to lead the funeral procession to St Matthew's Cathedral. The haunting cadence of muffled drums, the reverberations of the twenty-one-gun salute, the military drills, and the clattering hoofs of the riderless horse stirred the nation to idolatry.

Holding the hands of her children, both dressed in light blue coats and red lace-up shoes, Jacqueline Kennedy radiated a majestic presence which was both awe-inspiring and soothing to a country racked with grief. Standing erect behind her black veil, she kept control and fought for repose, shedding few public tears. She listened reverently to Cardinal Cushing's prayers and seemed quite moved when the prelate slipped from traditional Latin into English, crying out, 'May the angels, dear Jack, lead you into Paradise.'

Outside the cathedral, as the cortège began the final trip to Arlington, the band saluted the dead President with one final rendition of 'Hail to the Chief'. As parade soldiers snapped to attention to salute their fallen leader, Jackie bent over and whispered to her son. 'John, you can salute Daddy now and say goodbye,' she said.

The three-year-old stepped forward, raised his right hand stiffly, and cocked his elbow at precisely the right angle. The image of that little boy giving his father a final salute was the most heart-rending of the day. The country was reduced to tearful spasms as it watched the small saddened face of John Fitzgerald Kennedy, Jr, his dimpled knees and bright red shoes, saying goodbye to his father. Words cannot recapture the poignancy of that moment, but with that little salute the President's son moved the nation from crippling despair to total devotion.

Clad in the same black suit she wore when her husband announced his Presidential candidacy, Jackie lit the eternal flame over his grave and passed the torch to his brothers. Then she returned to the White House, passing throngs of people sobbing in the streets. At the Executive Mansion she held a reception for the visiting heads of state. Emotionally spent, she coasted on nervous energy, reverting helplessly to the sudden mood swings that characterized her complex personality.

These volatile shifts became most obvious during her private meeting with President de Gaulle. As the royal First Lady, she gave him a sharp ticking-off on 'this France, England, America thing', chastising him for hampering Franco-American relations and sabotaging her husband's grand design. Then, moments later, she reverted to the childish coquette. Taking him by the hand, she said, 'Come, let me show you where your beautiful commode is.' On the French chest that de Gaulle had given to the Kennedys stood a bouquet of fresh daisies. Jackie picked a flower from the vase and handed it to him, 'I want you to take this as a last remembrance of the President,' she said. De Gaulle later told aides he was quite perplexed by this disturbing performance of Jacqueline Kennedy.

After all the state visitors had left the White House, Jackie gathered her family and friends in the private dining-room to celebrate the birthdays of Caroline and John-John.

On Thanksgiving Jackie flew to Hyannis Port to see Ambassador Kennedy, who was not allowed to attend his son's funeral. The old man's nurse, Rita Dallas, remembers a loud terrible scene as the Kennedys tried to prevent Jackie from going upstairs to the Ambassador's room. 'She was aggravated at the smothering attempt of the family to get her to rest,' said Mrs Dallas.

'I'm here to see Grandpa,' Jackie screamed. 'I'll rest later – just leave me alone now and let me see Grandpa.'

Carrying the flag that was furled over John F. Kennedy's coffin, Jackie asked Mrs Dallas to give it to Joe Kennedy. Then she walked into his room and, putting her arms around the paralysed patriarch, began talking to him. 'Grandpa, Jack's gone and nothing will ever be the same again for us. He's gone and I want to tell you about it.' Then for the next hour the thirty-four-year-old widow poured her heart out to her enfeebled father-in-law, telling him in bloody detail the most harrowing experience of her life.

Two days later she returned to the White House to begin packing. Frightened by her sudden aloneness, she clung to her staff for support. Embracing Nancy Tuckerman, she said, 'Poor Tucky. You came all the way down from New York to take this job, and now it's all over. It's so sad. You will stay with me for a little while, won't you?'

Depressed and weeping, she turned to her personal secretary, Mary Gallagher. 'Why did Jack have to die so young? Even when you're sixty, you like to know your husband is there. It's so hard for the children. Please, Mary, don't ever leave. Get yourself fixed for salary on my government appropriation – just don't leave me!'

'Mr West,' she said to the White House usher, 'will you be my friend for life?'

During those last days in the White House Jackie swung between thoughtlessness and tenderness. She moved her husband's valet to tears by presenting him with the President's rocking chair inscribed with a bronze plaque saying, 'For George Thomas – The Rocking Chair of John Fitzgerald Kennedy – 35th President of the United States. It was always in his bedroom – I know he would want you to have

216

it – JBK.' Yet she was cavalier towards Maud Shaw, the nanny who had tended her children since Caroline was eleven days old. Instead of giving her a treasured keepsake from the President's belongings, Jackie handed her one of Kennedy's old shirts. 'I couldn't believe it,' said the nanny later, 'but then what could I say?'

Then came the real wrench. The White House which she once detested suddenly became her greatest security. Although Eleanor Roosevelt had vacated the Executive Mansion the day her husband died, Jacqueline Kennedy could not bear to relinquish her position as First Lady. She dreaded leaving. The day before her departure she ordered another inscribed bronze plaque placed over the fireplace in the President's bedroom, proclaiming to the world her proprietary rights as the President's wife. The plaque said: 'In this room lived John Fitzgerald Kennedy with his wife Jacqueline – during the 2 years, 10 months and 2 days he was President of the United States – January 20, 1961–November 22, 1963.'

No other First Lady in history had ever done such a thing. Only one other such plaque existed, and that was the one on the President's mantle which read: 'In this room Abraham Lincoln slept during his occupancy at the White House as President of the United States, March 4, 1861–April 13, 1864.' Jackie placed her plaque right beneath Abraham Lincoln's.

Chapter Seventeen

'When Jack quoted something it was usually classical,' said his widow, 'but I'm so ashamed of myself – all I keep thinking of is this line from a musical comedy. At night before we'd go to sleep Jack liked to play some records, and the song he loved most came at the very end of this record. The lines he loved to hear were: "Don't let it be forgot that once there was a spot, for one brief shining moment, that was known as Camelot."

'Oh, there'll be great Presidents again,' she continued, 'and the Johnsons are wonderful, they've been wonderful to me – but there'll never be another Camelot.'

Transfixed by this thought, she repeated it again in her small whisper. 'Don't let it be forgot that once there was a spot, for one brief shining moment, that was known as Camelot – and it will never be that way again.'

Shrouded in widow's weeds, Jackie proclaimed a year of mourning for herself in which she vowed to enshrine the memory of her husband in the minds of all Americans. As time went by she brooded about the assassination and began to feel more and more inadequate as a wife and helpmate. She became fixated with making amends to him. First there was the eternal flame. 'Whenever you drive over the bridge from Washington to Virginia,' she said, 'you see the Lee Mansion on the side of the hill in the distance. When Caroline was very little, the mansion was one of the first things she learned to recognize. Now at night you can see his flame beneath the mansion for miles away.'

Then, before leaving the White House, she approached Lyndon Johnson and asked him to rededicate Cape Canaveral in Florida so that when Americans reached the moon they would arrive in rockets from Cape Kennedy. Knowing her husband's total commitment to the space programme, this seemed a fitting first memorial to him. Lyndon Johnson immediately rechristened the space launch site in honour of the late President.

Jackie had named her home in the hunt country Wexford in honour of the county in Ireland where Kennedy's ancestors were located. She began referring to herself as Bridey Kennedy among Jack's Irish lieutenants. Days before, she asked that Irish songs be played outside the White House as the caisson left for St Matthew's Cathedral. On the day of his funeral, mourners listened to the lilting strains of 'The Boys from Wexford' and 'Come Back to Erin' in honour of America's first Irish Catholic President. His widow took shamrocks to his grave on St Patrick's Day. On 17 March she mailed 900,000 black-bordered prayer cards to acknowledge the sympathy messages she had received. 'I felt St Patrick's Day was the appropriate time to acknowledge those letters,' she said.

She swore she would live in Washington to pursue the dreams of Camelot. 'I'm never going to live in Europe,' she said. 'I'm not going to travel extensively abroad. That's a desecration. I'm going to live in the places I lived with Jack. In Georgetown and with the Kennedys at the Cape. They're my family. I'm going to bring up my children. I want John to grow up to be a good boy.'

For the next year she dedicated herself to the John F. Kennedy Memorial Library, opening exhibits and sponsoring displays. She encouraged more than a hundred people associated with the New Frontier to record their recollections, and gave her full cooperation to William Manchester in documenting the death of her husband for a book he was writing. She spent ten hours with the author tape-recording her thoughts about those horrible days. She appeared on television to thank the hundreds of thousands of people who wrote to her. The day she chose to make this appearance happened to be the same night Mrs Johnson was holding her first White House dinner, which meant that the next day's papers were full of Jackie, not Lady Bird.

Speaking with great difficulty, Mrs Kennedy said, 'The knowledge of the affection in which my husband was held by all of you has sustained me, and the warmth of these tributes is something that I shall never forget. Whenever I can bear to, I read them. All his bright light gone from the world. All of you who have written to me know how much we all loved him and that he returned that love in full measure. Every message is to be treasured, not only for my children, but so that future generations will know how much our country and peoples in other nations thought of him. Your letters will be placed with his papers in the library to be erected in his memory on the Charles River in Boston, Massachusetts. I hope in years to come many of you and your children will come to visit the Kennedy Library.'

More than one million condolence letters poured in after that broadcast. In less than a year a devoted populace raised over 10 million dollars to honour the memory of the late President. Congress allocated $50,000 a year to Mrs Kennedy to staff her office, appropriated $10,000 a year to her as a widow's pension, passed a resolution giving her free postage under her personal frank, and voted funds to continue Secret Service protection for her and her children the rest of her life, or until she remarried.

The United States Senate approved a bill to establish the John F. Kennedy Center for the Performing Arts as a national monument to be built in Washington. Congress authorized 15 and a half million dollars in Federal funds to match the same amount in private donations. Soon, other countries, big and small, began making donations to the Center.

New York renamed Idlewild Airport in memory of the late President, and cities across the nation dedicated an avenue, a school, or a square to him. Dallas, Texas, was one of the first to establish a John F. Kennedy Plaza. Memorials sprang up around the world – Kennedy Platz in Berlin, Corso Kennedy in Rome, Avenue Kennedy in Paris. Then there was the silver Kennedy 50-cent piece, and the designation of his Brookline birthplace as a national historical landmark. Soon gifts arrived by the thousands for his widow and children. Princess Lala Aicha of Morocco flew to Washington on behalf of her brother King Hassan to present Jackie a century-old palace in Marrakesh.

Still, none of the presents or memorials filled the ugly emptiness she felt during those awful days. She told friends she suffered implacable loneliness and nightmares of despair. 'I'm a living wound. My life is over. I'm dried up – I have nothing more to give and some days I can't even get out of bed,' she confided. 'I cry all day and all night until I'm so exhausted I can't function. Then I drink.'

Jackie begged her secretary to stay in the room with her as she began unpacking her husband's personal folders. 'It's so much easier doing it while you're here than at night when I'm alone,' she said. 'I just drown my sorrows in vodka.'

When the decorator Billy Baldwin arrived from New York to help her redecorate the Harriman mansion, he found Jackie putting books away in the living-room. 'I had never seen anyone looking so bereft,' he said.

'Look,' said Jackie, opening some boxes. 'I have some beautiful things to show you.' Producing small pieces of Greek sculpture and precious Roman figurines, she said, 'These are the beginning of a collection Jack started. It's so said to be doing this. Like a young married couple fixing up their first house together. I could never make the White House personal – so many rooms around me that I knew were empty ...'

Then in front of the decorator she broke down, sobbing in desolation. Excruciating minutes passed before she looked at him. 'I know from my very brief acquaintance with you that you are a sympathetic man,' she said. 'Do you mind if I tell you something? I know my husband was devoted to me. I know he was proud of me. It took a very long time for us to work everything out but we did, and we were about to have a real life together. I was going to campaign for him. I know I held a very special place for him – a unique place ...'

She talked on and on, very quietly and very sadly, about her life with Jack Kennedy, trying to rationalize their marriage into something special and enduring. She had to tell herself and anyone who would listen that she had indeed been a good wife to her husband and that, despite his flagrant philandering and constant pursuit of other women, he did love her in his own way. Jackie agonized over this more than anything. Throughout her mourning she kept repeating pathetically that her years with Jack Kennedy in the White House had been the happiest of their ten-year marriage. 'The room filled with her terrible loneliness,' said the decorator.

'Can anyone understand how it is to have lived in the White House, and then, suddenly, to be living alone as the President's widow?' she asked him. 'There's something so final and passé about it. And the children. The world is pouring terrible adoration at the feet of my children, and I fear for them, for this awful exposure. How can I bring them up normally? We would never even have named John after his father if we had known ...'

Wallowing in self-pity, Jackie frequently lashed out at the secretaries trying to help her. Screaming at Evelyn Lincoln, she said, 'Oh, Mrs Lincoln, all this shouldn't be so hard for you, because you still have your husband. What do I have now? Just the Library ...'

Mrs Lincoln had made the mistake of requesting larger accommodations. 'She wanted to know why I needed such a large office,' said Kennedy's secretary, 'and I told her that since all the people loved the President so much, I felt his things should be displayed in a nice office for them to see. Then she burst out with, "But these things are all mine," and told me what she wanted done with them, not to give them to this one and that one.'

Jackie criticized her husband's secretary for taking so long to complete her records for the Kennedy archives. 'Why, Mrs Lincoln,' she said, 'I could sit down and in a half day index all these items on cards myself.'

Although she wrote a letter of tribute to the Secretary of the Treasury commending the Secret Service, and stood beside Clint Hill as he received a medal for 'exceptional bravery', Jackie complained bitterly about the protection in Dallas. She mentioned one particular agent who had not acted during the crucial moment. 'He might as well have been Maud Shaw,' she said. 'Well, what can I do now? Send a blast – write a memo – Oh, well, I guess Jack would only have gotten more reckless as time went on anyway ...'

She rehashed the shooting in Dallas with Dave Powers and

Kenny O'Donnell, wondering if there was an interval of at least five seconds between the second and third shots. She was convinced that if the Secret Service men in the front seat had reacted more quickly to the first two shots, and if the driver had stepped on the gas before instead of after the fatal third shot was fired, her husband would still be alive.

Wallowing in her own private misery, she shunned friends who were trying to be kind. Wayne Hays, the former Ohio congressman, tried to offer a special gesture but was rebuffed. He had visited the Kennedys in the White House and remembered Jackie showing him an exquisite antique crystal inkwell sitting on a desk in the Green Room. She had told him then that of everything in the executive mansion that was the only object she truly coveted, the one thing she wanted to take with her when she left.

Later Hays saw a picture of the inkwell in an antique magazine and recognized it as the exact duplicate of the one Jackie loved. So he called the dealer in London and asked him to hold it. On his next trip to Europe he made a special trip to England and paid $1,500 for the treasure which he planned to present to the First Lady when she returned from Dallas.

After the assassination he waited several weeks before telling Sargent Shriver that he had a gift for Jackie and would like to give it to her. Shriver said he would check with his sister-in-law. Months passed and Hays never heard a word. The next time he saw Shriver he again mentioned the gift he had for Mrs Kennedy. Shriver called him back a few days later to say that he had talked to Jackie who suggested that Hays stick his gift in a brown paper bag and send it to her by messenger. Enraged by the rebuff, the congressman decided to keep it for himself.

At that time Jackie felt beset by financial worries and began scrutinizing her expense accounts. Seeing the vast amounts of money spent on food and liquor, she became convinced that her staff was taking unfair advantage of her. 'I think the employees are taking food home with them,' she said. Spotting a petty cash allotment that Mary Gallagher had made to a Secret Service man, Jackie exploded. 'What're they doing,' she snapped, 'using my money for their accommodations?'

When she noticed that Mrs Gallagher had paid $900 to Provi, her personal maid, for overtime, she screamed. 'Overtime? Do you mean to say that for every little thing extra someone does around here, I have to pay them?'

'Yes, Jackie,' replied Mrs Gallagher. 'That's usually the way it works.'

'Oh, Mary,' said Jackie. 'About Provi's salary – I just think $100 is too high … And you,' she said, whirling on her secretary, 'demanding $12,000 salary. Why, I just can't afford it.'

Most people assumed that John F. Kennedy's widow inherited millions upon his death. The fact of the matter is that she only received a lump sum payment of $25,000, plus all her husband's personal effects, including furniture, furnishings, silverware, china, glassware, and linens. In addition, she was paid $43,229.26, representing the total due the President's estate from Navy retirement pay and allowance, death benefits from the Civil Service retirement system, and salary owed him as President for 1–22 November 1963. In terms of capital she received less than $70,000. Although John F. Kennedy was the wealthiest man ever to occupy the White House, his taxable assets at the time of his death totalled only $1,890,640.45.

The two trust funds he established for his wife and children were estimated at 10 million dollars, but Jackie's share as a widow was limited to yearly payments from the principal of one trust which could not exceed 10 per cent of the value at the beginning of the calendar year.

Two months after her husband's death she sat down with the Kennedys' financial advisor to review her money situation. Afterwards she began receiving $200,000 a year, approximately $17,000 a month, from the trust fund. She continued sending her bills to the New York office, which handled everything for her.

'Jack left her an income but not capital,' said Betty Spalding, who visited Jackie after the assassination. 'He provided for the kids but Jackie only got a widow's income. I visited her at Wexford, and we stayed up talking until 3 am one morning. She wondered where she was going to live and

18 December 1970. Jackie, Caroline and John Jr eating ice cream after school in New York.

Jackie and Pat Lawford at the "21 Club", New York.

3 January 1971. Jackie and Caroline leaving Central Park after Caroline had been sleigh riding with her brother.

17 January 1971. Jackie and Ari walking in New York.

6 October 1971. Jackie leaving
Central Park after walking around
the reservoir.

5 June 1975, Jackie Onassis and Caroline Kennedy at her graduation from Concord Academy.

8 May 1976. Jackie Onassis mobbed by the press at the Star Spangled Gala benefiting the New York Public Library at the Metropolitan Opera House.

18 September 1977. Jackie Onassis and Pete Hamill.

worried about how to raise her children and how she was going to hack it alone.'

As a woman who could spend $40,000 on department stores in three months, Jackie now felt strapped. In December 1963 she bought a house in Georgetown across the street from the Harrimans for $175,000. A few weeks later the house on N Street where she lived before moving to the White House was put on the market for $225,000. 'God, that enrages me,' she told a friend. 'Jack and I bought that house in 1957 for $78,000. We sank a lot of money into it for renovations and only got $105,000 for it three years later. We barely made a profit at all, and now the Ausbrooks are going to make $120,000 on the deal because it was our house, and they only lived there three years.'

In her grief Jackie leaned heavily on her brother-in-law, Robert Kennedy, who visited her and the children in Georgetown every afternoon. She asked Dave Powers to stop by at noon every day to have lunch with John-John and play soldier games with the little boy, marching about and saluting as they did in the White House. Caroline's nursery school continued classes in the British Embassy until summer. 'Bobby and I spent some time with Jackie almost every afternoon,' Kenny O'Donnell recalled, 'both of us so troubled and uncertain about the future that she probably was more consoling to us than we were helpful to her.'

The sledgehammer blow of John Kennedy's death devastated Robert Kennedy, who secretly requested the protection of US marshals for his family. 'He was not entitled to Secret Service protection at the time, but since he was Attorney-General and a good friend of Jim McShane, the director of the US Marshal Service within the Department of Justice, agents were sent out to Hickory Hill for around-the-clock protection,' recalled one of the marshals. 'We were out there for six months after Dallas, and Bobby was so distraught some days he couldn't even talk to us. Other days he might say hello, but none of us ever carried on a real conversation with him. He was so undone by the assassination that he could barely talk to his wife. I still remember the nights when he couldn't sleep. He'd get up at 3 am and climb into his convertible and drive off by himself with the top down in that freezing weather, speeding out of the driveway and peeling down the deserted streets. He never allowed any of us to accompany him so we never knew where he went. He'd be gone until six in the morning. Then he would come back, go in the house, change his clothes and go off to work.

'Most of his kids were so young they didn't really comprehend what had happened to the President, but once when we were driving Bobby, Jr, some place, he began horsing around and grabbed the transmitter in the car. Before we knew what was happening, he started talking over the broadcast mike, saying, "This is Bobby Kennedy, the Attorney-General's son, and I've just been kidnapped." Those transmitters alert every security force in Washington, and we nearly had a real catastrophe on our hands until we could get the mike away from him and radio back that he was only kidding and we weren't actually on an emergency alert.'

Bobby Kennedy spent more time with his sister-in-law and her children than with his own, and Jackie leaned on him for everything. She even considered at one point asking him to adopt Caroline and John-John, feeling she could never raise them by herself, but Bobby told her the idea was crazy, that she had to go on. He gave as much as he could at the time, offering her all his love and support and protection. 'I think he is the most compassionate person I know,' said Jackie, 'but probably only the closest people around him – family, friends, and those who work for him – would see that. People of a private nature are often misunderstood because they are too shy and too proud to explain themselves.'

Jackie often visited Hickory Hill during her mourning so her children could play with their cousins. She was plagued by crowds of staring people who daily lined the sidewalks in front of her house. Each morning busloads of tourists arrived flashing their cameras. Curiosity seekers camped out, waiting to catch a glimpse of her and the children.

'They actually sit there and eat their lunch and throw sandwich wrappers on the ground,' she sobbed. 'I'm trapped in that house and can't get out. I can't even change my clothes in private because they can look in my bedroom window.'

'It was awful the way the press hounded her after the assassination,' said Betty Spalding. 'They burst into her house, stared at her constantly, and just made her life miserable.'

One night Jackie tried to dine out in Washington with her sister Lee, Marlon Brando, and his business manager, George Englund. Lee, who was a friend of Englund, suggested that the four of them have a quiet dinner at the Jockey Club, Jackie's favourite French restaurant. Minutes after they arrived reporters and photographers descended, forcing Jackie and Lee to run out of the kitchen exit. Brando and Englund walked out of the front door by themselves.

'It was a gross error,' Brando mumbled to reporters. 'I am in Washington for a conference with the American Indians. I don't even know Mrs Kennedy.'

'Mr Englund is helping to plan the Kennedy Foundation dinner in New York,' said Pamela Turnure, 'and I think the dinner was in connection with that. They didn't want to leave her alone, so they asked her to join them for dinner.'

Jackie felt that the press dogged her every step, making it impossible for her to go anywhere. Finally Lee Radziwill persuaded her sister to consider moving to New York, where she would not be such a tourist attraction. 'You've got to get out of this gloomy city,' she said. 'Washington is too full of painful memories for you.' Jayne Wrightsman, Jackie's Palm Beach friend, also argued in favour of the move, and told her of someone selling a five-bedroom cooperative apartment at 1040 Fifth Avenue. Jackie flew to New York to visit the grey granite building overlooking Central Park. After seeing the fifteenth floor apartment with its own private elevator and twenty-three windows, she decided to make the move. 'It's perfect,' she told André Meyer, her financial advisor and chairman of the banking firm of Lazard Frères, 'and if you think it's a good investment, I'll buy it.' The purchase price was $200,000.

While Jackie was spending the summer in Hyannis Port, her office made the official announcement. 'Mrs Kennedy feels that the change in environment in New York from Georgetown, and its many memories, will be beneficial to her and her children,' said Pamela Turnure, who was making the move along with Nancy Tuckerman to work in Jackie's Manhattan office.

During that summer Jackie continued talking about the assassination, unable to forget the savagery and violence of Dallas. 'I will never go there again,' she said. 'You can't imagine how I felt when I was going through Jack's things in the White House and found a set of cuff links in his drawer, emblazoned with the map of Texas. Oh, God – it's awful. I try not to be bitter but I know I am.

'I was so fiercely loyal to him I once said thoughtlessly he should be President for life! No, he said, even if he were re-elected, eight years in the Presidency is enough for any man.

'I never had or wanted a life of my own. Everything centred around Jack. I can't believe that I'll never see him again. Sometimes I wake in the morning, eager to tell him something, and he's not there ... Nearly every religion teaches there's an afterlife, and I cling to that hope.

'Jack was something special, and I know he saw something special in me, too ... The three years we spent in the White House were really the happiest time for us, the closest, and now it's all gone ...'

At Robert Kennedy's insistence Jackie tried to be happy. She flew to Stowe, Vermont, to go skiing, took a holiday in the West Indies with the Paul Mellons, shopped in New York, and went on a cruise with the Wrightsmans. 'When I go on a trip it's all right,' she said, 'but it's so empty and depressing to come home.' Then Teddy Kennedy was injured in a private plane that crashed in a fog near North-ampton, Massachusetts, killing two of the other passengers. In critical condition with a fractured vertebra and broken ribs, the youngest Kennedy remained hospitalized for weeks. Jackie flew with Bobby to visit him. Later, in the hospital cafeteria, she looked at her brother-in-law and said, 'Oh, Bobby, we have such rotten luck.'

In his own abyss of despair, the Attorney-General was struggling with what to do about his own future, knowing he could no longer work effectively in Lyndon Johnson's administration. The man from Texas was considered an unworthy successor to his brother's Presidency – a crude, vulgar interloper who would never be sitting in the White House if it had not been for the Kennedys. How he despised him.

While President Johnson was gearing up to run for the office on his own, Bobby Kennedy, the heir apparent, was determined to continue his brother's dreams, to perpetuate the Kennedy dynasty. Riding a wave of mass appeal as the successor of his martyred brother, Bobby decided to seek the Senate seat from New York. From that political base he would proceed towards the Presidency. When he appeared at the Democratic National Convention in Atlantic City that summer, he deified his brother by quoting Shakespeare to the delegates. To applause and tears he introduced a film on John F. Kennedy, saying, 'When he shall die, take him and cut him out in little stars, And he will make the face of heaven so fine that all the world will be in love with night, And pay no worship to the garish sun.' Lyndon Baines Johnson was garish. For the rest of his life Bobby referred to his adored older brother as 'The President', never Jack. Lyndon Johnson was always 'him', or 'Johnson', or 'that man'. He lived constantly in the glorious shadow of Camelot and devoted himself to recapturing the dreams of John F. Kennedy's Presidency.

Jackie also went to Atlantic City that summer, to attend a reception in honour of her husband for 5,000 guests, but she did not go within a mile of the convention hall. That fall she refused to vote in the Presidential election. She had been prepared to accept Lyndon Johnson as a successor to her husband so long as the Texan continued to live in the shadow of John F. Kennedy. In the beginning she had no animosity towards him. She corresponded regularly with him, talked to him frequently on the phone, and accepted his visits to her home to console her and the children. In fact, when friends commented about how awful it was that Lyndon Johnson should have succeeded her husband as President, she said, 'Oh, he's not as bad as all that – after all, he's got all Jack's advisers. So how can he go wrong?' But when Johnson began overshadowing her husband in the public mind, achieving legislative triumphs in Congress that Jack Kennedy never had, her emotional subconscious erupted. She would not accept Johnson's overwhelming success as President. She began to hate him.

Feeling that she had failed her husband in his life, depriving him of the unstinting support she could have given and that he expected her to give, she now dedicated herself to making amends. 'And the clearest and easiest way to do this was to help her brother-in-law, whom she clearly identified with her husband, to carry on, re-creating the dream so dear to her husband,' said Robin Douglas-Home, 'and which he had been prevented from achieving by his premature death.'

Jackie, now the most famous and admired woman in the world, gave her full support to her brother-in-law. At his request she agreed to meet with Dorothy Schiff, publisher of the *New York Post*, a powerful liberal newspaper whose endorsement Bobby desperately needed to win the New York Senate seat.

'He must win. He will win. He must win. Or maybe it is just because one wants it so much that one thinks that,' she told Mrs Schiff, referring to herself in the third person. 'People say he is ruthless and cold. He isn't like the others. I think it was his place in the family, with four girls and being younger than two brothers and so much smaller. He hasn't got the graciousness they had. He is really very shy, but he has the kindest heart in the world.'

From Bobby, the conversation naturally moved to reminiscences about her husband. As she talked, her eyes filled with tears. 'I never told him anything or showed him anything unpleasant,' she said, 'and when he got home I always had his favourite drink, a daiquiri, ready for him, and his favourite record playing, and perhaps a few friends.

'People tell me that time will heal. How much time? Last week I forgot to cancel the newspapers and I picked them up and there was the publication of the Warren Report, so I cancelled them for the rest of the week. But I went to the hairdresser and picked up *Life* magazine, and it was terrible. There is November to be gotten through ... Maybe by the first of the year ...'

She continued talking disjointedly, moving from one random thought to another without logical sequence.

'I don't want to be Ambassador to France or Mexico,' she said. 'President Johnson said I could have anything I wanted. I would like to work for somebody, but the list is ... One is expecting someone to come home every weekend, but no one ... I left Washington because of the old haunts. I just couldn't bear to be reminded all the time. I wanted to move into the house I had lived in when Jack was a Senator, but I could not get it because someone else had it ...

'I offered Jack peace, tranquillity, and serenity, but now the board has moved, all the little pieces changed places ... People all over ask me to write ... there are a lot of requests from magazines which I've barely looked at ... They all want me to write about gracious living or fashion – but I am interested in the same things Jack was interested in ...'

Mrs Schiff remembered how difficult it was to keep the conversation going. 'It was hard talking to her. She let silences go on. She is odd and different, very much less the queen than she was.'

Her hairdresser, Rosemary Sorrentino, remembers when Jackie came into Kenneth's beauty salon around the first anniversary of Kennedy's assassination. 'Walking down Fifth Avenue she saw pictures of him in every store window with black mourning drapes and by the time she got to the salon, she was almost hysterical. She came in and broke down and sobbed.'

'Oh, Rosemary,' Jackie cried. 'It was so awful in Washington. They'd follow me everywhere and sit out there in front of the house all day and eat their lunch and throw papers on the lawn. I thought that moving to New York would make it easier for me. If God had only let my baby live. I walk down the street and see his picture in every window. I can't stand it. Why do they remember the assassination? Why can't they celebrate his birthday?'

'She was crying so hard that I put my arms around her and tried not to cry myself,' said Mrs Sorrentino. 'She was just sobbing. And then later she began to change. Jackie cooled to us after the assassination. She was almost frozen when she came into the salon. I don't know why. Maybe because it was us who reminded her of the happy times. We had been doing her hair for years when she was a Senator's wife and then through the Presidential campaign and then the Inauguration and during her White House days. Maybe she was trying to forget all that now. I don't know.

'When she was First Lady she came to visit the salon and put her arms around me and kissed me and was very warm and affectionate. But after the assassination she withdrew. Her hair was in terrible condition, because of the trauma, I'm sure. Once when she walked in, Liza Minnelli was getting her hair done and she walked up to Jackie and said, "Hello, Mrs Kennedy. I'm Liza Minnelli. I met you a few months ago." Jackie didn't say a word to her. She just smiled a cold smile and walked away. Her best friends would be sitting in my room having their hair coloured and never say a word to her for fear of being snubbed. They knew she didn't like to be approached. After the President's death, she continued coming to Kenneth's but she was cool and aloof.'

Living to keep alive the memory of John F. Kennedy, Jackie became a national monument. Neither resigned to her public role nor anxious to be a mere private citizen, she continued to have a seismic effect on the world. She tried to do the things that other Fifth Avenue mothers do, walking her children to school, attending their plays, taking them on the carousel in Central Park, buying them ice cream from the Good Humor man. (Once she stopped to ask a policeman on a bright red motor scooter for directions. The officer recognized her and asked for her autograph. 'I'll give you an autograph if you'll take John for a ride on your scooter,' she said. The policeman refused, saying he couldn't violate department regulations.)

She surrounded herself with New Frontiersmen, who constantly reminisced about her husband and the good old days when they came to visit. Her office, not listed in the telephone book, nor on the roster of tenants in the lobby, functioned behind an unmarked door on the 14th floor of a Park Avenue building where Nancy Tuckerman and

Pamela Turnure continued answering the letters that poured in, some of which were merely addressed to 'Lady Kennedy, USA'. Even without an address they unerringly found their way to her office.

Within that suite were shelves of Jackie's White House scrapbooks. Her thousand days as First Lady were chronicled in seven volumes marked *Flowers*, containing photographs of every vase for every White House occasion. There were two scrapbooks on *China* with photographs of every dinner plate, salad plate, and wine glass used for every state occasion. The two volumes on *Linen* contained pictures of every placemat, napkin, and finger bowl doily she used as the President's wife. There were two *Material* scrapbooks cataloguing every scrap of fabric and paper used in the White House restoration for curtains, chairs, and wall coverings, listing the manufacturer, stock number, and price. The scrapbook labelled *Rose Garden* documented every phase of redoing that spot of land outside the President's office, with photographs of stones and bulldozers and trees wrapped in burlap.

Unseen by the public, this office represented Jackie's shrine to herself as First Lady. A compulsive archivist, she saved everything pertaining to her days in Camelot, insisting that they be kept in her office as precious reminders of her past. Yet she could not bear to visit the office for months after her husband's death. 'She couldn't let go of her great interest for all the good taste she brought to the White House as First Lady,' said her friend, Paul Mathias, 'and it was, after all, a big success. But she is an eternal contradiction. She lives in an eternal contradiction. She loved being Mrs Kennedy and, thinking she had had the best of life, she has now given up. But at the same time she was Mrs Kennedy and the President's wife, she withdrew from it all. In history people become legends after they die. She, by surviving and being with him when he died so dramatically, became a legend in her own lifetime, and she cannot live up to it because no human being could.'

Jackie tried desperately to carve a new life for herself and did all she could to help Bobby campaign for his New York

Senate seat. She even gave him permission to use Caroline and John-John in the campaign, knowing that the President's children would lend him a magic aura. She continued providing access to William Manchester in researching his book, instructing her secretaries to call everyone associated with the Kennedy administration to assure them that she was behind the project all the way and wanted them to give the author their full cooperation.

But, no matter what she did, she still felt overshadowed by death. 'I can't escape it,' she told a relative. 'Whether I'm helping with the Kennedy Memorial at Harvard, or taking a plane from Kennedy Airport, or seeing a Kennedy in-law, I always think of Jack and what they did to him.'

Chapter Eighteen

Finally the official period of mourning passed. Jackie celebrated by shedding her widow's weeds. For the rest of the year her every move was chronicled in the society pages. Every time she set foot out of her Fifth Avenue apartment her photograph appeared in newspapers around the world.

In January she refused to fly to Washington to attend President Johnson's inauguration and swearing-in ceremonies.

In February she flew to Mexico.

In March she took her children to Florida with her sister, Lee, to holiday at Hobe Sound. She appeared in white mink and diamonds at the Metropolitan Opera to hear Maria Callas sing *Tosca*. That month the Johnsons invited her to Washington for the dedication of the Rose Garden in her honour. Again, she refused their invitation, sending her mother instead.

The garden was financed by a $10,000 donation from the White House Historical Association which Jackie organized as First Lady. A plaque attached to a pillar of the arbour reads: 'This garden is dedicated to Jacqueline Kennedy with great affection by those who worked with her in the White House, 23 April 1965.'

Janet Auchincloss barely held back her tears during the ceremony. 'I know you will understand why I cannot express how I feel about this tribute to my daughter today,' she said. 'President Kennedy loved gardens very much and planned this with Jacqueline. I know it would make her happy to have it dedicated to her today. I can't think of anything more meaningful to all the people who care about Jacqueline than to have this beautiful garden as a memorial to the years she shared with him there.'

What she didn't say, of course, was that her daughter flew into a rage when she received Lady Bird's invitation and screamed that she would rather go to Dallas, Texas, than ever return to Washington while Lyndon Johnson was in the White House.

In May Jackie flew to London for the Queen's dedication of Runnymede in memory of her husband.

In June she dined at The Colony in New York and attended the opening of 'Leonard Bernstein's Theater Songs'.

In July she celebrated her thirty-sixth birthday with the Kennedys at Hyannis Port.

In August she sunbathed on the cabana terrace at Bailey's Beach in Newport, Rhode Island, visiting Kennedy's former Ambassador to New Zealand.

In September she flew to Boston with Rose Kennedy to dance at the Golden Trumpet Ball. Then she flew back to New York to attend a formal dinner party hosted in her honor by Mr and Mrs Charles Engelhard.

In October she threw her own party in honour of John Kenneth Galbraith, President Kennedy's former Ambassador to India. Choosing white, Jackie appeared in a sleeveless ermine jacket and long silk gown to welcome her guests. She rented The Sign of the Dove in New York for a late night dancing party and midnight supper. New Frontiersmen converged on the restaurant like homing pigeons: the Robert McNamaras, the Robert Kennedys, the Stephen Smiths, the William van den Heuvels, Marietta Tree, Lee Radziwill, Teddy Kennedy, Truman Capote, Bunny Mellon, Pierre Salinger, Mrs David Bruce, Richard Goodwin, Arthur Schlesinger, Jr, Theodore Sorenson, Roswell Gilpatric, McGeorge Bundy, the Alphands, William Walton, the Douglas Dillons, Pat Kennedy Lawford.

Almost all the guests were in some way connected with the Kennedy administration. They represented the glittering façade of Camelot, the touch-football games, the parties at Hickory Hill where people were thrown into the swimming pool with their clothes on. They were the beautiful people. They arrived in Cadillac limousines. Their common bond was idolatry to the memory of John Fitzgerald Kennedy. They ridiculed Lyndon Johnson and poked fun at his

Secretary of State, Dean Rusk. They danced the frug to Killer Joe Piro's discotheque music. They toasted the dowager queen in her white fur jacket. They feasted on French pastries and *pâté de foie gras*. One guest, Aristotle Onassis, only stayed a few minutes. Everyone else drank and danced into the night, refusing to leave until 3:30 am.

Also in October Jackie leased a country home in New Jersey's fox-hunting area.

In November she accompanied Mr and Mrs Franklin D. Roosevelt, Jr, to the opening of *The Eleanor Roosevelt Story*. She privately visited Princess Margaret and Lord Snowdon in the home of John Hay Whitney. Then came the second anniversary of the assassination. She spent the day by herself in her New York apartment, refusing to read the newspapers or watch television. The next day she flew to Hammersmith Farm to have Thanksgiving with her mother and stepfather and celebrate the birthdays of her children.

In December she dined with Alan Jay Lerner, the lyricist of *Camelot*. She ordered a strapless white silk jersey gown from Mme Grès in Paris. She spent Christmas in New York and the next day flew with her children to Sun Valley to ski with the Teddy Kennedys.

Later she made a secret trip to Washington to stand in driving rain at seven in the morning at Arlington Cemetery. There she cried as Cardinal Cushing blessed the new resting place to which John F. Kennedy's casket had been moved during the night, reinterred alongside his two children – the daughter born dead in 1956, and Patrick Bouvier Kennedy, the son who only lived thirty-nine hours.

She spent the entire year wrapped around the Kennedys, enfolded in the security of their name and their associations. Then Jackie struck out on her own. She began travelling and shopping, frenetically filling her days with elegant lunches, horse shows, and socialites. She flew to Gstaad, Switzerland, to ski with the Galbraiths. In New York she went disco dancing with producer Mike Nichols. She was named to the Fashion Hall of Fame and once again proclaimed the most famous and admired woman in the world. She lunched with Kenny O'Donnell and Vivi Stokes Crespi at The Colony, went dancing again with Mike Nichols, and nipped into El Morocco with Arthur Schlesinger, Jr. She flew to Spain for the bullfight in Seville and dined with Her Serene Highness Princess Grace and Prince Ranier of Monaco. She angrily denied rumours that she planned to marry Spanish diplomat Antonio Garrigues, a sixty-two-year-old widower with eight children.

Photographs flashed around the world showing Jackie dressed in Andalusian riding garb, Jackie dancing the flamenco, Jackie waving to adoring crowds. Relishing the adulation, she smiled radiantly and bowed graciously. She seemed to be having a wonderful time. Actually, she ached with boredom. In Seville she told Howell Conant, 'I'm a relatively young woman and never a day passes I don't think about dear old Jack, but ... It depresses me still because every day someone sends me a picture of him. Thank God you came to sit by me. I was so bored. All these Spaniards. They drive me crazy.'

Then back to New York, off to Hawaii for six weeks with her children, back to New York, and up to Newport, Rhode Island, for the wedding of her stepsister, Janet Jennings Auchincloss. There Jackie attracted so much attention from the press that the wedding was mobbed by reporters and photographers, causing the bride to burst into tears. Frenzied crowds swarmed St Mary's Church, screaming 'Jackie, Jackie, Jackie', practically stomping each other to catch a glimpse of John F. Kennedy's widow. Jackie, on the arm of Stas Radziwill, smiled radiantly.

The next month she flew to Cape Cod for a belated birthday party in her honour hosted by her mentor, Bunny Mellon. 'This friendship which she has cultivated so assiduously over the years tells you a lot about Jackie,' maintains a friend, who describes Mrs Mellon as an awesome perfectionist worth hundreds of millions of dollars and Jackie as the beneficiary of her mammoth generosity.

'Bunny gleefully characterizes Jackie as a witch, and only half in jest attributes supernatural powers to her. She has told me often that I'd better not get on Jackie's wrong side because, if I do, Jackie will cast a spell on me and I'll never get out from under.'

Mrs Mellon is known to phone her friends six times a day and lavish them with $5,000 Schlumberger bracelets from Tiffany's. 'Over the years she has given Jackie envelopes of cash containing hundreds of thousands of dollars. She offered to build a house for her in Antigua. In the White House Bunny spent millions on Jackie, donating heavily to her restoration project. For the Mount Vernon dinner she provided all the gold vermeil cachepots on the tables and every single one of the chairs, recovering them in fabric which cost $24 a yard just so they would flawlessly match Jackie's decor. Then, when Jackie moved to New York, Bunny gave her a $17,000 bed for her Fifth Avenue apartment, but Jackie didn't like it, and Bunny, who is so sensitive, cried for days.'

The Bunny Mellon birthday party for Jackie was packed with Kennedys and their friends – Bobby and Ethel and Teddy and Joan, Ambassador and Mrs David Bruce, Dick Goodwin, John Kenneth Galbraith, Arthur Schlesinger, Jr, the Robert McNamaras, the Averell Harrimans, and Katherine Graham, the publisher of the *Washington Post*. Mrs Mellon also invited Jackie's hairdresser, Kenneth, and her decorator, Billy Baldwin. Knowing her affection for J. Bernard West, Chief Usher of the White House, Mrs Mellon invited him, too. Unfortunately, the party was being held the night before the wedding of Luci Baines Johnson, the President's younger daughter. Mr West thought it would be impossible for him to fly to the Mellon estate in Osterville, Massachusetts, and be back at the White House in time for the Johnson wedding the next day.

'You've got to come,' urged Mrs Mellon. 'I'll make all the arrangements for you.'

When Mr West arrived, the guest of honour pounced on him with glee.

'Oh, Mr West!' giggled Jackie. 'What's Luci doing without you? If this were the French Revolution you'd be the first one on the guillotine.'

The tension between the Kennedy and Johnson forces had reached such a pitch that Jackie was complaining bitterly

239

about 'that goddamned Lyndon'. 'Do you know he won't even let the Secret Service men wear their PT-boat tie clasps any more?' she said. That summer she received a letter from William Manchester in which he said he had finished writing his book, *The Death of a President*. 'Though I tried desperately to suppress my bias against a certain eminent statesman who always reminded me of somebody in a Grade D movie on the late show,' he wrote, 'the prejudice showed through.' Jackie didn't care. She felt that Lyndon Baines Johnson deserved whatever Manchester dished out.

Before publication the manuscript was submitted to Bobby Kennedy, who turned it over to his Justice Department aides John Siegenthaler and Ed Guthman as well as to former JFK aides Arthur Schlesinger, Jr, and Dick Goodwin to read. Each man made extensive revisions which the author agreed to. Bobby, looking towards his Presidential campaign in 1968, felt the book should be published in the fall of 1966, ahead of the contracted deadline. He was concerned about the timing of the book, not the contents. Manchester had signed a contract with the Kennedys giving them full right of review and revision before publication, so Bobby was not worried about the book because he had full control over the material. The author also promised that all royalties from the book would be donated to the John F. Kennedy Library. 'Jackie felt these clauses were necessary because she wanted to avoid commercialism and sensationalism,' said a Kennedy aide. 'But when she found out that *Look* magazine was paying $665,000 to Manchester for serialization rights, she began raising hell, saying that he was just cashing in on her husband's death and she would stop him, even if she had to take him to court.'

And so began the Battle of the Book.

Earlier Jackie had objected to Maud Shaw's book, *White House Nannie*, and sent Sol Linowitz to London to threaten an injunction against the publisher unless certain changes were made in the text. She strongly objected to telling the world that it had been the nannie, and not Jackie, who told Caroline of her father's death. Then there was Paul Fay's book on John F. Kennedy entitled *The Pleasure of His*

Company. 'Jackie sicked Ken Galbraith on that one and made Fay delete thousands of words from the text,' said a Kennedy aide.

Fay deleted everything Jackie wanted out, but she was still furious with him for writing the book in the first place. He sent her a $3,000 cheque from the royalties for the Kennedy Library. Jackie sent it back. He was one of Jack Kennedy's closest friends, but – because of the book – she never spoke to him again.

'She cooperated with Ted Sorenson and Arthur Schlesinger, Jr, on their Kennedy books, but she insisted in both that she be referred to only as Jacqueline or Mrs Kennedy – never Jackie,' said the aide. 'You'll notice in both books that her marriage to JFK is described in loving terms, and never once do they hint at the painful truth behind their relationship. Or, God help us, any of Jack's other women.'

In the Manchester book, Jackie objected to the personal references to her vanity; to searching the mirror for wrinkles in her face; to her sleeping arrangements with the President their last night in Texas; to his head wound descriptions; to her thoughts and actions when she returned to the White House and went to sleep under sedation. She also wanted to delete the description of how she slipped her wedding ring on his finger. She wanted no mention of her chain-smoking or her drinking.

Although she had given the author ten hours of tape-recorded interviews, she now insisted that he not use any of the material in his book. She demanded that the tapes be locked up in the Kennedy Library and not released to the public for fifty years. She also insisted that the letters she had shown Manchester which she wrote to her husband from the Onassis yacht not be quoted in the book. No one realized at the time just how serious Jackie was about her objections.

Still reeling from the tragedy in Dallas, the country revered John F. Kennedy's widow. They remembered seeing her through the mist of their tears, marching to muffled drums and holding the American people together with her dignity. They had no idea of the imperiousness which lay behind that black veil. Not even her brother-in-law realized the extent of her determination in this matter.

Involved in the ugly tangle were friendships of many years' standing. Manchester's publisher, Harper and Row, was headed by Cass Canfield, the stepfather of Michael Canfield, who once was married to Lee Bouvier, Jackie's sister. Despite their divorce, Canfield retained his close ties to the Kennedy family. His company published John F. Kennedy's Pulitzer Prize-winning book, *Profiles in Courage*, as well as Bobby Kennedy's book, *The Enemy Within*, Theodore Sorenson's book, *Kennedy*, and General Maxwell Taylor's book, *The Uncertain Trumpet*. Harper and Row was the obvious choice for the Kennedys' authorized version of the death of the President.

When excerpts from the book were sold for serialization, the Kennedys preferred *Look* magazine to *Life* magazine. 'I'm glad it's *Look*,' said Bobby Kennedy, 'because they have been so nice to the family and Luce has been such a bastard.' Gardiner Cowles, the publisher of *Look*, was a good friend of the Kennedys, and his editor-in-chief, Bill Attwood, had been appointed by President Kennedy as Ambassador to Guinea.

So from the beginning the Kennedys were dealing with people they trusted, friends who had served them well in the past. Jackie was prepared to prevail upon those friendships. When she objected to the magazine serialization, she assumed that she had merely to call the publisher and explain how she felt, and he would abide by her wishes. So she phoned Gardiner Cowles. 'November is always a difficult time for the children and me,' she said.

Cowles understood. He promised to postpone serialization until the following year. She insisted that he cancel it altogether. He explained that he could not do this because the magazine had already contracted to run the excerpts and was legally obligated to do so. Jackie said she didn't care: cancel it anyway. Cowles refused. So Jackie hired Simon H. Rifkind to represent her and called Cowles back, insisting that he fly to Hyannis Port with his attorney to meet with her. 'If you don't come,' she told him, 'I know it will be only because you are afraid to face me.' Gardiner

Cowles flew to Hyannis Port with his lawyer.

There Jackie tried to prevail upon friendship again. 'I simply don't understand why you would proceed with serialization when I don't want you to,' she said. The publisher replied that he felt *Look* magazine had bought the manuscript with full consent of the Kennedys. 'I'm willing to reduce the number of instalments from seven to four,' he said, 'and we won't start publication until the first of the year, but I don't see how I can legally do much more than that.'

'If it's money, I'll pay you a million,' said Jackie.

Cowles's attorney spoke up, saying it wasn't just the money. '*Look* thought it was a fine book worthy of serialization,' he said.

'You're sitting in the chair of my late husband,' said Jackie. 'I demand that both book and magazine serialization be stopped.'

The meeting ended with confusion on both sides. Realizing she was getting nowhere with the magazine people, Jackie summoned William Manchester to Hyannis Port, and the author, who adored her, went willingly. Once again Jackie tried to prevail upon friendship. 'I think the behaviour of Cowles is despicable and I hate all those rats at *Look*,' she said. 'I still like you, though, and it's us against them. Your whole life proves you to be a man of honour. Everyone is telling me not to read your book, but I'm going to read every word. I'm tougher than they think I am. I want you to stand with me against *Look* magazine.'

The most famous and admired woman in the world then made the point as clear as she could. 'Anyone who is against me will look like a rat unless I run off with Eddie Fisher,' she told Manchester.

At this point the author was teetering on the edge of nervous collapse. He had left his position at Wesleyan University and at Jacqueline Kennedy's request moved his wife and children to Washington to work on a book that would take two years of his life. He received a $40,000 publishing advance for the project and, when that money was gone, began draining his meagre savings to continue researching and writing. He spent months interviewing everyone connected with the assassination, flying back and forth to Dallas, reliving every excruciating moment of those days. Now his book was being shredded apart by publishers and editors and lawyers, and the widow he idolized was asking him to rewrite history and forfeit the only possible profit he could ever make. Days later he was hospitalized for nervous exhaustion. In the end the book earned more than one million dollars, all of which went to the John F. Kennedy Memorial Library.

The vicious free-for-all between the Kennedy family and the author and the publisher of *The Death of a President* remained front page news for weeks. A battery of lawyers deliberated, begging for compromise and suggesting paraphrases for the personal material that so offended Jackie. She remained adamant, refusing to compromise on the intimate revelations which she felt invaded her privacy. She threatened to sue and prepared to go to court to block publication of the book and the magazine serialization. After a month-long struggle, a settlement was reached. The magazine agreed to delete or tone down a dozen passages from the 60,000-word excerpt. In the end the net loss to *Look* added up to only 1,621 words, but Jackie technically emerged the winner. She had managed to suppress and censor parts of William Manchester's work. However, all the poignant vignettes she desperately wanted deleted had already been leaked to the press and printed in newspapers around the world. Everyone found out what she had been trying to hide, and the weight of public opinion suddenly shifted against her.

For five consecutive years she had topped the George Gallup poll as the one woman in the world most Americans admired. Now the pedestal began to crack and the beloved icon almost tumbled.

The Kennedys were so concerned about the public reaction against them as a result of the book debacle that they insisted Jackie forfeit the federal money that had been appropriated to maintain her office. Within days the announcement was made by Senator Edward Kennedy's office in Washington. The letter his staff wrote for Jackie was released to the press. 'Now the work at my office, although still considerable, has diminished enough so that I can personally assume the burden of my own official business,' it stated. 'Therefore I no longer wish a government appropriation for this purpose.'

Jackie insisted on maintaining her privacy on her own terms. This compulsion extended to everyone around her. Secretaries clammed up. New Frontiersmen refused to talk to reporters about her. Friends who even mentioned her name to a journalist became enemies. Employees were bound by legal affidavits.

When Jackie read that her young German cook, Annemarie Huste, planned to write a cookbook and publicize it by filming a television series, she fired her on the spot. Earlier Annemarie had written an article for *Weight Watchers* magazine that had nothing to do with Jackie, although her name was prominently displayed on the magazine cover: 'Jackie Kennedy's Gourmet Chef Presents Her Weight Watcher Recipes'. Jackie was starving herself at the time and taking diet pills to slim down from a size 12 to a size 8. She resented the implication that she hired a cook specifically to lose weight. Her lawyers tried to stop publication of the article, but the magazine was already on the newsstands. Then another article appeared a few months later describing how the pretty blonde cook rose in the ranks of the rich and famous, having once worked for multi-millionaire Billy Rose and now Jacqueline Kennedy. The article also mentioned that Caroline Kennedy was a better cook than her mother. This enraged Jackie even more than the fact that Annemarie was writing a cookbook. Jackie's lawyers tried to block publication of the book but finally settled for a guarantee that Jackie's name would not appear on the cover.

Annemarie worked for Jackie for two and a half years, earning $130 a week for a five-hour day. Like all Mrs Kennedy's employees, she was required to sign a contract swearing never to write anything about her employer or her children. Nancy Tuckerman, who initially recommended Annemarie to Jackie, called her after the article appeared. 'Mrs Kennedy feels it would be better if you didn't come back,' said Miss Tuckerman.

The young cook felt remorseful. 'I'm not bitter about being fired,' she said. 'I understand Mrs Kennedy's desire for privacy. I will never say anything unkind or disloyal about her and I shall miss the children very much. When you've worked for a family for two years, you become attached to the children. It's such a wrench that I don't think I could cook for another family again.'

Jackie's insistence on privacy also included the people who bought Wexford, the house she and her husband built in the Virginia hunt country. When she sold the house for $225,000 in 1964, she swore the new owners to secrecy by making them sign a legal contract binding them to silence and prohibiting them from allowing any publicity.

'It's the only house Jack and I ever built together and I designed it all myself,' she said. 'I don't want it to be exploited and photographed all over the place just because it was ours.'

The prospective buyers, Mr and Mrs Quing Non Wong, agreed to sign her unique contract. 'When we bought this place, we agreed to keep it completely quiet and free of all publicity for ten years unless Mrs Kennedy ruled otherwise,' said Mrs Wong. 'I forward all requests to photograph the home to our lawyer and he submits the requests to Mrs Kennedy's lawyer and Mrs Kennedy decides.' Jackie never once decided in favour of any request.

During the Battle of the Book Jackie tried to shield her children. 'We didn't talk about it, of course,' she said. 'But children pick things up. A word here, a word there, and they knew something was happening that involved them. There was no way to keep them from passing newsstands going to and from school. It was natural for them to look at the magazine covers and the headlines. Or be told something at school or on the street. It isn't always easy for the children. I still haven't gotten over that strange woman who leaped at Caroline as we came out of church on All Saints Day – a holy day of obligation ... Pounced on Caroline from nowhere. And she shouted at the poor child, "Your mother is a wicked woman who has killed three people. And your father is still alive!" It was terrible prying her loose ...'

Jackie spoke fondly of her children, who were both enrolled in private schools. 'Caroline is more withdrawn,' she said, 'but John, well, he's something else. John makes friends with everyone. Immediately. He surprises me in so many ways. He seems so much more mature than one would expect of a child of six. Sometimes it almost seems that he is trying to protect me instead of just the other way around.

'There was that day last November, the day of the anniversary,' she continued. 'As the two of us walked home from school I noticed that a little group of children, some of them from John's class, was following us. Then one of the children said, quite loud, "Your father's dead ... your father's dead." You know how children are. They've even said it to me when I've run into them at school, as if ... Well, this day John listened to them saying it over and over and he didn't say a word. He just came close to me, took my hand, and he squeezed it. As if he were trying to reassure me that things were all right. And so we walked home together, with the children following us.

'I sometimes used to say to myself, "He'll never remember his father. He was too young." But now I think he will. He'll remember his father through associations with people who knew Jack well and the things Jack liked to do. They will be getting to know his father. I tell him little things like "Oh, don't worry about your spelling, your father couldn't spell very well, either." That pleases him, you can bet.

'Then there will always be a Dave Powers to talk sports with him. John seems to know an awful lot about sports. He talks about someone named Bubba Smith, and about Cassius Clay ... I want to help him go back and find his father. It can be done. There was that stone his father placed on a mound during his visit to Argentina a long time ago, and then when I took the children there later John put a stone on top of his father's. He'd like to go back to Argentina and see his stone, and his father's stone – and that will be part of knowing his father.

'This coming summer at Hyannis Port, John will sail in his father's favourite boat, with Ted. And that will help, too.

And even smaller things than that bring him closer to Jack. The school insists that children even as young as John must wear neckties to classes. That was all right with him. It gave him a chance to wear his father's PT-boat tie pin ...'

'I don't want the children to be just two kids living on Fifth Avenue and going to nice schools,' said Jackie. 'There's so much else in the world, outside this sanctuary we live in. Bobby has told them about some of those things – the children of Harlem, for instance. He told them about the rats and about the terrible living conditions that exist right here in the midst of a rich city. Broken windows letting in the cold. John was so touched by that he said he'd go to work and use the money he made to put windows in those houses. The children rounded up their best toys last Christmas and gave them away.

'I want them to know about how the rest of the world lives, but also I want to be able to give them some kind of sanctuary when they need it, some place to take them into when things happen to them that do not necessarily happen to other children. Caroline was knocked down by a charge of photographers when I took her out to try to teach her how to ski. How do you explain that to a child?

'And the stares and pointing, and the stories ... the strangest stories that haven't a word of truth in them, great long analytical pieces written by people you never met, never saw. I guess they have to make a living, but what's left of a person's privacy or a child's right to privacy?'

Jamie Auchincloss remembers the happy times his older step-sister tried to create for her children. 'One night she was having a birthday dinner party in her apartment for the Crown Prince of Morocco and his little sister,' he said. 'I was going to school at Columbia University at the time and Jackie asked me to stop by. She liked me to visit to bring a male presence into the house for Caroline and John.

'That night the apartment was filled with Moroccan Secret Service men and a disgruntled nurse who was a real pain in the ass. Jackie went into the kitchen and brought out the birthday cake with those candles that don't blow out. And then she began singing. Now Jackie has the worst voice in the world and laughs about the awful way she carries a tune. But she went ahead and started singing, "Happy birthday to you, Happy birthday to you, Happy birthday dear Crown Prince, Lion of Judah, Heir to the Throne, Leader of the People." She threw in all the kid's royal titles and some Jewish and Irish and French ones as well. We all howled with laughter because it was very funny. The kid's nurse got terribly upset. The Crown Prince tried to blow out the candles and couldn't do it, which was also quite amusing when you consider that he's a direct descendant of Mohammed and the royal descendants of Mohammed never fail at anything. The kid went into a real royal rage. The nurse berserked, too, and began accusing Jackie of being a terrible person. Jackie was quite taken aback by the nurse because she's never really talked to that way, but she managed to act quite royal herself and said, "This is my house and my party and it is full of humour. No child should be so uptight and intimidated. I want him to have a good time." '

Complicating Jackie's struggle for privacy during this time were the ambitions of her younger sister, who suddenly announced she was going to be a star. 'I've made up my mind to give all the gossips their chance,' Lee said. 'I'm going to ... uh ... become an actress. I have agreed to play the leading role in *The Philadelphia Story*, opening at the Ivanhoe Theater in Chicago. I just hope people won't think I'm trying to cash in on the late President's name and fame ... Jackie has known for some time now and hasn't expressed the slightest objection.'

Actually, Jackie was mortified. 'She was terribly annoyed over Lee's going into acting,' said Paul Mathias, 'but she restrained herself and said, "If it's what she wants – she deserves a chance." But she was irritated. She knew it just stirred up publicity that involved her and the Kennedys.'

The Princess planned to make her stage debut as Lee Bouvier in the title role of Tracy Lord made famous by Katharine Hepburn in Philip Barry's play. With the help of her friend, Truman Capote, she began rehearsals. 'Noel Coward, the playwright, also gave me tips,' she said. 'And so did Dame Margot Fonteyn and Rudolph Nureyev.' George Masters flew from Hollywood to do her make-up and Kenneth flew from New York to style her hair. Yves St Laurent designed her costumes. Still the play flopped. The only compliment from the critics was that Lee learned her lines remarkably well.

On opening night, as Lee was basking in the spotlight, Jackie and her children were in Ireland on holiday with the Murray McDonnells and their eight children in their Regency mansion in Waterford. 'It's strictly a private holiday,' said her hosts, who later confided that Jackie was secretly relieved to be out of the country while Lee took her curtain call. Jackie very correctly sent her a good-luck cable on opening night and a tiny eighteenth-century Battersea enamel gift box.

The pilgrimage to Ireland was to introduce her children to the heritage of their father, and Irish eyes smiled on them when they arrived to tour Kennedy's ancestral home in Dunganstown. 'I am so happy to be here in this land my husband loved so much,' said Jackie at Shannon airport. 'For myself and the children it is a little bit like coming home, and we are looking forward to it dearly.'

Jackie spent a month in Ireland. The Irish Prime Minister hosted a state dinner in her honour at Dublin Castle, and Jackie made her entrance wearing a bright green full-length gown of chiffon and a white ermine stole. In County Kildare she sat in the presidential box in a green dress watching the Irish Sweepstakes Derby. She attended a performance of the Dunhill Players and received a Waterford crystal bowl just for being there. She visited Twomey's Irish pub, ordered Irish tweed riding habits for herself, and spent the Fourth of July watching her son try to play Gaelic football.

During this visit Lord Harlech, the former British Ambassador to the United States, flew to Ireland to be Jackie's houseguest for a few days. His wife, Sissie, had died in a car accident that May, and Jackie flew to London for her funeral. So did Bobby and the rest of the Kennedys. Now she wanted to offer her old friend a few days of relaxation. This act of friendship to the man who had been one of John F.

Kennedy's closest friends started a spate of rumours that would plague them for the next year. In newspapers around the world the hawknosed nobleman was heralded as the new man in Jackie's life and the man most likely to be her next husband.

Lord Harlech, known as Sir David Ormsby-Gore during his four years in Washington, inherited his father's title and lands when the elder Harlech died in 1964. His first cousin, the Marquess of Hartington, was married to Kathleen Kennedy, the late President's sister who died in an aeroplane crash over France. His ties to the Kennedy family were strong. As Ambassador he was closer to the President than any other diplomat. Kennedy once said, 'I trust David as I would my own Cabinet officers.' The ex-envoy had sailed with the President at Hyannis Port, played golf with him in Palm Beach, and dined frequently at the White House in the family's private quarters. Minutes after he heard of the assassination, he dispatched a letter to Bobby Kennedy saying, 'Jack was the most charming, considerate and loyal friend I have ever had, and I mourn him as though he were my own brother.'

It was only natural that Jacqueline Kennedy should try to comfort her friend after his wife's death. They knew each other well, and now shared a common bond of grief. As much as she wanted to remarry, she never considered Lord Harlech her next husband, and neither did her family or close friends.

'He's charming but he's boring,' said Paul Mathias. 'She's afraid about the children. She thinks Caroline might turn against her due to the loss of her father. Caroline is simply besotted with memories of her father, and her life is like a shrine to him. Jackie makes an enormous father cult for the children, maybe too much. Stas Radziwill asked her why she didn't make Caroline remove some of the pictures of Jack from her bedroom walls. Jackie said, "Oh, Stas. I couldn't ask her to move a single one." '

'Jackie will never get married again,' said her step-sister, Janet Auchincloss Rutherford. 'Both Mother and I don't think she will ever marry again because anybody who married Jackie would be "Mr Kennedy" and we don't think any man would want that. It's too bad. Jackie wants to get married again because of the children. All the family wants her to. Bobby does. Teddy does. I do. All of us do. But we're afraid it will never happen.'

As Jackie continued being seen in public with Lord Harlech, going to the ballet, to the theatre, to dinner, and flying to Harvard to confer on the Kennedy Library, the speculation increased. Embarrassed by the worldwide press coverage, Lord Harlech issued a statement: 'Mrs Kennedy and I have been close friends for thirteen years but there is no truth to the story of a romance between us. I deny it flatly.' Jackie publicly denied the rumours as well as privately reassuring her friends that she would never marry Lord Harlech. (Martha Barlett recalled her saying, 'Cuddling up to him is like cuddling the encyclopedia.') Her sister, Lee, laughed uproariously when asked about the relationship. 'Are you kidding?' she said. 'Have you ever seen him?' Lee thought the hawk-nosed Harlech looked ridiculously unattractive.

Despite the denials the speculation persisted, especially when Jackie asked Lord Harlech to accompany her to Cambodia in the fall of 1967. 'It was Jackie who decided to go,' said Paul Mathias. 'She said she would be damned whatever she did, so why not.' Having always wanted to visit the magnificent ruins of Angkor Wat, Jackie invited Lord Harlech to go with her.

'We expected the world's press to make the most of our trip, and they certainly did, but happily it was something we had foreseen,' he said afterwards. 'Before we started on the visit we discussed what to do and the whole question of what the press would make of it. We knew it would probably happen. It is quite true they photographed us together as much as they could with the obvious innuendo, but as we were prepared for it, we did not mind much. Certainly Mrs Kennedy took it very well.'

Royal honour guards in sampots bowed low to Jackie when she arrived in Cambodia wearing a green mini-skirt and short white gloves. Schoolgirls carrying silver bowls sprinkled the red carpet she walked on with rose and jasmine petals. A gilded throne under a gold-tipped canopy awaited her as she received the honoured Buddhist welcome reserved for visiting potentates. Even American flags were flown in her honour, a major concession considering the break in diplomatic relations between Cambodia and the United States. Throughout the trip Jackie refused to talk to reporters. She made only one public pronouncement, and that was when she dedicated Avenue J. F. Kennedy.

Speaking in French, she said: 'President Kennedy would have wished to visit Cambodia. He would have been attracted by the vitality of the Khmer people, a quality he showed in himself and which he so admired in others. By your commemoration of his name you have shown that you recognize his dedication to peace and understanding between all peoples.'

The next year Jackie made a similar trip with Roswell Gilpatric to Mexico to visit the Mayan ruins in the Yucatan. Again the trip received worldwide publicity, and rumours swirled that Gilpatric, then sixty-one and separated from his third wife, would be Jackie's next husband. Jackie, now accustomed to the speculation, gave up trying to deny the rumours. 'She cares less and less about what is written of her because she can't fight against all the things that are said,' confided Paul Mathias. 'First she used to want to fight everything. Now she says to hell with it.'

Roswell Gilpatric, who admitted knowing Jackie well, was too much of a gentleman to dignify rumours of their love affair. 'She's always been attracted to men as intellectual companions as well as for other reasons,' he said. 'She is a person in her own right. When she came out from the ether of death she found that she was a personal figure and she rather enjoyed it. The only thing she shrank from was the peephole type of publicity like *Women's Wear Daily*. She relished her dealings with the press. She'd make a deal with them, and she'd prepare herself carefully. She knew just what costumes to wear, just what light she looked best in. When she wasn't prepared to get off the plane in Mexico to meet reporters, the aircraft circled until she was prepared.

'Jackie is extremely perceptive about people,' he said. 'I wouldn't exactly say that she was two-faced, but she wouldn't let people know how she felt about them if she didn't like them. If she found a person was trying to profit from his or her acquaintance with her in any way, she could be acid in her comments to others about it. Jackie might say about one woman, "She helps you on with your coat so that she can look at the label in it and tell *Women's Wear Daily.*"

'Jackie writes extremely well, and on the trip to Mexico she really became interested in pre-Columbian art and did a great deal of reading about it, and about the Mayans. I tried to get her to write a piece about it, and illustrate it with some of the marvellous pictures a photographer took, but she lacks follow-through. She can drop an interest as she might drop an individual.'

While in Mexico Jackie received word that Robert Kennedy was going to run for President. She immediately composed a short statement for the press: 'I will always be with him with all my heart. I shall always back him.'

Rumours continued to fly regarding her relationship with Lord Harlech and Roswell Gilpatric, and Jackie continued to be seen with both of them in public. She frequently borrowed other women's husbands for escorts, and men like Franklin D. Roosevelt, Jr, Richard Goodwin, Robert McNamara, and John Kenneth Galbraith were glad to take her to the theatre or the ballet. The other men she was seeing at the time – Mike Nichols, Chuck Spalding, Michael Forrestal, William Walton, Arthur Schlesinger, Jr, Truman Capote – were all connected in some way with the Kennedy administration. Some were single. Some were gay. All were safe.

'The men were either members of the family – Bobby particularly at that time – or close family friends and associates,' said Rose Kennedy.

There was only one relationship that was beginning to matter to Jackie, and that was with Aristotle Onassis, the Greek shipbuilder who continued to be a close friend throughout her mourning. He often visited her alone in her New York apartment, each time bringing lovely gifts for her and the children. He was charming company, and Jackie looked forward to seeing him, but in the beginning she refused to go out in public. When she finally told Bobby Kennedy about her fondness for the man he always referred to as 'The Greek', he threw up his hands. 'It's a family illness,' he said, referring to Onassis's close friendship with her sister, Lee Radziwill.

'He's been wonderful to me, Bobby, and so good to the children,' said Jackie.

The political impact of having Aristotle Onassis married to his brother's widow left Robert Kennedy momentarily speechless – but only momentarily. He explained that any plans for remarriage could be talked about in five months, after he won the Democratic nomination for President. He made Jackie promise she wouldn't do anything rash until then. And, thinking of her ailing father-in-law, she agreed. 'I know this is what the Ambassador would want me to do,' she said.

Chapter Nineteen

All the Kennedys committed themselves to Bobby's presidential campaign. Ethel, Joan, Eunice, Pat, Jean, and Rose were ready to stump the primary states. Restoring the family name to the White House became the overriding ambition of these women who served their power-hungry men so faithfully. Steve Smith began organizing behind the scenes, and the New Frontiersmen lined up to help the heir apparent. Dick Goodwin, who had been working for Senator Eugene McCarthy's presidential campaign, immediately packed his bags to join Bobby.

In 1968 the issue was Lyndon Johnson's escalation of the war in Vietnam. McCarthy was the only Democrat to oppose the President on the war. In the beginning he tried to persuade Bobby to lead the opposition, but Bobby refused publicly to challenge Johnson. Convinced the war was morally wrong, McCarthy ran himself. He was so successful in the New Hampshire primary that Lyndon Johnson acknowledged defeat by announcing he would not accept the Democratic nomination for a second term. For the first time in history an incumbent President was forced to step down by a member of his own political party. McCarthy became a national hero – a lone symbol of courage. The day after his successful showing in New Hampshire, Bobby decided to run for President. Naturally, he expected McCarthy to step aside so he could run unopposed, but McCarthy refused, declaring instead that he was in the race to the end. The Democratic primaries thus became a bitter contest among the liberal anti-war McCarthy and Kennedy movements, and the conservative forces which supported Lyndon Johnson's war. Kennedy's constituency were the poor, the blacks, the Indians, the disenfranchised – plus New Frontiersmen eager to be reinstated under the mantle of their martyred President's brother. All the Kennedys threw themselves into Bobby's campaign except Jackie. She alone remained reluctant.

'Early in the winter I was having dinner with Jackie,' said Arthur Schlesinger, Jr, 'and I told her how important I thought it was for Bobby to run. She listened very quietly. Then she said, "I hope Bobby never becomes President of the United States." I said, "Why?" She said, "If he becomes President, they'll do to him what they did to Jack." '

Within a month an assassin's bullet tore into Martin Luther King, Jr, as he stood on the balcony of a motel in Memphis, Tennessee. Bobby Kennedy was campaigning when he heard that the black preacher had been murdered. Immediately he chartered a plane to bring King's body back to Atlanta. Then he arranged for extra phones to be installed in Coretta King's home and flew to Georgia to be at her side.

'Jackie sends you her sympathy, and really wanted to come,' Bobby told King's widow. 'This would be very hard on her because of her own experience, but if it meant anything to you perhaps she would try to come.'

'Oh, yes,' said Mrs King. 'It would mean a great deal to me if she did come.'

Bobby called his sister-in-law in New York, and Jackie reluctantly agreed to fly to Atlanta to attend the funeral. She arrived with Bunny Mellon. 'Jacqueline Kennedy came to my house just a few minutes before I was to go to the ceremony,' said Mrs King. 'She came back to the bedroom, and we met for the first time. We exchanged greetings, and I thanked her for coming and also for what her family and her husband had meant to us … I told her that I felt very close to her family for this reason … and I said, "for our people".

'She was very gracious. She said something about how strong I was and how much she admired me. I said the same thing back to her because I did feel that way. Then she said to me, "And you're such a good speaker. You speak so well." That's what she said.'

Jackie resented having to attend the funeral of the slain civil rights leader, but she did it for Bobby because she knew her presence was politically important to him. She felt uncomfortable among the wailing and weeping black mourners whose soulful spirituals filled the Ebenezer Baptist Church. Before the funeral Richard Nixon leaned over his pew to say hello to her and received an icy stare in return. As soon as the service ended she headed back to New York in a chartered jet.

Back in her own social milieu, Jackie attended the New York wedding of George Plimpton with her daughter Caroline. Days later she flew to Palm Beach on the private plane of Aristotle Onassis to spend Easter with her children in the villa of the Charles Wrightsmans. Onassis remained on board the plane, refusing to get off to be photographed, and then flew on to Nassau with his daughter, Christina. Jackie had already made plans to join him the next month for a Caribbean cruise aboard his luxury yacht and was looking forward to the elegant vacation.

She enjoyed the jet-set life of the Beautiful People. She was most at home in their pleasure domes, and she thrived on the company of other celebrities. Posh little soirées were her best distraction. To help her fight her depression and loneliness, Richard Goodwin asked his friend Norman Podhoretz to give a party for her to meet some interesting people. 'He wanted to cheer her up, expose her to someone besides café society,' said the intellectual writer.

'So I had the Edmund Wilsons, Bayard Ruskin, Mrs Robert Lowell, Philip Roth, and the Jules Pfeiffers. But it was traumatic. We were ill chosen. The guests were intimidated by her. The party was stiff.'

'She is like a very bright, open, young girl,' said Podhoretz. 'She is one of the best listeners I've ever met in my life. Fixed with those eyes, she listened like she's never heard human speech before. She asks good questions. She wants to learn. But she is a rich girl. And if she'd never married Kennedy she'd be something like her sister. She is fantastically snobbish. She conceals it usually, but I've seen it erupt.

'I thought at first she really wasn't. I was completely conned by her. She is most comfortable with people of her own class. Again, like a lot of those girls of her set, she is easily repelled by things and people out of her ken. She is more curious, perhaps more vulnerable than the girls of her world. She is a great flirt and coquette, has a wonderful teasing way about her with men. Doesn't really like women at all. In fact, she can be quite rude to them.

'I remember at a party in her apartment the men and women separated after dinner. Jackie soon excused herself from the ladies and said she'd be right back. Then, alone, she went in and joined the men. It wasn't a move to make the other women like her. But she shows a visible sense of superiority to other women. I had a tremendous crush on her. It went on for about a month or six weeks. We'd be on the phone three and four and five times a day, but nothing ever came of it. I could kick myself now. I'll always regret I was too chicken to make the final pass, but I could see myself doing it and her saying, "Why, you poor little thing. Did you think you could sleep with the President's widow? Oh, poor darling." I couldn't take that thought. So I let it slip by. I don't know what happened. I got dropped. Maybe because I didn't make a move, or maybe because I might have made one. It was very dangerous for me. My wife hated her.' (Mrs Podhoretz later described Jackie as 'the brightest sixteen-year-old in America'.)

'Jackie can be sarcastic about the Kennedys, though she loves them and somehow considers them more her family than her own family,' said the writer, adding that Bobby Kennedy viewed his famous sister-in-law as an important entrée to influential people. 'Bobby is very interested in who Jackie knows and he uses it. If she meets a new person, the new person is soon to find him or herself being invited to lunch by Bobby and gets the feeling that he or she is being looked over. Jackie is not self-conscious, nor is she aware of her motives. But Bobby does use her, and this puts off some of the intellectual community in New York. They felt she was being used to get to them for Bobby's ambitions.'

Bobby and Jackie were being seen together in New York so much that people began to gossip that their friendship might be more than familial. Jackie not only ignored the vicious rumours but fuelled them by embracing her brother-in-law in public, holding his hand, and kissing him. Although she publicly committed herself to his campaign, she privately remained aloof. 'Psychologically, it will be hard for her to see Ethel in the White House as another Mrs Kennedy,' said Paul Mathias. 'What will Jackie be then, the Queen Mother? Naturally, this is hard for her to accept. She wants good things for Bobby, but she hasn't really lent herself to his campaign as some people think. On the contrary. Perhaps she will before it is through.'

Jackie never had the chance. On 5 June 1968, Robert Francis Kennedy was shot in the Ambassador Hotel in Los Angeles, minutes after he won the California primary. Pregnant with her eleventh child, Ethel dropped to the floor to cover her fallen husband. 'Please give him room to breathe,' she cried. 'Please move back.' Someone slipped rosary beads into his fingers. Hordes of campaign workers and reporters, jammed into the hotel ballroom, were devastated by the horror of yet another assassination.

Roosevelt Grier, the beefy tackle for the Los Angeles Rams, grabbed the gunman's arm. Olympic decathlon champion Rafer Johnson lifted the assailant and spread him on a steel kitchen table. 'Nobody hurt this man,' they shouted. 'We want to take him alive!'

Screams filled the room as people pushed and shoved in panic. The gunman, Sirhan Sirhan, was hauled away by police. Minutes later Kennedy was lifted on a stretcher and rushed by ambulance to Good Samaritan Hospital, where six neurosurgeons tried to save his life.

At 3:45 am the telephone rang in Jacqueline Kennedy's New York apartment. Stas Radziwill was calling from London moments after he learned of the shooting. 'Jackie,' he said, 'how's Bobby?'

'He's fine. Terrific,' she said. 'You heard that he won California by 53 per cent, didn't you?'

'Yes, but how is he?'

'I just told you. He won California.'

'But Jackie,' said Stas, 'he's been shot. It happened just a few minutes ago.'

'No. It can't have happened,' she screamed. 'Not again.'

'She just didn't know the real story behind it all,' Lee

said later. 'It was the middle of the night in America and she had been asleep. She was terribly stunned.'

Jackie immediately flew to Los Angeles and stood with Ethel at Bobby's side during the agonizing hours he fought to live. When he was pronounced dead, she wept uncontrollably. She made no effort to be heroic this time. Giving in to her overwhelming grief, she sobbed until she was spent. Then she tried to comfort her sister-in-law.

'He's in Heaven now with Jack,' said Ethel, whose religious faith was unshakeable.

'Oh, Ethel,' Jackie murmured. 'You believe so strongly.'

The legacy of love surrounding the memory of John Fitzgerald Kennedy now embraced his younger brother as the two Kennedy widows began planning once again for a Kennedy funeral. Before leaving the West Coast, Jackie called Leonard Bernstein.

'We're all sitting here,' she said, 'trying to figure out what would be the best music to do at the funeral. We naturally thought of you. You're the only one whose taste and judgment should dicate what goes on.'

President Johnson sent a White House plane to bring Bobby's body back to the East. Jackie called Bernstein again. 'I'm sitting here on the plane next to Ethel,' she said. 'She has certain wishes about the funeral.'

'I told her what I had arranged so far, which was the Mahler, and she thought that would be beautiful,' said Leonard Bernstein. 'I told her I was having trouble with the other things, and she said, "No. You just insist. You just tell them that you are in charge. The family has given you this authority." '

'Ethel's first wish,' Jackie told Bernstein, 'is that the nuns from her old school, Manhattanville School, sing certain things that she remembers from her days there ... from her youth: In Paradisum – I forget what else. There were two things that she wanted the nuns to sing.'

Bernstein protested that females were not allowed to sing in St Patrick's Cathedral. Jackie remained firm. 'You tell them that that's Ethel's wish. She would also like "The Navy Hymn" to be sung ... You know it will make her feel so much better and bring her such comfort if she can have these things.'

Ethel insisted that Andy Williams be allowed to sing 'The Battle Hymn of the Republic', one of Bobby's favourite songs. Leonard Bernstein disagreed vehemently, saying it was in bad taste.

'If there's one thing about our faith, it's our belief that this is the beginning of eternal life and not the end of life,' said Ethel. 'And I want this Mass to be as joyous as it possibly can be.'

Jackie, supporting Ethel on every point, visited Cardinal Spellman to urge him to do exactly what Ethel wanted regardless of church traditions. The Cardinal finally gave in. The funeral stressed the Resurrection, the beginning of life. It was in English, and the vestments were violet instead of black. The Kennedy children, dressed in white, carried the Communion articles to the altar. Teddy, the last surviving male of the Kennedy family, delivered the eulogy. In a wavering voice he described his dead brother as 'a good and decent man, who saw wrong and tried to right it, saw suffering and tried to heal it, saw war and tried to stop it'. Andy Williams, unaccompanied, began singing 'The Battle Hymn of the Republic' from the choir loft. The poignancy of that one lone voice reverberating through St Patrick's Cathedral reduced the congregation to tears. Even Leonard Bernstein was impressed. 'It turned out to be *the* smash of the funeral. I say this in my own disfavour because I would have done anything I could to avoid it.'

Afterwards a funeral train carried Robert Kennedy's body from New York to Washington to be buried alongside his brother in Arlington Cemetery. Crowded with Bobby's school friends, his political associates and family, it crept along the Eastern seaboard for eight hours. People lined the tracks to wave goodbye. Truman Capote called it 'the ride of the century'.

Ethel walked through the train trying to comfort everyone. People were speechless when they saw her come by, cheering up the mourners, encouraging them to be happy and not cry. 'That was the first time I broke, on the train,' recalled Pete

Hamill. 'Of all the people, she was the one that had the right to grieve ... and yet she was worried about our grief more than anything else. Remarkable! She's really some woman. Jacqueline was wandering around with a tray at one point, and looking sort of icy; it was an interesting contrast.'

Actually, Jackie was in a state of shock. Suffering terribly from Bobby's death, she suddenly felt all alone in the world and completely unprotected. With the strong emotional support of her brother-in-law now gone, and her father-in-law unable even to feed himself, there was no one around to shield her, no one strong she could lean on, no one she could turn to for help.

'Jackie was very bitter after Bobby's death,' said a Kennedy aide. 'She became quite hysterical at one point and said, "I hate this country. I despise America, and I don't want my children to live here any more. If they are killing Kennedys, my kids are the number one targets. I have the two main targets. I want to get out of this country and away from it all!" She was terrorized, but then the whole family was for a while. Teddy spent at least two hours on the phone every night talking to his nieces and nephews, assuring them that he was not going to be shot. He told them that he would be there alive and well for them in the morning. Each one of those twenty-seven kids was traumatized by Bobby's assassination and each of them needed good psychiatric counselling. They had severe emotional problems. It was a terrible experience for everyone. No one knew exactly how to cope with it. Some of us rented a boat after the funeral and went out on the water and got very, very drunk and cried a lot.'

After the funeral, Jackie called Aristotle Onassis and asked him to bring his daughter to spend the weekend with her and her family at Hammersmith Farm in Newport. 'I still remember that weekend,' said Jamie Auchincloss. 'It was terrible. We were all in shock over Bobby's death. Jackie called Mummy and asked if she could bring a house guest with her. Mummy said, "Yes. Who is it?"

' "Aristotle Onassis," said Jackie.

' "God, no. Jackie, you can't mean it. You just can't mean it."

'Mummy almost died,' Jamie said. 'She was absolutely fit to be tied. She couldn't believe it. When Onassis arrived, Mummy treated him very badly. The reason for this goes back a couple of years before, when Mummy was in London staying at Claridges and wanted to see Lee. She was told that Lee, who was still married to Stas at that time, was in Onassis's suite at the hotel. Mummy went up there and knocked and knocked and knocked. But no one answered. She banged and hollered and finally noticed the door was ajar.

'Now, Mummy is the kind of person who opens other people's mail and walks through doors she's not supposed to. She's so snoopy that I once said to her after she had opened some of my mail, "If I ever catch you doing that again, and I'm of such a mind, I may just take you into court because there are laws against people who pry like you do."

'Anyway, the door was open, so Mummy barged right in and walked down a long hall with a raised platform at the end. Sitting there at a Napoleonic desk in his silk bathrobe and wearing sunglasses was Aristotle Onassis with his feet up on the desk, talking on the phone.

'My mother took one look at him and shrieked. "Where's my daughter?" she screamed.

'Onassis looked up, quite puzzled by this distraught woman standing in the middle of his private suite. "Pardon me, ma'am," he said, "but just exactly *who* is your daughter?"

' "My daughter is Princess Radziwill," screamed Mummy.

' "Oh, I see," said Onassis. "Well, she left here a half hour ago."

'Onassis went back to his phone conversation and Mummy stormed out of his suite without even saying pardon me or goodbye or thank you or anything. Naturally, she thought the worst. Knowing Onassis was a name hunter and Lee a fortune hunter, Mummy suspected trouble and a lot of it. She never got along well with him afterwards because of that one incident. She always treated him in a contemptible fashion.'

Janet Auchincloss was disgusted that Jackie would turn to Onassis in her grief, but she had no idea that her daughter soon would want to turn to the sixty-two-year-old Greek for the rest of her life. That weekend in Newport passed with strained cordiality on all sides of the Auchincloss family. 'Ari was a simple man but really quite brilliant in his way,' said Jamie. 'I enjoyed him thoroughly. He loved Chopin and melodic things. But Christina was absolutely impossible to be with. Jackie was on her best behaviour and tried desperately to get along with her, but she was just so difficult. Christina was terribly possessive of her father and wouldn't talk to anyone else. When she did, she constantly put down Americans, saying they drank too much and were so boring.

'I had to escort her around and she was awfully hard to please. Impossible, actually. She wanted to go here and go there, but after she said what she wanted to do and see, she clammed up and was uncommunicative. I was glad when she finally left and so was Mummy, I can assure you.'

A few days later Jackie and her mother received thank-you notes from Onassis accompanied by exquisite reproductions of ancient Macedonian jewellery. Throughout the summer he visited Jackie in Hyannis Port, getting acquainted with Caroline and John and the rest of the Kennedys. He especially looked forward to talking to Rose. He was charmed by Jackie's stories of the matriarch, of her economizing in the midst of wealth. 'Jackie told him how Rose scrimps and saves and cuts corners,' said a friend. 'How she once painted the Palm Beach house in front but not in back because it was too expensive. She told him about Rose's "wrinkies", those brown tapes she puts between her eyebrows to keep away wrinkles, and how she was always sending Jackie reminders to make the children drink their milk and go to Mass. She told him how Rose wouldn't hire a maid or an extra cook because she wanted to save money.'

Ari liked these eccentricities. He laughed about Rose's response to claims that Bobby was spending too lavishly to win in the Presidential primaries. 'It's our money and we're free to spend it any way we please,' Rose declared. 'It's part of this campaign business. If you have the money, you spend it to win. And the more you can afford, the more you'll spend. It's something that is not regulated, therefore it's not

265

unethical … The Rockefellers are like us. We both have lots of money to spend on our campaigns.'

Once they met, Rose found Onassis charming but not very attractive. She said privately that he did not know how to dress well and his trousers were too baggy. Recalling his visit to Hyannis Port, she said: 'I have a memory of him one summer day on our front porch sitting rather scrunched up in one of our tall, fanback white wicker chairs. Several of us were in white wicker chairs, too, and others were seated, reclining or sprawled out on cushions which were somewhat the worse from the summer sun and wet and fogs and hard use from grandchildren. The white paint on the wicker was beginning to flake, as it always does. Everything was pleasant, attractive, practical, but far from elegant. And knowing of Onassis's fabulous wealth and style of life – islands, yachts, and villas with retinues of servants – I wondered if he might find it a bit strange to be in such an informal environment as ours. If so, he showed no sign of it. He was quietly companionable, easy to talk with, intelligent, with a sense of humour and a fund of good anecdotes to tell. I liked him. He was pleasant, interesting, and, to use a word of Greek origin, charismatic.'

During his stay Onassis invited Teddy to escort Jackie on the *Christina* for a week's cruise in August. Teddy accepted, knowing that Jackie was planning to marry the tycoon. He wanted to discuss the financial future of his sister-in-law and her children and talk to Onassis about their trust funds. He also wanted an opportunity to try to change his mind. Marriage to a man who enthusiastically supported the military dictatorship of the Greek junta could only reflect negatively on the politically ambitious Kennedys.

Before leaving, Teddy flew to Hyannis Port to talk to Rose Kennedy.

'Mother,' he said, 'I'm going to take a cruise on Onassis's yacht.'

'Well, what's so extraordinary about that?' asked Mrs Kennedy.

'Onassis is very much in love with Jackie,' said Teddy, preparing his mother for the worst.

Minutes passed before Rose Kennedy responded. 'I've known Onassis for fifteen years,' she said finally. 'He's a fine man.'

As one of the richest men in the world, Aristotle Socrates Onassis was also one of the most notorious. He had been arrested, indicted on criminal charges in the United States in 1954, and released on bail; he escaped jail only by paying a seven-million-dollar fine. He sailed his ships under foreign flags to escape taxes and buried his business dealings in a web of questionable corporations. Professionally reprehensible, he also alienated the establishment by flaunting his personal life. For ten years he conducted a tempestuous love affair with Maria Callas, the opera star who cast aside her Italian husband in 1959 to follow Onassis around the world. Months later, Onassis was sued for divorce by his wife, Tina. The public eagerly followed the relationship between the singer and the shipping magnate, devouring details of their melodramatic fights, their separations, their romantic reconciliations.

The fiery, raven-haired Callas was an accomplished artist of major proportions. Her voice was remarkable, and she infused her music with the emotional dynamics of a great actress. For twenty-five years she gave electrifying performances which made her the most important opera singer in the world. Legions of idolators followed her.

The Kennedys were hardly opera lovers, but they knew of Maria Callas from her public liaison with Onassis. Over the years they had seen the front page photographs of the couple cruising on his yacht, entertaining celebrities like Winston Churchill, Elizabeth Taylor, and Greta Garbo, kissing over champagne glasses, dancing and dining in Paris, Monte Carlo, and Athens. They saw the pictures of Onassis attending bouzouki parties in Greece and throwing plates on the floor, smashing thousands of dollars worth of crockery for sheer entertainment. They read about the lawsuit involving a challenge by Maria Callas and Onassis against another shipbuilder in a dispute over a tanker. Soon it became public knowledge that Onassis had invested three million dollars in the tanker just so his mistress could have a controlling interest. Onassis and Callas went to court to protect their interest, and once again their relationship was spread all over the front pages.

What the Kennedys did not know was that in March 1968 the couple were about to legitimize their longstanding affair by getting married. At the last minute the tempestuous diva and the shipping magnate quarrelled violently, and he stormed out. He started seeing Jackie more frequently in New York. They met regularly in her apartment and even dined out occasionally. But few paid much attention. It was assumed that Onassis, a renowned celebrity seeker, was merely paying homage to America's most famous woman.

Jackie felt secure with this man, who was in many ways like her father-in-law, Joe Kennedy. She enjoyed his company, felt energized by his vitality, and appreciated his attention and his lavish generosity. She began to confide in him, unleashing her feelings about her marriage, about living in the White House and being First Lady. She told him how difficult it was to be emotionally and financially shackled to the Kennedys. They reminisced about the first time they met, when Jack Kennedy was a Senator and they were visiting his parents in the south of France.

The *Christina* was docked at Monte Carlo, and Onassis invited the young couple aboard for cocktails to meet Winston Churchill. Published reports of the meeting described an enthusiastic rapport between the Presidential hopeful and the former Prime Minister, but actually Churchill was aloof and preoccupied. When they left the yacht, Jackie kidded her husband: 'I think he thought you were a waiter, Jack.'

She told Onassis how disappointing it was for Kennedy to meet his hero and then not be received well. She talked about her husband in terms of a little boy with big dreams and aspirations. Publicly she fought to perpetuate his untarnished image, but she had no illusions about the Kennedy myth which she helped create. She talked openly about her bitter disappointments as Jack Kennedy's wife, the death of her baby, and the horror of seeing her husband assassinated just when their marriage was starting to work. She confided her concern about her children. She was especially worried about her seven-year-old son not having a strong male influence in his life. John, Jr, was becoming a problem, showing off constantly, punching his schoolmates, and getting into squabbles. The headmaster at St David's School recommended that he repeat the second grade, but Jackie refused to hold him back. Instead, she changed schools and enrolled John in Collegiate, hoping that the discipline of a new private school would help him.

Onassis listened sympathetically. He ached for Jackie and knew how lonely she was as a widow and how she longed to be married again. He felt strongly that Jackie had been bruised by her husband's philandering and that Jack Kennedy never appreciated her great style but begrudged her spending. In the beginning he felt compassion for her and wanted to brighten her life. He also felt needed.

After Robert Kennedy's assassination, Jackie's world caved in. Plagued by fears and violence, she turned to her friend, the only man she knew who could offer her the protection and security she so desperately wanted. There were complications which had to be worked out, of course, especially regarding religion. Onassis, a member of the Greek Orthodox Church, was a divorced man. As a Roman Catholic, Jackie would risk excommunication by marrying him. For the sake of her children, she wanted to avoid a public denunciation from the Vatican. She also needed to cushion the blow for the Kennedys. But she was determined to marry Onassis with or without Church sanction and the Kennedys' support.

Firmly convinced that only Onassis could bring her the happiness and security she wanted for herself and her children, she made up her mind to marry him as soon as she could. She began inviting him to Hyannis Port so he could spend more time with Caroline and John, hoping that they would accept him as a presence in their life. She sought the counsel of Richard Cardinal Cushing, who officiated at her wedding, baptized her children, and buried her husband. His support would give her the confidence she needed to pave the way with the Kennedys. There was never any question of Onassis's adopting her children. She wanted them to retain their name and their close association with their father's family. They needed this identification for their own emotional security. Jackie needed Onassis for hers.

Onassis, meanwhile, had problems with his own children. Christina and Alexander adored their mother and resented any other woman in their father's life. They had always despised Maria Callas as being responsible for the divorce which separated their parents. Onassis never had the time to be a father to his children because he poured himself into his work and travels, but he loved them dearly and did not want to shatter the little emotional security they had.

To establish Christina and Alexander as his rightful heirs, he had to deal with the peculiar Greek law known as 'nomimos mira', which required a husband to leave at least 12.5 per cent of his wealth to his wife and 37.5 per cent to his children. The law was strictly enforced, making it impossible for a Greek to disinherit his family. If a Greek died intestate, the percentages doubled. Onassis wanted to protect Jackie financially, care for her children, indulge her expensive whims, and guarantee her comfort in case of his death, but he was not prepared to bequeath his vast fortune to her at the expense of his two children. Under the existing law Jackie would inherit at least 64 million dollars of Onassis's estimated 500-million-dollar estate. He asked her to waive this right under 'nomimos mira', and then he persuaded the Greek government to pass a law recognizing the validity of her signed agreement. In exchange for this concession, Jackie received three million dollars for herself and one million apiece for her children. The agreement was worked out between Teddy and Onassis during the August cruise. There was still no definite date for the wedding, just the understanding that it would be some time in the future.

When Jackie returned home from the cruise, she flew to Boston with a Secret Service man to talk to Cardinal Cushing. The highly emotional meeting lasted two hours as Jackie unburdened herself to the prelate, going into painful detail about her life with Jack Kennedy and her five lonely years of widowhood. Years before, the Cardinal had been visited by Mrs Leonard Kater, the Georgetown landlady who tried so hard to keep Kennedy from becoming President. She brought along photographic evidence of the candidate's infidelity while his wife was out of town. So the Cardinal was partially prepared for Jackie's intimate revelations. She told him how good Onassis had been to her throughout the years and how kind he was to President Kennedy's children, caring for them like his own.

The Cardinal admitted that he had been besieged with calls from the Kennedy family, pleading with him to intercede and prevent her from marrying the shipping magnate. The Kennedys were so incensed by the prospect of the wedding that they sent Robert McNamara to New York to try to talk some sense into Jackie. She remained firm in her decision and bitterly turned aside each of McNamara's arguments.

Cardinal Cushing, the son of a South Boston Irish immigrant blacksmith, refused to cave in to the demands of the Kennedy family. Instead, he gave Jackie his full support. She told him she had been like a drowning person grasping for a straw before the Cardinal walked into her life years before. From then on, she said, she always felt she had somebody to go to when she felt abandoned by everyone else. The Cardinal explained that there was little he could do to prevent the Vatican from excommunicating her, but he promised to defend her publicly and said that no one had the right to call her a sinner. He told her that his own sister had violated church teachings by marrying a Jew, but that eventually the marriage was validated within the Catholic Church and they lived happily together for over thirty years. He also assured her that their meeting together would remain as confidential as a confession. 'My lips are sealed forever,' he promised. Jackie hugged the prelate and with tears in her eyes thanked him for being compassionate. Later she wrote him a long letter, thanking him again for understanding her. Neither realized then what the Cardinal's defence would eventually cost him in terms of public support.

By now all the Kennedys were aware that Jackie planned to marry Onassis. She also confided her plans to her sister, who in turn confided in Truman Capote. She told her financial advisor, André Meyer, who then spent two weeks trying to persuade her to change her mind. Meyer despised Onassis and felt strongly that Jackie was making a monumental mistake. Jackie ignored his pleas.

Labour Day weekend brought the family together at the Kennedy compound in Hyannis Port. 'Steve Smith was absolutely enraged about Jackie's plans,' recalled a Kennedy aide. 'He called her and Onassis every name in the book, screaming that they were going to ruin the Kennedy name politically. He was then thinking of getting into politics himself and running for governor in New York, and he knew the political fallout from that marriage would be disastrous to him. All those years he had to work in the background running all those Kennedy campaigns. Now that he had half a chance for himself, it was going to be flushed down the drain by his sister-in-law. God, was he mad. But Steve wasn't the only one. Everyone, including Teddy, was quite upset. They finally extracted a promise from Jackie that Caroline and John would be educated and raised in the United States no matter how much time she spent abroad. They also discussed how they should react publicly when the announcement was made, but they didn't know when that would be. Jackie wouldn't say.'

The secret of the marriage was already known by too many people to be contained much longer. On 15 October the *Boston Herald Traveler* ran a front-page story predicting a marriage in the near future between John F. Kennedy's widow and Aristotle Onassis. The story ran without any official confirmation from the Kennedy family, but Cardinal Cushing, refusing to lie, did not deny the rumour.

That day Jackie called Onassis in Athens to tell him that the story was out and they should get married as soon as possible. Onassis was engaged in delicate business deliberations with the Greek military dictator, George Papadopoulos, but he agreed with Jackie and dropped everything to begin making the necessary arrangements in Greece.

Next Jackie called her mother in Virginia. 'Hi,' she said. 'Are you free?'

'No, I'm not,' replied Janet Auchincloss. 'I'm quite busy right now working on Stratford Hall.'

'Mummy, please. I want you to come to Greece.'

'How ridiculous, Jackie. I've got too much to do here.'

'I also want you to announce my engagement to marry Ari, and then we'll leave from New York with the children for Athens and get married on Sunday.'

'Oh, God, Jackie. You can't mean that,' screamed Mrs Auchincloss. 'You're not really serious, are you? How can you do this? What about the children? Please, Jackie, I think you should –'

'Sorry, Mummy. It's too late.'

Unaware until then of her daughter's plans, Mrs Auchincloss was stunned by the phone call. 'Mummy was hysterical,' recalled Jamie Auchincloss. 'She did everything she possibly could to talk Jackie out of that marriage. She was just incensed. But it was no use. Jackie had made up her mind and there was nothing anyone could do about it. Mummy kept saying, "She's finally getting back at me for divorcing her father. That's what she's doing. I just know it." Mummy felt quite reticent about calling the press herself, but she did as Jackie ordered and released a statement through Nancy Tuckerman in New York. Then she had to get her passport and started getting hysterical again because she had left it in Newport and no one up there could find it. Finally she called Frances Knight in the Passport Office in Washington, and Mrs Knight, who was from Newport herself and always loved Mummy and Jackie, issued her a new one in fifteen minutes.'

Nancy Tuckerman was equally flabbergasted. 'I can't quite believe it,' she told Jackie.

'Oh, Tucky, you have no idea of how lonely I've been all these years,' Jackie replied. 'Please give me your support. I need you now more than ever to handle things.'

Then Jackie called her sister-in-law, Jean Smith, to tell her that the marriage had to be rushed now that the news was out. She asked Jean to come to Greece with her and bring her children, but Steve Smith refused to allow the kids to go. Instead, he sent them to spend the weekend with

273

Ethel Kennedy's family at Hickory Hill. Then Jackie asked Jean to call Rose Kennedy to tell her the news before Jackie called her later in the day. The call to her formidable mother-in-law, the woman she always referred to as Belle Mère, was her toughest. She refused to call her cold and needed Jean's intercession to prepare her.

Rose Kennedy was as astonished as Janet Auchincloss and Nancy Tuckerman. 'I was completely surprised,' she said. 'In fact, I was rather stunned. And then perplexed. I thought of the difference in their ages. I thought of the difference in religion, he being Greek Orthodox, and the fact that he had been divorced; and I wondered whether this could be a valid marriage in the eyes of the Church. I thought of Caroline and John, Jr, and whether they could learn to accept Onassis in the role of stepfather so that he could give them the guidance that children need from a man. There were many things on my mind – my thoughts were awhirl – but I began trying to sort them out, give the various factors some order of priority.'

By the time Jackie called, the Kennedy matriarch had composed herself enough to offer her daughter-in-law good wishes, telling her to make her plans as she chose to do. It wasn't a loving endorsement, but it was as much as the fervently religious Rose could offer. Jackie tried to reassure her by saying that she had talked to Cardinal Cushing and that he had given her his support. Rose was pleased that Jackie had consulted the Kennedys' spiritual adviser, but she refused to attend the wedding in Greece, using as her excuse her husband's declining health. Jackie understood and did not press her.

She then phoned Lee in London and told her why she had to hurry her plans. Lee assured her that she and Stas and their two children would be waiting for her in Athens.

At 3:30 pm on 17 October 1968, Nancy Tuckerman made the announcement in New York to the press. 'Mrs Hugh D. Auchincloss has asked me to tell you that her daughter, Mrs John F. Kennedy, is planning to marry Aristotle Onassis sometime next week. No place or date has been set for the moment,' she said. The statement was intentionally ambiguous because Jackie wanted to keep the place and date a secret to avoid an avalanche of reporters and photographers.

Two hours later she walked out of her Fifth Avenue apartment, wearing a grey jersey dress and holding the hands of her two children. Accompanied by Bunny Mellon and a group of Secret Service men, she entered a waiting limousine which whisked her to the airport.

There she met her mother and stepfather, Jean Kennedy Smith, and Pat Kennedy Lawford and her daughter. Onassis had arranged for the wedding party to fly on his airline, Olympic Airways, and bumped ninety scheduled passengers in order to give them complete privacy during the eight-and-a-half-hour flight to Greece.

Chapter Twenty

Camelot started collapsing moments after the wedding announcement. The news of Jacqueline Kennedy's re-marriage hogged front pages around the world with head-lines registering shock, dismay, and indignation. 'SHE'S NO LONGER A SAINT', screamed Oslo's *Verdens Gang*. 'JACKIE, HOW COULD YOU?' demanded the *Stockholm Expressen*. 'JOHN KENNEDY HAS DIED A SECOND TIME', claimed the *Daily Morninger* in Istanbul. Then followed the personal comments of people close to the couple, some of whom strained to offer best wishes, and others who held nothing back.

Rose Kennedy: 'I'm never really surprised my by family any more.'

Teddy Kennedy: 'I talked to Jackie several days ago and she told me of her plans, and I gave her my best wishes for their happiness.'

Steve Smith: 'No comment.'

Sargent Shriver, then in Paris serving as Ambassador to France: 'I do not know anything about it. But I feel it's not appropriate for me over here to make any comment.'

Eunice Kennedy Shriver: 'No comment.'

Alexander Onassis: 'My father needs a wife, but I don't need a mother.'

Lewis Auchincloss: 'Well, we assume that she needs the money. After all, how can she lived on $250,000 a year?'

Gore Vidal: 'I can only give you two words – highly suitable!'

Maria Callas: 'She did well, Jackie, to give a grandfather to her children. Ari is as beautiful as Croesus.'

President Lyndon Johnson: 'No comment.'

Lady Bird Johnson: 'I feel strangely freer. No shadow walks beside me down the hall of the White House or here at Camp David ... I wonder what it would have been like if we had entered this life unaccompanied by that shadow?'

Tish Baldrige: 'You know, it's her life and it's hers to lead, and let's just everybody be glad she's happy.'

George Smathers: 'I think she did it just so she'd never have to be beholden to the Kennedys again.'

Nancy Tuckerman: 'I'm very excited.'

Larry O'Brien: 'No comment.'

Mrs Larry O'Brien: 'It just can't happen. They're just too disparate.'

Roswell Gilpatric: 'She once told me that she felt she could count on him. It was an attribute she looked for in all her friends.'

Lord Harlech: 'Mrs Kennedy has been a very close friend for fourteen years. I hope she will be very happy.'

Bill Walton: 'She deserves great happiness and I hope she finds it.'

Truman Capote: 'I've known about it for a long time – at least six months. Let's say, I've known for six months that they were going to be engaged. Harlech never pretended to be anything more than a friend. The romance just came from the press. As for the official announcement, I'm happy for anything that makes her happy. We're great friends.'

Paul Mathias: 'I wish her great happiness. She deserves to be happy.'

Coco Chanel: 'Everyone knew she was not cut out for dignity. You mustn't ask a woman with a touch of vulgarity to spend the rest of her life over a corpse.'

Joan Rivers: 'Come on, tell the truth. Would you sleep with Onassis? Do you believe she does? Well, she has to do something – you can't stay in Bergdorf's shopping all day.'

Bob Hope: 'Nixon has a Greek running mate. Now everyone wants one.'

Monsignor Fausto Vallaine, chief of the Vatican press office: 'It is clear that when a Catholic marries a divorced man, she knowingly violates the law of the Church.'

The only person to step forward with heartfelt good wishes was Cardinal Cushing. 'Why can't she marry whomever she wants to marry?' he said. 'And why should I be condemned and why should she be condemned? ... I turn on the radio and all I hear are people knocking her head off, as it were, criticizing her and so forth, and they are so far from the truth that no one would believe me if I ever got on a radio programme and revealed what I know. Few people understand Jacqueline Kennedy ... I encouraged and helped her in every possible way. I had a letter from her that would be worth hundreds of thousands of dollars if I allowed any of the national secular magazines to publish it, but I burned the letter. That letter was thanking me for understanding her.

'I have been contacted by many of those who are identified in high places with the administration of the late President Kennedy and I have been contacted by others immediately related and associated with the Kennedy family to stop all this from taking place, namely that Jack's widow, God bless him, would marry Aristotle Socrates Onassis ... All I know that I am able to tell you is this: caritas, charity.'

Reaction to Cardinal Cushing's remarks was hardly charitable. He was besieged with hate mail and outraged calls. He was so overwhelmed by the outcry that he decided to announce his retirement two years earlier than planned.

'I've had it,' he said a few days later. 'What the future status of Jacqueline's marriage in the Catholic Church is not for me to decide. But of one thing I am certain, when my dearest friend, John Fitzgerald Kennedy, the 35th President of the United States, asked me to take care of Jacqueline and the children – if anything happened to him – I can salute him today in memory and say, "Jack, I have fulfilled my promise", but it has showered upon me so many mail deliveries, some of which are in the language of the gutter, if I may so characterize them, that I have decided to change my own plans.

'As of 24 August 1970 I propose to retire as Archbishop of Boston. At that time I shall be about 50 years a priest, about 30 years a bishop, of which about 25 years have been spent as Archbishop of Boston. Now I propose after the publicity I have received in recent days in my own native city, which publicity has been going all over the world, to offer my resignation to His Holiness Pope Paul VI at the end of this year.'

The climate of hate feeling around Cardinal Cushing in

Boston was not felt in the tiny Chapel of Our Lady on the Greek isle of Skorpios. There under falling rain – a Greek good luck sign for a wedding – the American queen of the world married the multi-millionaire king of international society in the most celebrated nuptials of the twentieth century.

Clutching the hand of her solemn ten-year-old daughter, Jackie walked into the chapel wearing a beige chiffon and lace two-piece Valentino dress with long sleeves that fell three inches about her knees. It was the same dress she had worn to the wedding of Bunny Mellon's daughter in Washington a few months earlier. A hairdresser was flown in from Athens to style her long brown hair in a flowing bouffant around her shoulders and a single braid falling in the back, held by a beige ribbon that matched her dress. Despite her beige low-heeled shoes, the five-foot-seven bride towered over her short, squat bridegroom, who wore a baggy blue double-breasted suit, a white shirt, and a red tie. John, Jr, and Caroline, who was dressed in white organdy, stood next to their mother holding ceremonial candles and looking quite serious and somewhat dazed. The only flower in the church was a gardenia plant bearing two blossoms. The former First Lady's Secret Service agent, wearing a John F. Kennedy PT-boat tie clasp, stood squarely in the door to bar reporters from entering.

At 5:15 pm on 20 October 1968, a bearded Greek Orthodox Archimandrite stepped forward, clad in a gold brocade vestment and a towering black hat, to perform the thirty-minute ceremony. Hugh D. Auchincloss gave his step-daughter in marriage much as he had fifteen years before when she walked down the aisle of St Mary's Church in Newport to wed John F. Kennedy.

'Do Thou now, Master, send down Thine hand from Thy holy dwelling place and unite Thy servants, Aristotle and Jacqueline, for by Thee woman is united to man,' intoned the priest.

In Greek he told the couple that the wife should obey and fear her husband and the husband should love his wife as Christ loved His Church. Onassis's sister, Artemis, then stepped forward to place delicate leather wreaths of lemon buds and white ribbons on the couple's heads. As the priest chanted in Greek, she criss-crossed the wreaths three times. Simple gold wedding bands were placed on their fingers and passed between them three times, the number three symbolizing the triumvirate God in the Holy Trinity. Assisted by three cantors, the priest offered the couple a silver goblet of red wine to kiss before drinking. Throughout the ceremony Jackie watched the priest intently. When he started the Dance of Esiah, she took his hand and Ari's hand and led them in a promenade three times around the altar, as is the custom for a Greek wedding. There was no kiss to signal the end of the ceremony. Only the priest's words: 'The servant of God, Aristotelis, is betrothed to the servant of God, Jacqueline, in the name of the Father, the Son, and the Holy Ghost.'

Jammed into the little chapel, Jackie's wedding party stood throughout the service, crowded alongside Onassis's two children; his sister, Artemis Garofalides; his half-sister and her husband; his niece, Mrs Panos Drakos, and her husband; his friends and business associates from Monte Carlo, Mr and Mrs Nicholas Kokims; and Joannis Georgakis, the managing director of Olympic Airways, and his wife. Only twenty-two persons were allowed inside to witness the wedding.

Onassis spared no effort in protecting his bride's privacy. He hired two large helicopters equipped with electric bullhorns to guard the island. A security force of two hundred armed men held back the mobs of journalists and photographers who arrived earlier in the day. Patrol boats, reinforced by cruisers and helicopters from the Greek navy, circled the island to keep the reporters from getting closer than 1,000 yards.

Besieged by journalists, Jackie released a statement that morning pleading for privacy and promising to pose for pictures once the ceremony was over. 'We know you understand that even though people may be well known,' she said, 'they still hold in their hearts the emotions of a simple person for the moments that are the most important of those we know on earth – birth, marriage, and death. We wish our wedding to be a private moment in the little chapel among the cypresses of Skorpio with only members of the family present – five of them little children. If you will give us those moments, we will so gladly give you all the co-operation possible for you to take the pictures you need.'

The post-wedding cooperation was limited to a few minutes of picture-taking. The resulting photographs, which circled the world, showed a serenely smiling thirty-nine-year-old bride with her hand through the arm of a slouching sixty-two-year-old groom. Glum expressions on the faces of Alexander and Christina Onassis made them look as if they had emerged from a funeral instead of a wedding. There was not one smiling picture of Caroline or John F. Kennedy, Jr. Both youngsters kept their little heads bowed, refusing to smile for photographers.

The wedding party left the chapel in jeeps and drove to Onassis's luxury yacht *Christina* to change clothes for the reception and dinner. Named after his only daughter, this three-million-dollar sea palace exceeded the length of a football field, was staffed by a crew of fifty, and contained lapis lazuli balustrades and solid gold fixtures in every bathroom. Basic operating costs totalled $1,140,000 a year. From stem to stern the opulence was dazzling. There were nine cushioned guest rooms and luxurious suites named after different Greek islands, each containing a marble bathroom and ornate dressing room. The children's playroom, decorated by Ludwig Bemelmans, contained dolls dressed by Dior, a rocking horse, a specially designed slot machine for children, and exquisite hand-carved musical toys.

Onassis's private quarters at the top of a circular staircase consisted of a three-room suite. The huge study contained a $2,500,000 painting by El Greco hanging over an Empire desk alongside Russian icons and swords in golden scabbards which were gifts from King Ibn Saud of Saudi Arabia.

The bedroom was adorned with eighteenth-century Venetian mirrors. Upon the dresser sat a bejewelled Buddha, the oldest statue of its kind in the Western world and valued at $300,000. A mirror-lined dressing room led into a Siena marble bathroom that looked like a temple. The bath, inlaid with flying fish and dolphins made by mosaic artists in Berlin, was an exact replica of the one in King Minos's lost Palace of Knossos in ancient Crete.

In one salon there was a landscape painting by Winston Churchill, and in another a private cinema room for watching movies. Paintings of Marcel Vertes circled the white dining-room. A grand piano sat in the huge smoking-room near an open fireplace of lapis lazuli which was installed at a cost of $4 a square inch. The *pièce de resistance* was the *Christina*'s swimming pool, decorated with an enlarged reproduction of another mosaic from the Minos palace. The bottom of the pool could be raised electronically to deck level and used as a dance floor.

The yacht boasted forty-two phones, plus inside lines on which guests could ring the servants' quarters for maids, valets, seamstresses, and masseuses. There were bars and pantries and lounges as well as a ship's hospital with surgical and X-ray equipment. The yacht carried eight speedboats, two lifeboats, three dinghies, one sailboat, two kayaks, one glass-bottom boat, and a hydroplane.

More than a floating palace, the *Christina* served as the executive mansion for an international business empire and catered to the whims of a man of rare wealth, power, and influence.

The Kennedy sisters, though accustomed to luxury, were astonished when they first stepped aboard. 'My God,' exclaimed Pat Lawford. 'I can't quite believe it.'

'Almost makes you feel poor, doesn't it?' giggled Jean Kennedy Smith.

Janet Auchincloss was equally overwhelmed. 'Yes, it's quite fabulous,' she told a friend later. 'Almost too much so, if you know what I mean.'

With or without his stupendous yacht, Janet Auchincloss was not about to accept a man older than herself as her son-in-law. Especially this man, with his sunglasses and baggy suits, who fled from Turkey to Argentina with $60 in his pocket and eventually created the largest shipping empire in global history. Even with his 500-million-dollar fortune,

Aristotle Socrates Onassis did not measure up to her standards. 'Of course, it wasn't the marriage I wanted for my daughter,' she said. 'He's hardly the type of man I hoped she'd remarry, but there was nothing I could do about it. Believe me, I tried.'

Ethel Kennedy, awaiting the birth of her eleventh child and still in mourning four months after the assassination of her husband, surprised Jackie with her good wishes. The night before the wedding she sent Ari a cable. 'Are there any more at home like you?' she wired. But from Eunice Kennedy Shriver there was only a frosty silence. Nor were there congratulations from Teddy. A few days later Rose finally managed to say that she wished her former daughter-in-law happiness, but there was no message of good wishes from the Kennedy matriarch on the wedding day.

After a quick toast of pink champagne in the lounge of the yacht, the guests retired to their suites to prepare for the wedding feast. Jackie spent an hour with Onassis in their private quarters while her personal maid and Lee Radziwill's governess readied the children for bed. Caroline and John, Sidney Lawford, Tina and Tony Radziwill changed into their pyjamas and nightdresses and dressing-gowns, then went downstairs to join the adults in the living-room.

Jean Kennedy Smith walked in first, wearing silver lamé pyjamas. Patricia Kennedy Lawford followed her minutes later, dressed in a spectacular tunic dotted with platinum blobs the size of silver dollars. Then came Jackie, radiant in a floor-length white skirt, a black blouse, and the gold be-jewelled caftan belt which the King of Morocco gave her while she was First Lady.

What she wore on the third finger of her left hand stopped everyone. Gone was the gold wedding band from John F. Kennedy worn throughout her widowhood. In its place was a huge heart-shaped cabochon ruby the size of an Easter egg, surrounded by dozens of one-carat diamonds. Dangling from her ears were identical heart-shaped rubies framed in diamonds. Transfixed by Jackie's $1,200,000 cache of jewellery, no one said a word. Finally Caroline ran up to her mother and broke the silence.

'Mummy, mummy, mummy,' she cried. 'They're so pretty – you're so pretty.' She held up her hand to Jackie's face and pushed aside her mother's long dark hair to look closely at the dazzling earrings. Jackie laughed at Caroline's pleasure in the jewels and took the ring off so her daughter could try it on her own fingers. The ten-year-old tossed the unfaceted ruby in the air, delighting her cousins as the gem twinkled and flashed against the light like a squadron of fireflies. Onassis also gave his bride a mammoth gold bracelet with rams' heads studded with rubies.

No guest ever left the *Christina* without a precious memento from the host, and this evening Onassis gave everyone treasures from Zolotas, the jeweller in Athens, the equivalent of Tiffany's in New York. Lee and Jean and Pat each received jewelled zodiac rings and the mother of the bride a diamond clip. Caroline and Sidney and Tina squealed with delight as they opened their velvet boxes containing little gold bracelets set with diamonds and sapphires. John, Jr, and Tony Radziwill each got an Acutron clock with instruments for telling the time, weather, date, latitude and longitude. 'You'll need these if you're going to captain this yacht,' quipped Onassis.

Getting down on his hands and knees, the tycoon began tumbling around with the youngsters, who climbed all over him shrieking with laughter. Jackie watched them lovingly and everyone watched Jackie. Guests were then ushered into the dining-room and seated for the wedding dinner. The bride and groom sat side by side. On Onassis's left sat his daughter, Christina, and next to Jackie sat Alexander. 'There were toasts and tears all around,' remembers one guest.

The most moving tribute came from Jean Kennedy Smith, who arose and held up her glass of wine to say, 'I want to toast my dear sister.' Jackie cried as she listened to her former sister-in-law who had overcome her husband's objections to be with her on this day.

Janet Auchincloss kept dabbing her eyes as guests stood to toast the bride and groom. Finally she arose, looked directly at her son-in-law, and said, 'I know that my daughter is going to find peace and happiness with you.'

Onassis rose and toasted the seven sisters assembled around his table, saying this was a good omen for a family now united by love and marriage. Then Jackie stood and lifted her glass. 'I wish to make a toast to the only brother at this table,' she said, referring to her new stepson, Alexander. Tears filled his eyes. Christina Onassis cried and hugged her father.

By the time the wedding cake was served there was not one dry eye at the table. Onassis's sisters smiled through their tears as they watched their brother enjoy himself. When the waiters brought in the cake plates, Onassis called down the table for the Kennedy sisters to look closely at the design. Imprinted on the china was an ancient Greek symbol that looked exactly like an American dollar sign, a touch Joe Kennedy's daughters readily appreciated.

Jackie and Ari cut their cake with an antique Greek knife. After everyone was served, Caroline and John, Jr, and their cousins scooped up the sugary decorations. Soon the children were hugged and kissed and sent to bed, and the adults went into the smoking room for after-dinner drinks and dancing. Jackie and Ari sat together holding hands. They never kissed, but just looked at each other occasionally and smiled secretly, as if sharing a special bit of knowledge the rest of the world would never know.

The next day the wedding guests left the *Christina* to fly home. Ari flew to Athens to continue the business negotiations which had been interrupted by the hurried preparations for the wedding. Jackie kissed her children goodbye and remained in Greece to begin her honeymoon with her new husband. She called Billy Baldwin in New York and asked him to fly to Greece at once to begin decorating the house on Skorpios so it would be ready for Christmas.

When the decorator arrived he was shown the house and then given a tour of Onassis's yacht. He was appalled. 'Inside it was the ugliest thing I had ever set eyes on,' he said. 'Entirely covered with thick wall-to-wall carpeting, with tacky canvas runners ... Dinner was elaborate and very good, but the table was hideous, set with bad china and fancy glasses and silver, and the flowers were overdone.'

The fastidious little man was dismayed when Jackie led him into the salon for coffee. 'Apple-green French-panelled walls and French reproduction furniture everywhere,' he gasped.

He immediately set to work trying to get the house in shape for the holidays. Onassis gave him complete freedom, insisting that he did not want to be involved in the details. 'Billy,' he said, 'I will help you all I can with getting the house complete, but you have to get one thing straight. This house I want to be a total surprise. I trust you and Jackie, and I don't want to know anything about it. I have only one request. Can there be a long sofa by the fire so I can lie and read and nap and watch the flames?'

The decorator gave Onassis his one request and then spent over $250,000 ordering from London the furniture, curtains, and slipcovers Jackie wanted.

Reaction to the wedding continued unabated, with news of the nuptials claiming front pages for weeks. Few women in history have had the power to stop the world simply by getting married. For five years the widow of John F. Kennedy had been the hallowed object of people's admiration and overwhelming guilt. The minute she chose to marry a man outside her church and her culture, she dashed the hopes of those who had elevated her. By becoming the wife of an international buccaneer with a sixth-grade education, who fell far short of the inflated myth surrounding the late President, she broke the spell. But even as she tumbled from her pedestal, Jackie remained the cynosure of an insatiable curiosity and the subject of endless speculation.

Her picture appeared on the covers of *Time* and *Newsweek* with stories describing her as the new First Lady of Skorpios with seventy-two servants on call, the new mistress of a villa in Glyfada with ten servants, of a penthouse in Paris with five servants, of a hacienda in Montevideo with thirty-eight servants, and of a Fifth Avenue apartment in New York with five.

Other articles psychoanalysed her as the daughter of a drunken divorcé who never paid his bills and then the stepdaughter of a wealthy man who refused to indulge her. As an adult she became the wife of the most powerful man in the world, a President who had mastered all manner of adversity – except for Jackie's quirks and wild extravagances. Now she was the wife of one of the richest men on earth, a man who would willingly give her anything.

The press played so heavily on the age difference that Jackie looked like an ingénue and Onassis an old croaker gasping his last. The public ridiculed the marriage with a series of Jackie jokes which circulated for weeks. In a typical quip, John-John goes up to Onassis and says, 'Will you do a frog for me, please?'

'A what?' asks the tycoon.

'A frog,' says the youngster. 'Will you imitate a frog?'

Onassis did not understand what the seven-year-old meant, so he asked him again.

'I want to hear you do a frog,' says John-John, 'because Mummy says when you croak, we will be the richest people in the world.'

The jokes became increasingly macabre. One was repeated by Congressman Morris Udall during his presidential campaign: A reporter interviewing Russian Premier Nikita Khrushchev mentions that Lee Harvey Oswald had once been in Russia. The reporter asks the Russian leader if the course of world events would have been different if Oswald had stayed in the USSR and shot him instead of Kennedy. Khrushchev thinks a minute. 'Well, yes,' he finally replies. 'For one thing, I don't think Aristotle Onassis would have married Mrs Khrushchev.'

Later, a book written by a steward on Onassis's yacht claimed that the servant had seen a 170-clause marriage contract signed by the couple. According to the book, it stipulated separate bedrooms for each, a $585,040-a-year allowance for Jackie while they were married, plus a 20-million-dollar settlement for her in the event of divorce. The story made headlines around the world, and even Jackie's closest friends assumed it was true.

'It's a lie, a complete lie,' she told Truman Capote. 'I don't have any money. When I married Ari, my income from the

Kennedy estate stopped, and so did my widow's pension from the US government. I didn't make any premarital financial agreement with Ari. I know it's an old Greek custom, but I couldn't do it. I didn't want to barter myself. Except for my personal possessions, I have exactly $5,200 in a bank account. Everything else I charge to Olympic Airlines.'

Onassis was dissected in the press as a driven, ambitious man hell-bent on buying the world's most famous woman to add to his collection of celebrities. 'He's obsessed by famous women,' said Maria Callas. 'He was obsessed with me because I was famous. Now Jackie and her sister, they have obsessed him and they are even more famous.' Later the diva moaned, 'First I lost my weight. Then I lost my voice. Now I've lost Onassis.'

Lee Radziwill tried to defend her sister's remarriage by putting Onassis in the perspective of other wealthy Europeans who lived lavishly and spent gargantuan amounts of money, throwing it around for sheer pleasure. But instead of helping, Lee's words only fuelled more controversy.

'My sister needs a man like Onassis,' she said, 'a man who can protect her from the curiosity of the world. I think she's tired of having to exercise such enormous control over herself, not to be able to move without all of her gestures being judged and all her steps being traced, not to be able to live like other people. I think she's rather tired of being a public personality and a part of the political life. Politics has never been her dominant interest. Not at all. Nevertheless, in the past she knew how to assume public responsibilities quite well, it seems to me. She did it proudly and with honour. But it isn't fair that she should have to continue to force her nature. My sister is very jealous of her private life, very timid.

'You can call Onassis anything, but not old,' insisted Lee. 'On the contrary, he's very young, energetic, and vigorous. You only need to meet him to see that right away. In spite of the difference in their ages, I'm convinced that my sister will be happy with him. But people aren't used to men like Onassis who exhibit their wealth. The wealthy Europeans are ostentatious with their money. They want to show everyone how rich they are, to buy every good thing that money can buy, to enjoy themselves, and even, sometimes, to have the pleasure of wasting money. Rich Americans, on the other hand, are more strait-laced with their money. They establish libraries, they're philanthropic, they support political movements. It's as though they must buy forgiveness for having so much wealth. Americans can't understand a man like Onassis. If my sister's new husband had been blond, young, rich and Anglo-Saxon, most Americans would have been much happier, I suppose.'

The supposition was correct. Americans were devastated by Jackie's choice. As the royal coin of the realm she was suddenly devalued. She in turn was embittered by the public's outcry but also resigned to the furor swirling around her. She read thousands of words written about the wedding that weekend, carefully combing papers from around the world.

On the private island of Skorpios she sought refuge from the world's outrage, not knowing then that her wedding was the opening night of a Greek tragedy that would play for the next seven years – a drama that was to plague her with a series of deaths and family scandals that would eventually rob her of the happiness she so desperately wanted.

The fear she had experienced in marrying into the Kennedy family and coping with their pursuit of power nearly overwhelmed her as a twenty-four-year-old bride. She soon realized she was not emotionally equipped to deal with politics on their level, and the effort almost claimed her psychological equilibrium. She could never be recompensed for the murders of her husband and her brother-in-law. She directed her bitterness towards the country which stimulated such violence. Marrying a foreigner who had no stake in American politics seemed like an ideal escape from her lonely role as the enshrined widow of a martyred President. She could now wrap herself around a man who would indulge her and amuse her and treat her as the wife-child she always wanted to be. She would never have to account to him for the money she spent. She could begin another life removed and remote from the role of American heroine, an unnatural, even painful part she was forced to play on the world's stage. 'I'm an outsider – and that's uncomfortable in American life,' she had said months before.

Never knowing sustained happiness, she had always felt cheated. She naturally gravitated to a man who promised her a life free from care and concern and the Kennedys. The good luck rain that fell on the little chapel on Skorpios on her wedding day was to consist only of intermittent showers of happiness. There would be buckets of diamonds and $60,000 sable coats and priceless paintings, antiques and artifacts, but no real inner, spiritual happiness. In her more desperate moments, Jackie tried to forget how she really felt by going on wild spending sprees clocked at $3,000 a minute.

For the first time in her life she could shop and spend and buy without accounting to anybody for anything. She didn't even have to bother with cash. Her face was her charge plate. The bills were sent directly to the Onassis office, where they were paid by an indulgent tycoon who delighted in pleasing his wife. He could afford her compulsion to shop, her obsession to redecorate, her passion to accumulate. 'God knows Jackie has had her years of sorrow,' he said. 'If she enjoys it, let her buy to her heart's content.' He showered her with trips and vacations and cruises around the world, with first-class accommodations, with suites filled with flowers and fruit and champagne. He summoned perfumed tribes of international celebrities to entertain her, chauffeur-driven Rolls-Royces to transport her, bodyguards to protect her, and private planes to fly her wherever she wanted to go. All that money could buy rained down on Jackie the day she became Mrs Aristotle Onassis.

The only thing she could not afford was protection from the maelstrom of events which was to envelop her, wreaking havoc on her new marriage. The woman Jack Kennedy once described as 'fey' would soon know the darker definitions of that word: she would be marked by apprehensions of death and calamity. With her second husband she would have to face tragedy so often she would become almost unfeeling. She would agonize with him over the sudden death of his sister-in-law and the mysterious death of his first wife. Together they would bury his only son, Alexander. They would suffer the scandal of Chappaquiddick and the drowning of one of the young women with Teddy Kennedy. They would mourn the death of Ambassador Joseph Kennedy, the death of Cardinal Cushing, and the death of Stas Radziwill. Later they would be brushed by the cancer of young Teddy Kennedy and the amputation of his leg. They would survive the suicide attempt of Christina Onassis and her hasty nine-month marriage, but the tragedies would take their toll. Eventually they would lose everything they sought for themselves as husband and wife. In the end, only the death of Onassis would save Jackie from the shame of divorce, leaving the wife-child a widow once again.

Chapter Twenty-one

Jackie stayed in Greece with her husband nearly a month. Then she flew home by herself to be with her children, leaving him in Athens to do business with the Greek dictator, George Papadopoulos. He was in the midst of negotiating the biggest financial deal of his career, a 400-million-dollar investment package for Greece. The negotiations collapsed shortly after the junta fell. But Onassis went ahead with plans to build an oil refinery, a shipyard, an aluminium plant, several light industries, an air terminal and a string of tourist resorts which would completely revolutionize Greece while making him the richest man in the world.

He was severely criticized in the United States for wanting to become a partner in the dictatorial regime of the Greek junta, but he could not have cared less. His business dealings had never been hampered by any sort of moral scruples. He was a totally apolitical man interested only in empire building. 'It's not a question of money,' he said. 'After you reach a certain point, money becomes unimportant. What matters is success. The sensible thing would be for me to stop now. But I can't. I have to keep aiming higher and higher – just for the thrill.'

Days later he flew to New York to spend the weekend with his new family at Jackie's rented country home in Peapack, New Jersey. Before he arrived she had a photographer arrested for trespassing on her property and ordered barricades erected on every road leading to her house. Onassis teased her about setting up an armed camp.

Shortly after she returned from Greece her secretary, Nancy Tuckerman, called Rosemary Sorrentino at Kenneth's to ask her to go to Jackie's apartment to do her hair. 'I had to keep it a secret because the press was dying to get hold of her,' said Mrs Sorrentino. 'She couldn't come to the salon because traffic would have been backed up for blocks.

People actually stood outside for hours waiting to see her.

'Nancy told me I had to dress like a washerwoman with a scarf on my head and enter by the servants' entrance so reporters would not be alerted. She sent a limousine to pick me up at the salon and let me out about a block away from Jackie's. I entered the back way, was checked by the Secret Service men, and then went up the private elevator on the 15th floor of Jackie's building. I looked like a peasant when I arrived, just awful, but at least no one found out who I was.'

Mrs Sorrentino was not surprised by Nancy Tuckerman's instructions. As First Lady, Jackie always ordered the beautician to say she was a secretary so White House reporters would not know that she and Kenneth flew down from New York to do her hair. 'One time when the Jerome Robbins ballet was rehearsing for a state dinner, Jackie let me go downstairs and watch, but she made Kenneth stay upstairs in the family quarters because the press would recognize him,' said Mrs Sorrentino.

'I was so used to her little games that I really didn't pay much attention to it when Nancy called me. Jackie looked just terrific when I walked into her apartment. I congratulated her on her marriage and told her how gorgeous she looked. Bunny Mellon was there at the time and Jackie kept telling us both how happy she was and all about her honeymoon. She looked wonderful.'

At Kenneth's salon, Mrs Aristotle Onassis was not treated like an ordinary client. According to Mrs Sorrentino she was elevated to royalty. 'When she started coming back to the salon, she always came under a fictitious name so no one would find out that she was there. She had her own private room of the eighth floor where she had her hair straightened and coloured. She never wanted anyone to know that we had to dye her hair, so she made each of us swear we wouldn't ever talk to reporters. She got so mad when the word got out that she wore falls and wigs to make her hair seem fuller that she wouldn't speak to any of us for a while. She asked me to teach a little Greek girl how to wash and set her hair and then I didn't see her very much because she was always travelling with Mr Onassis.'

In December, Jackie flew to Washington to visit Ethel Kennedy. Before leaving, she visited the graves of her first husband and her former brother-in-law at Arlington National Cemetery. Then, with Caroline and John, Jr, she flew to Greece to spend Christmas with Onassis and his children on Skorpios. Before leaving she bought a sixteenth-century gold Annunciation scene for Ethel which Bobby had wanted to give her as his Christmas present. He had picked it out for her shortly before he died. Jackie gave her husband a painting of herself by Aaron Shikler. In return she received a set of earrings worth $300,000. Within the next few years Onassis showed his wife with well over three million dollars worth of jewellery. On her fortieth birthday he gave her a 40-carat diamond – one carat for each year, plus a diamond necklace and bracelet worth one million dollars. Knowing that President Kennedy had started the space programme in 1961 and wanted to put a man on the moon within the decade, Onassis's jeweller decided to give Jackie something special to commemorate the Apollo II mission, so he created a set of earrings consisting of a sapphire-studded earth at the ear and a large ruby moon hanging from a chain. The Apollo ship was attached to a thin gold thread which circled the sapphire earth and then dropped to the ruby moon. It was a unique if not ostentatious design, and the jeweller absorbed the $150,000 cost to please the wife of his best customer.

For specially designed jewellery, Onassis always went to Zolotas, but for larger, more expensive pieces like Jackie's 40-carat diamond he went to Van Cleef & Arpels in Paris. Usually he paid cash and asked that the baubles be gift-wrapped or sent with flowers. Before their marriage, he sent Jackie several bouquets wrapped with diamond bracelets. Other times he had jewellery delivered to Olympic Airways and someone there delivered it to her as a surprise.

Ilias Lalaounis, the designer for Zolotas in Athens, recalls frequent visits Jackie made to the store after her marriage. 'She said that jewellery is epoch making and she loves her own to be original. She simply insists on being the first to appear with something new and different.'

After the Christmas holidays Jackie flew back to New

York with her children, while Onassis flew to Paris where he dined quietly with Maria Callas at the country home of their friend, Baroness van Zuylen. Later he made the rounds of his favourite night clubs with Elsa Martinelli and her husband, Henri Dubonnet, the aperitif heir. He stayed in daily telephone contact with his wife. The next month the golden couple met in New York to spend time with Caroline and John before leaving on a cruise together in the Canary Islands.

Easter was spent cruising on the *Christina* with the children, Rose Kennedy, and Nancy Tuckerman, who was placed on Onassis's payroll at Olympic Airways to continue her secretarial duties for Jackie. During the cruise Onassis gave the Kennedy matriarch a gold bracelet with a serpent's head studded with diamonds and rubies. Rose, figuring her host had bought the bracelet at Bonwit Teller's as a token gift, assumed it was merely a piece of pretty costume jewellery with fake stones. Later she had it valued and learned it was worth $1,300.

As Mrs Aristotle Onassis, Jackie became closer to her former mother-in-law and frequently invited her to spend time cruising on the *Christina*. 'When I married Ari, she of all people was the one who encouraged me,' said Jackie. 'She said, "He's a good man." And, "Don't worry, dear." She's been extraordinarily generous. Here I was, I was married to her son and I had his children, but she was the one who was saying if this is what you think best, go ahead ... She comes and visits us. It's wonderful for Caroline and John. And Ari adores her. The first Easter after we were married she came to spend a few days with us in the Caribbean. That next summer she stopped over in Greece. She was on her way to Ethiopia to have a joint birthday celebration with Haile Selassie ... She came and spent the New Year with us.'

During Rose's trip to Greece, Jackie photographed her visiting the Acropolis and put the pictures in a photo album with amusing captions. She also wrote her former mother-in-law a letter saying how utterly unexpected life's chain of events was and that she and Rose, after all their experiences together, should now start to share new experiences in a different environment and atmosphere. No longer beholden to the Kennedy fortune, Jackie initiated a rapprochement with the woman she had resented for so many years.

After spending the New Year in Greece with Jackie and Ari, Rose said: 'I am thrilled by her assurances of welcome because this way I shall always be able to contact Caroline and John, and to know that all enjoy having me with them, including Ari and his relatives. And New Year was possibly a little less foreign to the children because I was there.'

Rose had good reason to be concerned about her grandchildren. Caroline never fully accepted Onassis as her stepfather and frequently made disparaging comments about him to her school friends. John got along better with him, but he, too, felt that Onassis was trying to buy their affection with ponies, sailing boats and other gifts. Onassis, genuinely fond of the children, tried to spend as much time with them as his schedule would allow. He was also generous to Jackie's aunt and first cousin, who lived in a dilapidated estate called Grey Gardens in East Hampton, Long Island.

In 1971, Edith Bouvier Beale, Black Jack's sister, and her spinster daughter, known as Little Edie, were almost evicted from their seaside mansion by the Suffolk County Health Department after inspectors found the twenty-eight-room house overrun by cobwebs, feces, raccoons and eighteen diseased and flea-ridden cats. The Beales had no heat, running water or food at the time, prompting public officials to declare their house unfit for human habitation.

A man from the sanitation department called Big Edie's son, Bouvier Beale, a New York lawyer married to a society girl and living on an estate in Glen Cove. He told Beale that his mother's house was about to be condemned unless he would give her the money to fix it up. He also warned Bouvier Beale that the next health inspection of Grey Gardens would create a national scandal. Bouvier Beale remained unmoved. 'If that's what it takes to get mother out of the house, so be it,' he said, refusing to help her.

Days later there were front page headlines: 'JACKIE'S AUNT TOLD: CLEAN UP MANSION'. Stories flashed around the world telling the sordid tale of Big Edie, whose husband walked out on her many years before, and Little Edie, who had devoted her life to her eccentric mother in the gloomy mansion covered with vines the size of boa constrictors. Their relatives, all rich, well-bred and socially prestigious, turned away from them in shame, preferring a scandal to parting with a penny of their fortunes to help rebuild the decaying estate which had once been a luxurious resort mansion. Jackie ignored the plight of the Beales for a month, saying through her secretary that they were living the way they wanted to and she was not going to interfere.

'Oh, it was just awful,' moaned Little Edie. 'The Bouviers hated us, mother and I, because we were the rebels in the family. We're the artists. We're descended from fourteenth-century French kings, you know. I can read and write French because I learned at Miss Porter's School in Farmington, but I can't speak it very well. The neighbours say we're crazy just because we have an overgrown Louisiana Bayou look to our old family house ... Oh, they hate our cats ... you know ... we would have perished without Mr Onassis.'

Unsynchronized by logic, the words tumbled out of Little Edie in pell mell fashion. Flashing from the past to the present, she talked about the Greek husband of her famous first cousin. 'He's a wonderful man. He called Mother and me. Mother has a gorgeous voice, you know, and Mr Onassis asked her to sing to him on the telephone and he sang beautiful love songs to Mother. They were on the phone for forty-five minutes. Oh, it was wonderful ... Jackie introduced us on the phone and she said she loved him very much.'

'She said, "Don't you think I'm lucky to be married to such a splendid person?" and I said yes. I wanted to meet Mr Onassis in person but you know I wasn't in very good shape then ... not thin like I used to be as a young girl ... I've lived in this hole all my life ... Jackie is always in good shape ... She told me that Nehru fell madly in love with her ... but she didn't like politics ... We knew she wasn't too happy with Kennedy.'

Onassis saved the women from eviction by spending over $50,000 to repair the gaping holes the raccoons had chewed in the ceilings. He bought them a new furnace so they wouldn't have to wrap themselves in newspapers at night to keep warm, he financed new plumbing throughout the house, and began paying all the utility bills.

'Jackie asked us, "What do you want to do with your life?" and Mother said, "I want to stay right here at Grey Gardens which is my home." So Mr Onassis fixed it up for us and gave Jackie the money to put in the bank for mother to pay for our oil and heat and water and lights,' said Little Edie. 'She came to visit us once and I met Caroline and John ... you know, Lee is a great beauty ... prettier than Jackie ... She is a princess ... I held her when she was a baby ... Lee came to see us, too ... I had to sell our silver to pay for food and I only got $6,000 and I had to give the dealer half just to sell it.'

Later, John Davis drove out to East Hampton to visit his aunt, who was then seventy-six years old and spending most of her time singing French operettas in bed with her cats who ate and voided on her dingy blue bedspread. 'When I arrived, she was wearing a perfectly magnificent silk dress,' he said. 'I told her how gorgeous it was and she said, "Oh, do you like it? It's a Givenchy. Jackie sent all her most expensive clothes out to me." ' The sight of his aunt running around her tumble-down house in haute couture unnerved John Davis. 'It was quite a vision, but I thought it was rather sweet of Jackie to give her clothes to her aunt. I think it tore her heart out to see them living the way they were and she wanted to help them in some way. Her hand-me-downs were quite lovely.'

Most of Jackie's time was spent flying back and forth to Europe. On holidays she took her children to Greece to join Onassis, then returned with them to New York, as Onassis stayed to tend his world-wide business empire. This pattern of separate lives continued throughout their marriage, mixed in with regular meetings on various continents. The long-distance relationship was ideal for Jackie, who never could bear to be with someone for any sustained period of time. With Onassis she found a man who made no demands on her while allowing her the freedom to live alone with her children.

'Jackie is a little bird that needs its freedom as well as its security,' he said, 'and she gets both from me. She can do exactly as she pleases – visit international fashion shows and travel and go out with friends to the theatre or any place. And I, of course, will do exactly as I please. I never question her and she never questions me.'

In New York Jackie began calling on old friends to escort her around town when Onassis was not there. She was frequently seen going to dinner and attending benefits with André Mayer, Bill Walton, Franklin D. Roosevelt, Jr, and Paul Mathias. 'She's marvellously contented and leading the kind of life she's always wanted to lead,' observed Walton.

Dubbed 'Daddy O' and 'Jackie O' by *Women's Wear Daily*, Ari and Jackie attracted the same frantic hordes of people who stampede royalty and idolize movie stars. They became the most famous couple in the world, knocking Elizabeth Taylor and Richard Burton off the front pages of the tabloids. Even alone, Mrs Aristotle Onassis emerged as the world's greatest living human tourist attraction, exciting more curiosity than any other woman alive.

No longer hemmed in by the political dictates of the Kennedys, Jackie began having fun for the first time in her life. She flaunted her new wealth, revelling in the diamonds and sapphires and rubies bestowed upon her by the indulgent Onassis. She discarded the little white gloves from her days as First Lady and romped around in skintight pants, T-shirts without a bra, wild calypso skirts and floppy hats.

As the most exquisite jewel in his collection, Jackie was encouraged by Onassis to shop and buy and spend for herself. He even suggested that she invest in some new lingerie and toss out the high-necked nightgowns from Elizabeth Arden and the cotton underpants which reminded him of a little boy's boxer shorts. To surprise her, he asked Halston to design some sexy lingerie and sent the designer a pair of her panties and one of her brassieres so he would know the right size. 'I could have auctioned off those undies for enough money to retire for life,' said Halston, who took the assignment and began creating transparent silk designs. When the collection was finished, he sent it to Jackie who was indeed surprised. And so outraged that she returned it unopened with a curt note.

Jackie enjoyed her fame and relished publicity, but only on her terms. Unexpected flashbulbs irritated her and prying lensmen threw her into a rage. One day a photographer snapped her leaving a movie house after seeing the pornographic film *I Am Curious Yellow*. She flipped him to the street with a quick bit of judo. Papparazzi enraged her, particularly one Ron Gallela who was in constant pursuit. She complained bitterly to Onassis about the photographer and he tried to persuade the man to leave her alone. Putting his arm around Gallela one evening, he asked, 'Why do you do this?'

'You have your job, I have mine,' said the photographer.

'She has had much tragedy in her life.'

'Yes, but life goes on. I'm not a sadist giving her pain. This will help her forget. If not for me, people would kill themselves with curiosity about her and the kids. There is a big void for an American papparazzi with courage and I am filling it.'

'Don't do it any more.'

'Then give me a job with Olympic Airlines.'

'Yes, and for that I will pay you one dollar.'

Jackie was angry with Ari for even talking to the photographer. Eventually she had Gallela arrested for harassment. Gallela filed a $1,300,000 countersuit charging her with assault, false arrest, malicious persecution and interference with his work. Jackie countersued him for $6,000,000 in damages charging him with invasion of privacy and mental anguish. She also got a court order temporarily restraining him from 'alarming and frightening' her. She claimed she was an 'absolute prisoner' in her New York apartment, living in 'dread fear' of him and his camera.

All of Gallela's 4,000 photographs of Jackie showed her looking exquisitely beautiful. Not one was unflattering. He never photographed her smoking or drinking, and always took his pictures in a bright light to camouflage her grey teeth and soften the wrinkles around her eyes. In one year he made $15,000 selling Jackie photographs to national publications. These pictures he took by vaulting over hedges, leaping from behind coatracks, and following her to Capri,

Naples, Skorpios, Peapack, New Jersey and Brooklyn Heights. Each picture showed an undisguised love of his subject.

The court case of *Gallela* v. *Onassis* dragged on for days as Secret Service men appointed to protect Caroline and John testified in favour of their mother. Finally the federal judge, who had been appointed by President Kennedy, ruled in Jackie's favour. He ordered the photographer to stay fifty yards away from the most newsworthy woman in the world and 100 yards from her apartment. His ruling was later reversed by the Court of Appeals and the distance was reduced to a mere twenty-five feet. Still it was enough for Jackie to claim another victory, adding the supression of Ron Gallela to the massacre of William Manchester.

'It serves him right,' she crowed to her friends. 'He has no right to harass me the way he does.' Onassis was not so pleased. When Jackie's lawyers sent him a bill for $235,000 he refused to pay it, saying 'I had nothing to do with the damn thing.' Jackie complained to friends that her husband was a cheapskate and a tightwad. Months later the prestigious law firm of Paul, Weiss, Rifkind, Wharton and Garrison sued Onassis to recover its costs. More months passed before it received a cheque for $235,000.

'In public Jackie is always on,' says her stepbrother Jamie Auchincloss. 'She's professionally Mrs John F. Kennedy and Mrs Aristotle Onassis twenty-four hours a day. She knows how to get out of a car like a movie star arriving at a première. Despite her screams for privacy, she has practised making a grand entrance so often that she now does it like a pro.'

'She knows exactly how to smile and warm up a crowd. In fact, she's exhausted at the end of the evening because she puts out so much energy being on. But that's when she liked to be photographed, and only then. What really drives her up the wall is having photographers take her picture when she is not prepared and then making money off her. Fashion models make thousands of dollars when their picture is on the cover of a magazine but Jackie doesn't get a penny when hers appears. That really gets to her.'

With millions of dollars at her disposal Jackie reverted to

eccentric economizing. She secretly sold her clothes at second-hand stores which accepted them on consignment and gave her 60 per cent of the price. Rather than donate the clothes to charity and ask a tax deduction, she sold them for cash. This niggling profit was important to Jackie because she rarely had any cash. Nancy Tuckerman often called Creon Brown, Onassis's financial supervisor, to ask for additional funds. Shortly after their marriage, Onassis gave Jackie 2 million dollars and recommended that she invest it in tax-free bonds. Instead she played the stock market and lost almost everything. She begged Ari to reimburse her but he refused, saying that he had advised her against putting her liquid capital into high risk securities.

Jackie was extravagant and spent thousands of dollars on her clothes, and she was equally indulgent with her children, and tried hard in the beginning to help her stepdaughter shop for clothes.

Christina was an awkward, gawky young woman given to frequent use of amphetamines to control her weight and tranquillizers to cope with her depressions. Accepting Jackie as her stepmother was unbearable. She always hoped that her father would reconcile with her vivacious, beautiful blonde mother who was only sixteen when she married the forty-year-old Onassis. Tina Livanos Onassis was married to the Marquis of Blandford when Ari decided to marry Jackie, but Christina and her brother, Alexander, still naively hoped their parents might be reconciled. In 1959 Tine testified in the New York Supreme Court when she began divorce proceedings on the grounds of adultery: 'It is almost thirteen years since Mr Onassis and I were married in New York City. Since then he has become one of the world's richest men, but his great wealth has not brought him happiness with me.'

From childhood Christina and Alexander were exposed to the panoply that surrounded their father's life. They lived through his feuds with oil companies, whaling associations, sovereign states, world leaders, rulers and potentates. They felt the bitter division between him and their uncle, Stavros Niarchos, who was married to their mother's dark and serious sister, Eugenie. They suffered through Onassis's ten-year liaison with Maria Callas and despised her.

Spoiled, indulged and pampered, they grew up meeting persons of note and notoriety across the world. Prince Ranier and Princess Grace of Monaco were considered members of the family. Sir Winston Churchill was a beloved friend, and Greta Garbo a frequent guest in their home. Their portraits were painted by Vertes, Domerque and Vidal-Quadros. Their ponies were a special gift from the King of Saudi Arabia. Money rained down on them from the Onassis and Livanos empires. The trust funds established for them by their father made them multi-millionaires by the time they were twenty-one. Yet both children seemed more cursed than blessed by their vast wealth.

Christina grew up with a father who never spent much time with her while never hiding his disappointment at not producing a second son. She wandered aimlessly through a lush life of penthouses and yachts, worrying about her unruly hair, her heavy figure and her large nose which she finally had bobbed. After her father married Jacqueline Kennedy, she tried to be cordial but there was little pretence. Soon she referred to Jackie as 'My father's unhappy compulsion'.

Close friends of Jackie say the feeling was mutual. 'Jackie told me that Christina was a spoiled monster with fat legs and chunky ankles who dressed like a Greek peasant,' said one woman. 'She made an effort in the beginning to please Ari by having little dinner parties for Christina in her New York apartment and taking her shopping for clothes, but it never worked.'

A friend of Christina concurs. 'Make no mistake about it, she hated Jackie from the start. At the best of times, they tolerated each other – were just barely civil.'

Less than three years after Jackie became Mrs Aristotle Onassis her stepdaughter, then twenty, eloped with Joseph Bolker, a forty-eight-year-old divorced American selling real estate in Los Angeles. Onassis was informed of the Las Vegas marriage by telephone as he celebrated Jackie's forty-second birthday on Skorpios. The call drove him wild, and he immediately disinherited his daughter, telling her that she

303

could never receive another penny from her 100-million-dollar trust fund as long as she remained married to Bolker. The thought of his only daughter married to a Jewish real estate broker with four grown children enraged him. Having always detested and distrusted Jews, Onassis was savage about Christina's marriage to one. His fury was uncontrollable. Witnessing his rage, Jackie drew back, afraid to say anything for fear of further triggering his inflamed anger. She saw then how vitriolic he could be when crossed.

Christina's marriage lasted only nine months before Bolker caved in to Onassis and started divorce proceedings in California. 'We were subjected to extraordinary pressures,' he said. 'She is a young woman and should not be alienated from her father.'

'He may soon be just my ex-husband, but he will always be my best friend,' said Christina. 'I am too Greek and he is too Beverly Hills. That's really the trouble.'

Onassis also berated his son, Alexander, for his romantic involvement with Fiona Thyssen. Onassis objected because Fiona, a divorced baroness with two children, was, despite her youthful beauty, almost old enough to be Alexander's mother. Alexander retaliated by baiting his father about Jackie: he made no attempts to hide his hostility towards her and was often openly rude in his remarks. One night at Maxim's the three began gossiping about a show girl who was taking an older man for all he was worth. Alexander turned to his stepmother and said, 'Jackie, you certainly don't think there's anything wrong in a girl marrying for money, do you?'

Embracing his father's feud with Stavros Niarchos as his own, Alexander felt betrayed when his mother married the man who was once married to her sister. At this point his relationship with his father improved considerably and they began discussing important business decisions. Onassis actually began to listen to, if not accept, his son's advice.

Alexander persuaded him to replace the faulty Piaggio aircraft in their fleet with helicopters, a decision that would eventually lead to his death. Growing more confident of his son's business acumen, Onassis accepted him as an equal and began to confide in him. He admitted that his marriage to Jackie had been pointless, and together they discussed the practicality of divorce and how much Onassis money it would cost.

On the evening of 21 January 1973, Alexander called Fiona from Athens and arranged to meet her the next night in London. He explained that he had to train a pilot for his father to fly the Piaggio which was on board the *Christina*. An American amphibian pilot had arrived from Ohio to make the test run and Alexander wanted to check him out personally before assigning him to the plane.

They took off from Athens the next day. Seconds after they were airborne the Piaggio banked sharply causing the plane to cartwheel and crash. Rescuers who rushed to the wreckage recognized Alexander only by his bloodstained mono-grammed handkerchief. His head reduced almost to pulp, he was rushed to the hospital for a three-hour emergency operation to remove blood clots, then placed in an oxygen tent on a life-support system. Only a miracle could save him.

The news reached Ari and Jackie in the United States. Christina was in Brazil. Tina and Stavros Niarchos were in Switzerland. Fiona was still waiting in London. They all flew to Alexander's bedside, praying for that miracle. But Onassis soon realized it was hopeless and said he could not torture his son any longer. He ordered the doctors to turn off the life-support system, then watched helplessly as his son died minutes later.

'We weren't killing him,' Onassis said. 'We were just letting him die. There is no question of euthanasia here. If he had lived, he would have been dead as a human being. His brain was destroyed and his features completely disfigured. Nothing could be done for him.'

Onassis was rocked to the core of his soul by his son's death. He lashed himself with guilt, feeling that if he had not demanded a trained pilot for the Piaggio his son would not be dead. He insisted that if he had only followed Alexander's advice sooner and replaced the Piaggio with a helicopter, he would still be alive. Onassis could not accept the death as an accident. He convinced himself that it was the result of sabotage by his enemies. He immediately began an investigation, offering a huge reward for evidence of foul play. This mania consumed him for weeks as he ignored his family and his business to build a web of suspicion and paranoia bolstered by imagined suspects and supposed motives. He was prepared to spend his fortune and the rest of his life to find out how Alexander had died.

Surrounded by his Greek relatives who indulged him, allowing him to wallow in his self-pity, his American wife felt like an outsider. Their wailing grief was beyond the range of her tightly controlled emotions. Her instinct was to bury the pain and forge ahead. Onassis wanted to revel in his misery and retreat to the past. There was only one woman who could possibly understand his suffering. She alone could console him and help him pull his life together enough to go on living. And so it was to Maria Callas that he turned in his time of most desperate need.

Twenty-two

In February 1970 all the letters Jackie had written to Roswell Gilpatric became public. Charles Hamilton, the New York autograph dealer, had received them from someone previously connected with Gilpatric's law firm where they had been locked in a safe. Hamilton began preparing to auction them for sale. Reporters learned the contents and printed what Jackie had written to the man who had spent the day with her at Camp David when she was six months pregnant. But that was all past history to Aristotle Onassis. It was a letter she had written to him from the *Christina* on her honeymoon that crushed him.

'My God, what a fool I have made of myself,' he told his friends. 'What a fool.'

The letters were immediately seized under subpoena and returned to Gilpatric, but not until their contents had been published around the world. Jackie's embarrassment heightened when Gilpatric's third wife, Madelin, filed separation papers the next day. The implication to everyone was that Jackie had been responsible for alienating the lawyer and his wife.

'That is so untrue and sort of unfair to both of them,' said Nancy Tuckerman. 'They are very close friends. He was at the Onassis's first anniversary party at their apartment in October. And he was a very good friend of President Kennedy's too.'

The third Mrs Roswell Gilpatric didn't think the implication unfair at all. She indicated on more than one occasion that there was more to the relationship than mere letters. Privately she told her friends that Gilpatric's sycophantic devotion to Jackie broke up their marriage. Publicly she left no doubt about it. 'I have my own feelings about that, but I won't go into them,' she said. 'They were certainly very, very close. Just say it was a particularly warm, close, long-lasting relationship.'

Onassis was humiliated by the speculation swirling around his wife's relationship with Roswell Gilpatric. Whether or not they had been lovers no longer mattered to him. He was stung by the knowing looks from his friends, the cackling remarks from his enemies, and the disgusted comments from his children. He was accustomed to being pilloried for his business dealings, but never had he experienced a situation which so threatened his manhood. It was an unintentional emasculation on Jackie's part but the damage to her husband's ego was not slight. She was terrified to face him and confided to friends that he would probably divorce her. When she finally called to explain and apologize, she was surprised by his reaction.

He smoothly reassured her that all was well and she wasn't to worry about a thing. He understood perfectly. He said it was just another example of the media blowing something out of proportion like it did the month before when he was in Paris with Maria Callas celebrating the première of her first film. Only his closest Greek associates knew that the letter to Gilpatric was the beginning of a breach.

With Madame Callas, as he called her, Onassis had a special relationship that was left intact despite his marriage to Jacqueline Kennedy. He continued seeing the diva regularly, at first only in the privacy of her Avenue Georges Madel apartment in Paris, then later publicly in nightclubs and restaurants.

Although her singing put him to sleep, Onassis enjoyed Callas's worldwide success and was proud of her highly acclaimed talent. She was bright, shrewd and beautiful in a sensual way. She was the perfect match for Onassis, appealing to him intellectually, emotionally, and sexually. Being Greek, he understood her as completely as she understood him, although at times there was no one who could infuriate him more.

Though annoyed by her stinging comments on his marriage, he visited her privately after the wedding and managed to soothe her hurt feelings. Onassis still needed a relationship with the singer, the one person who loved him without reservation and accepted his moods and rages as part of his personality. She knew how much he enjoyed the access his new wife provided to New York's social set. While she laughed at him for socializing with the likes of Bill and Babe Paley, the Murray McDonnells, and Peter and Cheray Duchin, she did not begrudge him their company. She knew what a coup it was for him to be accepted into the drawing-rooms of America's rich.

She also understood how protective Onassis felt towards Jackie, who, he said, did not possess Maria's kind of fiery strength and independence. He prided himself on being able to offer his wife a buffer zone cushioning her from a curious and often cruel world. He enjoyed making her laugh, amusing and distracting her as he once did Maria Callas.

She offered to become a friend to his new wife, but Jackie refused. So she continued seeing him whenever possible, meeting him privately at the homes of friends they had seen together in the past. In Paris they frequently dined at her apartment or at the country estate of Baroness van Zuylen. In New York, his business associate, Constantine Gratsos, provided them with the privacy they needed. Maria Callas was always discreet about these meetings, but she did not deny them.

'Onassis is my best friend,' she said. 'He is, was, and he always will be. When two people have been together as we have, there are many things that tie you together. The scandal comes about because I have never met his wife. It's not wished on the other side. Frankly, I don't understand why she doesn't come into my life. If we did meet, it would certainly stop all the gossip in the newspapers.'

When asked if such a meeting would not create a tremendous emotional strain, Maria shook her head. 'Oh, I don't know. It depends on whether the man needs you. There are many times that I am sure Onassis needs me as a friend because I will tell him the truth. He would always come to me with his problems, knowing that I would never repeat and he would find an objective mind. We share cheerfulness, mutual friends and honesty.'

A conspiratorial man by nature, Onassis trusted few people, but Maria had proved herself to be someone he could confide in. In many ways she was his female counterpart, having achieved her fame and her wealth on her own. He appreciated people who fought their way to the top, and in her he saw an ambitious woman who could match his drive and energy. She saw in him a remarkable man with a touch of genius for business, but she also recognized the unswerving opportunist and the amoral character who indulged in devious schemes and barbarous crimes to accomplish his goals. Unlike Jackie, she cared about his business dealings and was fascinated by the byzantine negotiations he thrived on. She was the only person who ever received a tanker as a gift from the shipping tycoon. Over the years she had watched him wage war on the American government, world oil interests, the Peruvian Navy and the principality of Monaco. He enjoyed these risks, feuds, and entanglements. 'Taking up these challenges has been most strenuous, dangerous, and expensive,' he once said, 'but I thank God that I have been able to afford it and that I have a strong stomach.'

Early in their relationship Callas recognized that her talent had been a vehicle for Onassis's self-promotion. She also realized that when she gave up her career to be with him she removed something vital from their relationship. After he married Jacqueline Kennedy, she concentrated on her voice again and prepared to make a comeback.

Shortly after Jackie's letter to Gilpatric was publicized, Onassis was seen in Paris on four successive evenings leaving Maria Callas's apartment at 1 am. Three months later he flew by helicopter to the island of Tragonisis where she was staying with the Embiricos family and gave her a pair of 100-year-old earrings. He was photographed kissing her on the mouth under a big beach umbrella, much as they had been photographed years before kissing over champagne glasses in Paris. He also kissed her poodle and laughed uproariously with her. The pictures appeared on both sides of the Atlantic. Asked for a comment, Callas said: 'I have great respect for Aristotle and there is no reason for us not meeting here since Mr Embiricos is a mutual friend.'

Jackie saw the pictures while on a plane bound for Greece to be with her husband. A few nights later she made a point of being publicly seen with him at Maxim's where they dined with friends and seemed to enjoy themselves. But for all his gregariousness and charm Onassis was no longer a happy man. His world had caved in with the death of his only son and his marriage brought him little comfort.

He began to complain openly about his wife and her constant spending, begrudging her excesses as much as he had earlier indulged them. He was irate when he found out that Jackie had taken twenty-three Olympic aeroplanes and helicopters out of service for her private trips. Exasperated by her continual tardiness, he repeatedly complained of the evening they invited people to her apartment for a dinner party at 6 pm and she didn't appear until well past 8:30. For more than two hours Onassis had to play host alone to Frank Sinatra, the Peter Duchins, the Leonard Bernsteins and Bill and Babe Paley. Minutes before New York's Mayor and Mrs John Lindsay arrived, Jackie finally came out of her room acting as if nothing was amiss.

He complained about her permissiveness with her children, specifically mentioning the way she let them wear dirty blue jeans. He felt strongly that she could have made more of an effort with his own children, who bitterly resented her. Though he spoke six languages fluently, Onassis never read a book and he could not understand why Jackie insisted on spending so much time alone reading. He continually ranted about her profligacy, especially for running up a $5,000 bill for messenger service for letters and gifts that she wanted personally delivered rather than mailed.

Soon he was spending more time away from Jackie than ever before. He pleaded the excuse of prolonged business dealings abroad but, in fact, he was fast losing interest in his far-flung empire.

Leaving Jackie in New York he took a long cruise with his daughter, Christina, his one last link with the destiny of the Onassis empire. He was naturally sceptical of a woman succeeding in a business dominated by men, but with his son gone he now had no choice but to prepare his daughter to take over. In grooming Christina to be his successor, he sent her to New York to work with his ship and insurance brokers.

He regularly took her to meetings with his executives, telling her not to say a word but to absorb all she heard so that she would be prepared one day to assume control.

For the first time in her life Christina had a sense of responsibility to something important. She curtailed her aimless life peopled with playboys and socialites and worked long hours each day, trying to learn the intricacies of her father's business. She still suffered deep depressions, especially since the death of her brother and, unlike her father, she could not bury herself in her work. Overwhelmed by her new duties, she began to withdraw from her family and friends, feeling she could no longer cope with anything. Weeks later in London she took an overdose of sleeping pills and was rushed to Middlesex Hospital under a fictitious name. There in the emergency ward, her life was saved.

She had barely recovered from her own brush with death when she received the news that her mother, Tina Niarchos, had died in the Hotel de Chanaleilles in Paris from an oedema of the lung. Onassis, receiving the news in Paris, immediately went to see Niarchos, his enemy for so many years. Their meeting was sad but without rancour. Christina arrived a few hours later and demanded an autopsy to find out exactly how her mother died. When her aunt, Eugenie, had died from an overdose of sleeping pills in 1970 the post-mortem examination showed fourteen injuries on her body that doctors claimed were caused by her husband's attempts to revive her.

The autopsy on Tina confirmed oedema, but Christina was unconvinced. She later said that if Stavros had been sleeping in the same room with his wife she might still be alive. Niarchos sensed her animosity. Filled with outrage, he told reporters that his wife had been depressed ever since she visited Christina in the hospital a few weeks before. He said that Tina had never recovered from the shock of her daughter's attempted suicide, making public for the first time what Christina so desperately wanted to keep private. Later Christina sued her former stepfather for the 300-million-dollar inheritance he received when Tina died.

Onassis could not bear to attend his former wife's funeral.

He felt tired and old and suddenly in touch with his own mortality. He had been experiencing difficulty keeping his eyes open and could not talk without slurring. Finally he checked into a New York hospital. His ailment was diagnosed as myasthenia gravis. He was assured it was not fatal.

The doctors, concerned that the disease might weaken his heart, insisted he be examined frequently. In a myasthenia gravis case, a defect in the body's chemistry impedes the connection of nerves and muscles, thus preventing the routine transmission of impulses. The only physical evidence of the disease in Onassis's case was his drooping eyelids, which had to be taped to his eyebrows to keep his eyes open. He hid the tapes behind dark sunglasses and made sport of his condition: 'If I spent as long with my make-up as Jackie, I could use invisible tape and no one would be the wiser.' The small jokes at his wife's expense grew in number as he stayed out later with his pals drinking until the small hours. Often, instead of returning to Jackie's Manhattan apartment at 4 am, he went directly to his suite at the Hotel Pierre and slept until noon.

Jackie had sincerely tried to ease his grief after Alexander's death. She invited Pierre Salinger and his wife to cruise with them on the *Christina* from Dakar in West Africa to the Antilles. For years she had told Ari that if he could just get away and forget his business and completely relax, he would feel much better. In the past this proved true. But now he seemed to take little enjoyment in the outings she planned. He did not talk about his grief but it permeated his days. He stayed up late every night by himself because he could no longer sleep.

'He did not really want to live any more,' said Costa Gratsos. 'He felt cheated. And he blamed himself for having been cheated. He felt responsible for Alexander's death. But there was no self-pity at all. There was an extraordinary degree of stoicism in the way he took everything.'

Sensing what was happening to her marriage, Jackie suggested again in January 1974 that they fly to Acapulco where she had honeymooned with Jack Kennedy, and he consented. Onassis had no illusions about that marriage and knew better than to be threatened by it. In the beginning the shadow cast by John F. Kennedy never seemed to affect him. He understood that Jackie felt she had to commemorate his life and career in order to establish an identity for her children, and he encouraged her to do so. Still, he was constantly reminded that her fame owed more to the slain President than to himself. Tormented by depression and failing health, he was infuriated when she told him on the plane to Mexico that she wanted a house built in Acapulco. The fact that she had honeymooned there with her first husband did not bother him as much as her compulsive need to acquire, now expressed in the wake of his business setbacks. Desperately wanting to break into the oil industry, he had proposed construction of a refinery in New Hampshire. For months he lobbied for it, only to be soundly rejected by the state legislature. For the first time in his life his powers of persuasion had failed him. The effort cost him dearly, sapping his diminishing energy. To make matters worse, Olympic Airways had been steadily losing money, and the Arab oil embargo nearly crippled his tanker business. No longer was he inclined to indulge his wife's luxurious frivolities, and he told her so. When she suggested building in Acapulco, he implied that her request was a new method of blood-letting.

Jackie lost her temper and screamed that he was hateful and mean to even suggest such a thing. She bitterly reminded him of what her marriage had cost her in terms of her image at home and abroad. She always came back to the fact that she had married him without a financial contract. She said that she had more than willingly put her signature to the 'nomimos mira' clause he wanted her to sign which waived all her rights to his estate. She did not want his goddamned money now, she screamed, and she never wanted it.

He replied acidly that she need not worry about it because she was never going to get it. Then, without another word between them, Onassis moved to the back of the plane and wrote in longhand his last will and testament. The document composed in the six-hour flight was designed to make his daughter, Christina, his major beneficiary. He also wrote a clause to establish a foundation in honour of his son,

314

Alexander. This in itself was significant because it was the first philanthropical instinct Onassis had ever shown.

He had made a career of shrewdly dodging taxes, sailing his ships under foreign flags and spreading his wealth through interlocking companies. Never before had he given his money to charity. Nor had he ever considered philanthropy a particularly worthwhile investment. Now he was endowing a cultural institution in his son's name 'to operate, maintain and promote the Nursing, Educational, Literary Works, Religious, Scientific Research, Journalistic and Artistic Endeavours, proclaiming International and National contests, prize awards in money, similar to the plan of the Nobel Institution in Sweden'.

He took care of Jackie by limiting her share of his estate to $150,000 a year for life, plus $150,000 a year to both her children for the rest of their lives. Aware that she might challenge this disposition, he added a clause instructing his executors to do all they could to stand in her way. 'I command the executors of my will and the rest of my heirs that they deny her such a right,' he wrote, 'through all legal means, cost and expenses charged on my inheritance.' If her legal challenge were to succeed, he decreed that she was to receive no more than 12.5 per cent of the total estate. That was the least he was allowed to leave her under the 'nomimos mira' law.

After the trip to Acapulco Onassis's health deteriorated drastically, and he resorted to cortisone treatments to keep the myasthenia gravis in control. His dwindling energy focused on the 95-million-dollar development of the Olympic Towers in New York, a 52-storey skyscraper with 250 condominium apartments and nineteen floors of office space overlooking St Patrick's Cathedral.

He no longer bothered to keep up the pretence of his marriage. The public appearances with Jackie were rare and always in the company of other people. Jackie continued to live her life entirely separate from him. She stayed in her Fifth Avenue apartment while he lived in his suite at the Pierre Hotel. Finally, encouraged by his daughter Christina, Onassis decided to explore the possibility of divorce.

315

Unbeknownst to his wife, he instructed his trusted aide, Johnny Meyer, to contact Roy Chon to ask if he would represent Onassis in divorce proceedings. 'He called me when Mr Onassis was with him,' said the lawyer, who in the 1950s was one of Senator Joseph McCarthy's key investigators on the House un-American Activities Committee. 'He said it was absolutely definite, and that Mr Onassis wanted to end the marriage.' Onassis also hired a private detective to follow Jackie, hoping to get evidence of adultery which could be used against her in court if she contested the divorce. The wily Greek knew that if he could prove his wife had been unfaithful, it would cost him less money. Since she wasn't sleeping with him, he reasoned she was sleeping with someone else.

While Onassis secretly arranged for a divorce, Jackie firmly denied rumours of the pending break-up through her secretary, Nancy Tuckerman. 'It's absurd,' she said, 'absolutely absurd.' Privately, Jackie told friends that her husband was sick and cranky and impossible to deal with at times, but there were no plans for a divorce.

Actually, Jackie knew better. Onassis's top aides were openly describing their boss's relationship with her as 'totally incompatible'. She knew they would not make such a public statement without his approval. Still, she made no effort to communicate with him and simply ignored him by going her own way.

In the fall she flew to Newport with her children and Lee to watch the America Cup races. Days later she was back in New York going to her exercise classes, seeing her dermatologist, jogging through Central Park and getting her hair done at Kenneth's. She bought her winter wardrobe from Valentino and purchased a $200,000 estate in Bernardsville in the centre of New Jersey's fox-hunting country. She took the children to Kenya for a vacation in a game lodge and lent her name to various benefits and charities. She joined a committee to save Grand Central Station. She visited the International Center for Photography and wrote an article about it for the *New Yorker*'s 'Talk of the Town' section.

Onassis bitterly decided to humiliate his wife by building a case that would justify the divorce. He asked his secretary to invite Jack Anderson to fly from Washington to New York for lunch. The syndicated columnist had never met Onassis, or even tried to interview him, and was surprised to get the call. He readily accepted and was met by a limousine and delivered to the 21 Club, Onassis's favourite restaurant.

In the past the shipping tycoon had maintained a love-hate relationship with the press. He made a point of courting society columnists like Suzy and Earl Wilson but he was not above slugging photographers or swearing at reporters. Sometimes he would cooperate by giving long interviews. Other times he would snap, 'Write or print anything you like about me. I don't give a damn.' He was amused when he read a premature report of his death. 'It helps to sell newspapers,' he said. 'I didn't deny the rumour. I just walked in the streets.'

Understanding the power of the press, he was now determined to turn it to his own advantage. Over lunch with Jack Anderson he began complaining about his wife. 'What does she do with all those clothes?' he asked. 'All I ever see her wearing is blue jeans.' He escorted Anderson to his office where he introduced him to his top aides, and then left them together so the reporter could get all the details he needed.

Anderson was shown piles of ledgers, memos and letters documenting Jackie's profligate spending. He learned that Onassis, after giving his wife a monthly allowance of $30,000, became so enraged by her astronomical bills that he transferred the account to Monte Carlo where he could watch it more carefully. Finally he cut her back to $20,000 a month and refused to give her any more money, ignoring pleas from Nancy Tuckerman that Jackie could not pay her living expenses.

By this time Onassis felt that he was being taken for all he was worth. Jackie felt victimized by his tyranny and hated him for suddenly withdrawing his money and trying to use it as a weapon against her. She despised having to beg him for anything but she refused to cut back on the life style he had once encouraged her to enjoy. They began to quarrel bitterly.

317

According to friends, an incident in Rome involving Elizabeth Taylor particularly enraged her.

Onassis and the movie star were lunching together when an intruder started annoying Miss Taylor. Onassis splashed a glass of champagne in his face to get rid of him and made news around the world. Jackie was furious.

'I am ashamed of you,' she said. 'The children read the news accounts of that incident and were humiliated. How could you be so tasteless?'

The peasant delights which had once been so charming now embarrassed Jackie. She cringed each time Ari boasted that his barstools were fashioned from the testes-skin of sperm whales. She was appalled by his public carousing and bored by his continual bouzouki parties on the *Christina*. She no longer joined in the singing and dancing he loved. Feeling trapped, she complained about 'being stuck on Skorpios all summer'. The British diplomat Sir John Russell, who frequently visited Onassis, described her as stiff and inhibited. 'There was nobody there who had much in common with her,' he said, 'nobody she could be completely relaxed with.'

Having once enjoyed receiving rubies the size of eggs, she now refused to wear her husband's jewellery. She told friends that his taste was crude and vulgar. To Onassis the jewels remained a way of showing the world what he could afford. They demonstrated his success and achievement. He expected his wife to show her gratitude by wearing them on occasion.

The next time Jackie asked him for money, he suggested that she sell her jewellery. He observed that the gems were only taking up space in a locked vault. She refused to parry his sarcastic thrusts and began staying away from him as much as possible.

Days later she received a call from Athens that her husband had collapsed with pains in his abdomen. Accompanied by a heart specialist, she flew from New York to Greece and went directly to Onassis's home in Glyfada. A few days later the doctor recommended that Onassis be hospitalized and Jackie agreed. His sisters argued in favour of keeping him at home and bringing in specialists to attend him, but Jackie insisted that he be taken to the American Hospital outside Paris. 'He's my husband and I believe this switch is necessary,' she said. 'Let's not argue.'

That afternoon Jackie and Christina flew with Onassis on his private plane to Paris. Throughout the flight he directed most of his conversation to the doctor accompanying him. 'You understand, professor, the meaning of the Greek word thanatos – death,' he said. 'You know I will never come out of the hospital alive. Well, please practise thanatos on me.'

At Orly Airport Onassis refused to be carried from the plane on a stretcher. He also resisted efforts to get him straight to the hospital, insisting instead on spending the night at his Avenue Foch apartment. From there he phoned Maria Callas. In the morning he left for Neuilly and entered the hospital by the back door.

For the next five weeks he lay in a semiconscious state, being fed intravenously and kept alive by a respirator. Doctors performed gall bladder surgery. Every forty-eight hours they replaced his blood. His sisters and his daughter stayed with him around the clock so that at least one would be on hand whenever he awoke. For the first few days Jackie stayed long periods with him, too, but the strain between her and his family became so unbearable that she soon was visiting the hospital only once a day. Depressed by the death watch of the Onassis family, she called her good friend Paul Mathias and went with him to see the Peggy Guggenheim art collection. They dined frequently at Les Deaux Maggots, a famous café on St Germain Des Pres, and took long walks together. Many of her hours were spent with her friends Peggy and Clem Wood. She ate dinner at Lucas Carter at the Place de la Madeleine. She saw *The Towering Inferno* on the Champs Elysées. She was photographed one night smiling over dinner with Francis Fabre, president of the French airline. She shopped for clothes and regularly had her hair done.

The pictures of Jackie meandering around Paris and out on the town while her husband lay dying in the hospital enraged Christina. No longer able to tolerate the presence of her stepmother, she moved out of the Onassis apartment and checked into the Plaza Athenee Hotel. She didn't even bother to pack her clothes.

In his few lucid moments Onassis talked to Christina about his business. She knew how relieved he would be if she were married to someone like Peter Goulandris, the scion of another Greek shipping dynasty. They had been engaged at one point and disappointed Onassis by not marrying. He felt that Peter, a Harvard graduate, was smart enough to mastermind his empire and that a merger of both family fortunes would make them the dominant shipping power in the world. Aware of all this, Christina told her father that she was seeing Peter again. Onassis smiled weakly and asked her to bring the young man to the hospital to see him. When she arrived holding Goulandris's hand, Ari sent everyone else out of the room so he could talk to the couple alone. Later they emerged with the news that they would marry. It was a loving deception on Christina's part, the least she felt she could do for her father whose life was slipping away.

By the end of the month Onassis seemed to make a slight recovery. He was hooked up to a dialysis machine because of his failing kidneys and placed in an oxygen tent to relieve the strain on his lungs. Doctors said he could linger that way for weeks, perhaps months. So Jackie decided to fly home to see the NBC-TV documentary that Caroline had worked on in Appalachia during the summer. When she told Ari of her plans, he made no effort to dissuade her. Assuming that she would be gone only for the weekend, Christina agreed to allow Maria Callas one final farewell visit to Onassis's bedside.

Jackie phoned on Monday. Told that her husband's condition had not changed, she decided to stay in New York. Towards the end of the week Onassis caught pneumonia and began slipping away. Still Jackie made no move to fly back. On Saturday, 15 March 1975, Onassis died with Christina at his side and his wife 3,000 miles away.

Twenty-three

The good luck rain that fell on Jackie on her wedding day now turned to torrents of abuse. She was ridiculed for not being with her husband in his final hours. The public hostility hit her like a burst of hail from a storm cloud. Once again she was a widow, but this time she did not have the consolation of a country deep in mourning. No one, least of all the Onassis family, could understand why she had left her husband in the hospital to die alone.

'There was an agreement that she had with Ari that she should spend part of the time with him and part of the time with her children,' said Nancy Tuckerman. 'He wanted it that way. And at this time she just felt she should be with John and Caroline.'

'She got a call from the doctors in Paris saying that Ari was very ill and that he was dying,' said her stepfather, Hugh Auchincloss. 'She was packing to leave when he passed away. I don't think his death came as a tremendous shock to her.'

'I think she felt terrible not to be there when he died,' said Lee Radziwill.

Jackie received the news early Saturday morning and stayed in her apartment all day. Unable to face the Onassis family alone, she called Teddy Kennedy and begged him to fly to the funeral with her children. That night, dressed completely in black, she left with her mother for Paris. Her children arrived later with their uncle. The only person to meet her at Orly airport was the family chauffeur, who drove her directly to the Onassis apartment, where she stayed for ten hours before visiting the hospital to see her husband's casket.

Throughout the day Onassis's aides avoided her and his relatives barely spoke, except to say that Christina could not see her because she was under sedation and resting. Jackie's best rapport had always been with Ari's sister, Artemis, but now even Mrs Garafoulidi shunned her, making no attempt to hide the family's animosity.

When Jackie offered to help with the funeral arrangements she was told that everything had been taken care of. Onassis has asked to be buried on Skorpios next to his son, Alexander, and his wishes for a simple Greek Orthodox service were being planned by his Greek family.

A few hours later Jackie went to the American Hospital in Neuilly. Accompanied by Onassis's private nurse and a bodyguard, she walked through the bronze doors of the chapel to pay her last respects to her husband. It was a quick farewell. There were no tears, no sighs, no anguished glances, no final kiss goodbye. She merely bowed her head to pray and left minutes later. Composed and controlled, she smiled at the photographers waiting outside the hospital.

There was no outpouring of affection for the forty-five-year-old widow as she went through the paces of her husband's funeral with a fixed but disconcerting smile.

The next day she flew with Ari's body to Actium airport in Greece. As she walked off the plane, she put her arm through Christina's and escorted her to a waiting limousine. Both sat in the back seat with Senator Kennedy as the funeral procession headed towards Skorpios. Even under sedation Christina could not control her emotions. The sight of her stepmother's continual smile to photographers along the way ripped her strained civility. 'Oh, God,' she moaned. 'Even now ... How can you ...'

'Hang on,' said Jackie with total control. 'It will all be over soon.'

Christina had spent the last forty-eight hours at her father's bedside watching him die. Now she gave way to her awful grief. She bolted from the car in tears – away from her father's widow – and ran ahead to ride with her aunts.

At the gravesite Jackie was forced to walk behind her husband's family and stand in the back with her mother, her children, and her former brother-in-law. Onassis's death had brought out all the repressed rage his family felt towards her, but behind sunglasses and a placid smile Jackie seemed impenetrable.

White lilies in white velvet-covered pots ringed the courtyard outside the little chapel on Skorpios. Sitting next to the huge wreaths on white tripods was a simple small bouquet with a card that said, 'To Ari from Jackie'. Out in the bay the *Christina* sat silently with her crew at parade rest and her flag at half mast. After a short service the coffin of Aristotle Socrates Onassis was carried outside and laid to rest in a freshly dug grave near his son's. Then the funeral party followed his daughter to his yacht, where Christina spoke to her father's crew in Greek.

'This boat and this island are mine,' she said. 'You are all my people now.'

Jackie smiled as she listened to her stepdaughter. Later Teddy Kennedy tried to approach Christina to talk about her father's will but she cut him off, saying, 'You better speak to my lawyers.' Jackie spent the night in Athens, then sent her son off with his uncle while she flew to Paris with Caroline to vacation at the country estate of Mr and Mrs Francis Fabre. Before leaving she gave reporters a short, controlled statement.

'Aristotle Onassis rescued me at a moment when my life was engulfed with shadows,' she said. 'He meant a lot to me. He brought me into a world where one could find both happiness and love. We lived through many beautiful experiences together which cannot be forgotten, and for which I will be eternally grateful.'

She declared that her ties with the Onassis family were as close as ever. 'Nothing has changed,' she said, 'both with Aristotle's sisters and his daughter, Christina. The same love binds us as when he lived.' She maintained she wanted her children 'to be brought up in Greece amidst Greek culture'. Then she was asked to comment on the reports that she was wrangling with her stepdaughter over Onassis's will.

'I'll answer with something my husband often told me,' she said. ' "Throughout the world people love fairy tales and especially those related to the lives of the rich. You must learn to understand this and accept it." '

With that the fairy queen began her second widowhood. This time she observed no official period of mourning. She shunned all the accoutrements of public grief. She made no pretence. Within hours she was photographed getting her hair done in Paris and watching the bullfights in Gageron. Returning to Skorpios a month later for a family memorial service at Onassis's grave, she again was shunned by her husband's family. She collected all her belongings and left. In the summer she returned again with her friend, Karl Katz, and Caroline to dedicate a new wing of a children's camp in memory of Onassis. 'My main purpose for coming to Greece, apart from loving the country, is to put into practice the last instructions of my late husband in order to preserve his name,' she said. That was her last trip to Skorpios.

Jackie's New York lawyers hired Greek counsel to ascertain exactly what she was entitled to from the Onassis estate. Published reports claimed she would inherit a minimum of 120 million dollars. Other so-called reliable sources insisted she would end up with 250 million. Actually, she was lucky to get an annual allowance. Publication of Onassis's will revealed that he had left his wife $100,000 a year from tax-free bonds and $100,000 a year in income, plus $50,000 for her children. Although too sick to pursue the divorce he wanted, he managed to demonstrate that he did not consider Jackie his wife in the truest sense of the word. She was taken care of only slightly better than his relatives and loyal retainers. The bulk of his estate went to his daughter.

Christina refused to raise the amount of Jackie's bequest and was determined to fight any future claim she might make on the Onassis estate. She ordered her lawyers to reach a settlement so she could obtain complete rights to the island and luxury yacht. So bitter was she towards Jackie that she refused even to consider the possibility of joint ownership. Her lawyers tried to suggest that she go along with the terms of the will which specified that she and Jackie share those properties, but Christina insisted she have total control herself. She never wanted to deal with Jackie again as long as she lived. She considered her stepmother a conniving opportunist who never cared as much for her father as for his money.

The lawyers advised Christina publicly to repudiate the fact that her father planned to divorce Jackie. They reasoned that a denial from the stepdaughter might establish better relations with Jackie until a final settlement could be reached. Onassis's will was susceptible to a legal challenge by his widow, and Christina's lawyers wanted to avoid a lawsuit at all costs. They pleaded with her not to antagonize her stepmother in any way until the legal matters were settled.

The day Jack Anderson's syndicated column appeared stating that Aristotle Onassis was indeed planning to divorce his wife before he died, Christina's lawyers released a carefully-worded statement through the office of Olympic Airways:

Miss Christina Onassis is very much distressed at the distorted stories and speculation which appeared in the international press about her late father and Mrs Jacqueline Onassis.

These stories are totally untrue and she repudiates them. In fact, the marriage of the late Mr Onassis and Mrs Jacqueline Onassis was a happy marriage and all rumours of intended divorce are untrue.

Her own relationship with Mrs Jacqueline Onassis was always and still is based on mutual friendship and respect and there are no financial or other disputes separating them.

It is the desire of Miss Christina Onassis and she understands it to be also the desire of Mrs Jacqueline Onassis that they both be left at peace and all detrimental and harmful speculations cease.

While Jackie's lawyers were negotiating on her behalf, she complained to her family that she was not receiving any money from Onassis's estate. 'She told my cousin that she was nearly broke,' said John Davis. 'She said, "Don't believe what you read in the papers. I'm strapped. I haven't been able to get a single cent out of Greece, not even my allowance. I've had to borrow money and sell stocks just to pay my bills." '

Jackie pushed hard for more money from the estate. If forced to give up her annual allowance, she insisted that she could take no less than 20 million dollars, plus her quarter interest in Skorpios and her share in the yacht. She asked her lawyers if she could challenge the 'nomimos mira' clause she signed which waived her rights to 12.5 per cent of the estate. If successful, she would receive close to 63 million dollars – which, under Greek law, was her fair share as the widow of a Greek man worth half a billion dollars. This was the veiled threat her lawyers used in negotiating with Christina, who still wanted Jackie to forfeit her rights to the yacht and the island.

The first offer Christina made was for 8 million dollars. Jackie refused it, stating again that she would not take anything less than 20 million. She even insisted on an additional six million dollars to pay US taxes on the 20 million. Finally, after eighteen months of costly negotiations, Christina agreed to her stepmother's demands on the condition that she break all ties with the Onassis family and abandon any further claim to their estate.

Jackie made her lawyers add a clause demanding the return of all the personal letters she had written to Ari over the years, plus a covenant prohibiting both women from ever publicly discussing the settlement. Then she signed her 26-million-dollar revenge.

Christina agreed because she wanted to cut all ties with Jackie, and, to her, 26 million dollars was cheap compared to the agony she would suffer battling her stepmother in court. After Jackie received the money from the Onassis Foundation, a board member said, 'Mrs Onassis is a woman who knows how to protect and augment her rights. She took advantage of Christina's wish to become controller of the part of the Onassis estate she was legally entitled to.'

News of Jackie's settlement made the front pages across the world. The Onassis empire was humiliated by the revelation and the Kennedys chose publicly to ignore it, refusing comment. They remembered well what Jackie had said to Joe Kennedy the day he was bragging about giving his children a million dollars when they turned twenty-one.

'I did this so they could be independent and turn around and tell me to go to hell, if they want,' said the Ambassador.

'Do you know what I would tell you if you gave me a

million dollars?' asked Jackie. 'I would tell you to give me another million.'

At the time the comment seemed nothing more than cute repartee on Jackie's part, but over the years her compulsion to spend became a source of embarrassment to the Kennedys. At one point Ethel upbraided Jackie over dinner, claiming her publicized shopping sprees were reflecting poorly on the family. 'Everything is always the family, the family, the family,' Jackie snapped back. 'That's all you ever think about.'

Undeterred by public opinion or the private feelings of the Kennedy or the Onassis families, Jackie secured her 26-million-dollar settlement from the estate of the man who wanted to divorce her. Blessed by fate, she emerged richer as a widow than she had ever been as a wife.

A year later Constantine Gratsos still had to fight for control when asked about Jackie. 'Please don't talk to me about that woman,' he said. 'I can't bring myself to even think about her. If it was something else I'd try to help you, but on this I can't. And don't even try to see Christina, because she can't bear the thought of that woman. She will turn you down flat. She never wants to see her again, or even hear her name. And you must admit she's paid dearly for that one consideration.'

Sitting in his executive suite in the Olympic Towers, Costa Gratsos looked like the epitome of an empire builder – a tall, distinguished man with white hair and black horn-rimmed glasses, fit and trim even in his seventies. The one threat to his controlled demeanour was mention of Jacqueline Kennedy Onassis, whom he referred to only as 'her', 'she', or 'that woman'. He could not bring himself to pronounce her name.

His hands clenched and his knuckles turned white as he thought about his best friend's second wife. Then he changed the subject. 'I knew the first Mrs Onassis well and loved her very much,' said Ari's top executive. 'And Maria Callas, I adored. She was a warm and beautiful human being full of giving, and the only woman in the world to truly love Mr Onassis. The only woman to ever really love him for himself.

'It was so sad,' he continued. 'How I ached for him and his disappointing marriage. He realized Maria's full worth only after he married. Then it was too late. But they continued their relationship. After his death, she secluded herself in her Paris apartment and wouldn't see anyone. She wouldn't even answer the phone when I called, and I was one of her closest friends. She literally died of a broken heart on 16 September 1977. Life for her was not worth living after he was gone.'

But for Jackie, finally free of her Greek albatross and financially independent for the first time in her life, living became a special pleasure. Six months after she buried Aristotle Onassis she went to work as a consulting editor at Viking Press, a job she secured through her friend Thomas Guinzburg, president of the New York publishing house.

'One is not unmindful of the range of contacts that lady has,' said Guinzburg, commenting on Jackie's wide circle of social, political, and international acquaintances.

Earning $200 a week, Jackie was given an office, but not required to work set hours. Her job was to attract new authors to Viking. 'I expect to be learning the ropes at first,' she said. 'You sit in at editorial conferences, you discuss general things. Maybe you're assigned to a special project of your own. Really, I expect to be doing what my employer tells me to do.'

Viking soon was swamped with bizarre unsolicited material, crank calls, and dozens of inquiries from all over the world. Letters poured in from people who merely wanted a reply signed by Jacqueline Bouvier Onassis, as she was now calling herself. Viking responded with printed forms. Jackie's co-workers squirrelled away her JBO office memos.

Jackie helped plan an exhibit about the changing role of women in the eighteenth century. She also travelled to Moscow with Thomas Hoving, director of the Metropolitan Museum of Art, and later edited *In the Russian Style*, a richly illustrated volume of photographs dealing with the fashions and furnishings of Imperial Russia. To launch her first book, Viking held an exclusive press luncheon in her honour in the Versailles Room of the Carlyle Hotel. The *New York Daily*

News, the largest circulated newspaper in America, was not included because Jackie said she didn't like the *News*. The six reporters invited to the luncheon were told they could not bring a photographer or a tape recorder. They were also instructed that questions unrelated to the book would not be allowed.

Jackie entered the room with her publisher and offered the reporters a fragile handshake and a dazzling smile. She wore a black cashmere turtleneck sweater, brown checked pants, little make-up, and no jewellery. She said she had selected all the gowns, headdresses, and accessories for the book's photographs. This prompted her publisher to say, 'Jackie wouldn't have allowed her name to go on the book if she hadn't been the prime mover behind it. She's not just a Hollywood type of star with a double doing the hard part of the job.'

After establishing that she had done most of the work on the book, she said: 'After I got out of college, I wanted to write for a newspaper or work for a publishing house, but I did other things. When the time was right, I did this. I would always have liked to. I see my future as staying on as an editor at Viking, hopefully. I love the work I do.'

Still, there were problems. Her secretary at Viking despised her and felt demeaned having to take her personal phone messages and type her letters. Others were polite on the surface, but there was an unspoken feeling that Jackie was not to be taken seriously, that this new job was merely a toy for her amusement. She was gently rebuffed in an editorial meeting when she suggested a colouring book on architectural ruins like Angkor Wat. Her suggestion that her friend Doris Duke write a book on her historical restoration project in Newport was also dismissed. She tried hard to bring in a major book – the memoirs of Lord Snowdon or the autobiography of Frank Sinatra – but, despite her friendships with both men, she failed. She wrote to Steve Roberts, who was in Athens with the *New York Times*, and suggested that he do a book on Greece, but nothing materialized. Later she flew over to talk to him about it. She mentioned how much difficulty she was having on the job. She said that being a celebrity hampered her effectiveness, and she sarcastically referred to the publicity she received her first day in the office as 'Nancy Drew goes to work'.

Aware that she was not being accepted as a professional, Jackie was almost defensive. 'It's not as if I've never done anything interesting,' she said. 'I've been a reporter myself and I've lived through important parts of American history. I'm not the worst choice for this position.'

In October 1977 Viking published Jeffery Archer's controversial novel, *Shall We Tell The President?* depicting Teddy Kennedy as the target of an assassination attempt. Jackie had known about the book for months. She was consulted about it at the outset and given the chance to stop publication if she felt it was tasteless, but she said she had no objections. Only when John Leonard reviewed it in the *New York Times* did she object. There was one passage from the critique that humiliated her: 'There is a word for such a book,' wrote Mr Leonard. 'The word is trash. Anybody associated with its publication should be ashamed of herself.' That pronoun was the pretext Jackie needed.

She conferred with her friends Richard Goodwin, the former Kennedy aide, journalist Pete Hamill, and Jann Wenner, publisher of *Rolling Stone*. Then she sent a handwritten letter of resignation to Tom Guinzburg. Later she issued a statement through Nancy Tuckerman, who was working at Doubleday, where Jackie would eventually go herself as an editor.

'Last spring, when told of the book, I tried to separate my lives as a Viking employee and a Kennedy relative,' she said. 'But this fall, when it was suggested that I had had something to do with acquiring the book and that I was not distressed by its publication, I felt I had to resign.'

Tom Guinzburg refused to be interviewed, but he issued a statement which said, in part, 'After being friends for more than half our lives, I more than ever deeply regret Mrs Onassis's decision to resign from the Viking Press without a personal discussion of the incident which resulted in her decision ... It is precisely because of the generous and understanding response of Mrs Onassis at the time we discussed this book and before the contract was signed which gave me confidence to proceed with the novel's publication.'

Jackie was firmly back in the Kennedy fold before she decided to resign from Viking. She had supported Sargent Shriver's ill-fated run for the Presidency in 1976 and contributed $25,000 to his campaign. She supported a textile factory in the Bedford-Stuyvesant area of Brooklyn because the project had meant so much to Robert Kennedy. To help promote the African fabrics it produced, she bought some for herself and allowed them to be photographed in her Fifth Avenue apartment. She arranged for Caroline to work a summer in Teddy's Senate office and she sent her son with Sargent Shriver's children to work on a poverty project overseas. She appeared for the ground-breaking of the John F. Kennedy Memorial Library in Massachusetts. She acted as honorary chairman of a benefit at the Kennedy Center in Washington and surprised many by showing up herself. She changed her legal residence to Hyannis Port after Onassis's death and frequently spent time there with friends like Pete Hamill and her children.

Hamill, a well-known columnist for the *New York Daily News*, had been living with Shirley MacLaine for several years, but moved out when the movie star said she didn't want to get married. About that time Jackie began her job at Viking. Although Hamill had been critical of her in the past, he began to feel sorry for her because of all the publicity she was getting. So he called her and offered to introduce her to writers around town. Jackie immediately accepted the offer and they became close friends and lovers. Their brief affair was widely publicized and pictures of the couple plastered all over the tabloids. Photographers dogged them, prompting Pete's brother to say that taking Jackie out is like taking out a big bright red fire engine.

They managed a few private moments together drinking beer and watching the boats come in to Sheepshead Bay. On the record Pete Hamill was too much of a gentleman to discuss his private life with a reporter. However, his previous lack of chivalry towards Jackie came back to bite him hard. When she married Aristotle Onassis, Hamill, a loyal

331

Kennedy supporter, was working as a columnist for the *New York Post*. Outraged by her remarriage, he took to his typewriter like Jack the Ripper to a meatcleaver.

His wrath vented at the typewriter, Hamill had second thoughts about submitting the column for publication. 'It was just too vicious,' he said later, 'so I told them not to run it, and I wrote something else which was published instead.'

The column was killed and filed away only to resurface six years later when Pete and Jackie were becoming serious about each other. In an attempt to humiliate the columnist, who was then writing for a competing New York paper, the publisher of the *New York Post*, Rupert Murdoch, revived the column and ran doses of it on Page Six, the paper's gossip section. For four days running readers were tantalized by nasty little snippets of the column which ran under the teasing caption, 'Who Wrote This?'

On the fifth day the *Post* ran a picture of Pete and Jackie together. It said: 'In 1971 Pete Hamill wrote of Jackie Onassis that it looked as if "no courtesan ... ever sold herself for more". He didn't approve of her marriage to Ari, you see. Times change, and so do Pete's opinions and now the gossips are saying that Mrs Onassis, 48, will make Hamill, 42, her third mate.'

Hamill was understandably incensed. 'The first day I saw that damn thing I knew exactly what the *Post* was trying to do. I immediately called Jackie and explained the whole thing to her and she understood perfectly. She wasn't mad at me but she was furious at that scumbag, Rupert Murdoch. She agreed with me that what he did was one of the dirtiest and cheapest deals ever pulled in journalism. That man is a total bastard and everywhere I go I'm going to get the message across that Murdoch is a first class sleaze.'

Jackie continued seeing Pete Hamill publicly and privately. He shared evenings alone with her and weekends with her children. He helped Caroline get a summer job at the *News*. He was staying with Jackie at Hyannis Port when they heard that Elvis Presley had died. He immediately headed for Memphis to cover the story, taking Caroline with him. Caroline gained interviews with the singer's family, and

Hamill helped her write her story. It was turned down by the *News* but later rewritten and used by *Rolling Stone* magazine.

Jackie was unquestionably enamoured of Pete Hamill's Irish charm, good looks and sense of humour. But his devotion to her children and theirs to him made him even more special.

'The things I care most about is the happiness of my children,' she said. 'If you fail with your children then I don't think that anything else in life could ever really matter very much – at least it wouldn't to me.'

Few people criticized Jackie's role as a mother. Her dedication to her fatherless children was genuine, and the relationship she developed with them over the years unique. She socialized with them, travelled with them, thrived on their company. After Onassis's death she began dating men much younger than herself so they could relate to her teenage children. Men like Pete Hamill, investment banker Skip Stein, and Jann Wenner were not father surrogates for Caroline and John, but they did provide Jackie with male company and another level of communication with her children. Each man considered her an exemplary mother. Her children's friends regarded her more of a pal than a parent.

'When Caroline was working as a copy aide at the *New York Daily News*, we used to go out a lot,' said one young man. 'One night we got absolutely smashed on beer and grass, and Caroline went home drunk out of her face. When I called her the next day, Jackie answered the phone. I couldn't believe it when she said in that sweet little-girl voice of hers, "I heard all about that wild party last night and I want to know why you didn't invite me to come along. You better take me with you next time because I don't want to miss out on any of the fun." She was really terrific and not upset at all that Caroline had come home bombed. Jackie is more of a friend to her kids than a mother. I know that's a cliché, but it's really true. They blow up at each other all the time and then they make up. It's weird but it's terrific.'

Jackie made her children very aware of who they were. Both cherished their Kennedy name and the fact that they were the children of the late President – the heirs of Camelot. They had no material need that could not be satisfied. From the trust funds established by Jack Kennedy and the Onassis settlement, both became millionaires before they were twenty-one years old.

Jackie became bitter and disillusioned as the wife of John F. Kennedy, but as the mother of his children she tried to consecrate his memory. For this reason, she told close friends, she would have paid any amount of money to suppress the revelations which came out in later years regarding the late President's private life.

'They have been more painful to her as a mother than a wife,' says Jamie Auchincloss.

'Each time a book or an article appears about one of Jack's mistresses, Jackie must tell Caroline and John that their father loved her and she loved him and they must love him, too,' he says. 'It's excruciating for her, but she's powerless to do anything about it. Everyone in the family has had to deny the stories because Jackie does not want her children to remember that side of him. She says it has nothing to do with his role as their father, and she has been successful in this deception because I don't think Caroline and John believe anything they have ever read about Kennedy's other women.'

The late President's friends and former aides also conspired to protect his children from the personal assaults on his private life. When Judith Campbell Exner was revealed in Senate testimony to be one of the many women who knew Kennedy intimately in the White House, Kenny O'Donnell, Evelyn Lincoln, and Dave Powers publicly denied any knowledge of her, although each helped arrange her visits to the President.

'I've never heard of her before,' said Kenny O'Donnell.

'I'm sorry I don't recall the name,' said Evelyn Lincoln.

'The only Campbell I know is Campbell soup,' said Dave Powers.

Powers later privately admitted to Mrs Exner's biographer that he did indeed know who she was, but he said he could never make such an admission publicly because he would lose his job as director of the John F. Kennedy Memorial Library.

Caroline and John were raised to revere their father. They returned only once to the White House since living there as the President's children, but it was a memory they cherished. In 1971 they came back with their mother for one evening to have dinner with President and Mrs Nixon. The invitation had been extended so that Jackie and her children could see the Kennedys' official portraits before they were unveiled to the public. Jackie wanted Caroline, then thirteen, and John, then ten, to see the paintings of their father and mother as President and First Lady.

'She told me she would like to slip in quietly,' said Mrs Nixon. 'She asked me not to tell anyone, not even the staff, that she was coming. She didn't want them buzzing around.'

At the time Jackie did not know that Pat Nixon was going to toss out the plaque she had soldered to the mantelpiece in the Presidential bedroom before leaving in 1963. The White House curator had decreed that Jackie's memorial to herself as the wife of the late President had no historical significance in the Executive Mansion, and it was quietly removed and placed in storage after her visit. When she arrived, the Monet painting the Kennedy family had donated in memory of President Kennedy was hanging in the Green Room, but that, too, was moved to a place of lesser prominence after her visit.

Caroline and John were thrilled to be inside the White House again. They said they hadn't remembered it as being so big and so elegant. They went into the Oval Office where their father had once sat as President and they saw the Jacqueline Kennedy garden dedicated to their mother as First Lady. They visited their bedrooms and the third floor solarium which had once been their playschool. It was an emotional return for both youngsters, and Jackie was grateful to the Nixons for giving them the chance to see the mansion which seven years earlier had been their home. She later wrote them a letter of thanks, saying, 'You have made it possible for the children and me to return to the White House privately, and for the children to see with you the portraits, where they hang, and to rediscover the rooms they used to know. For this moving experience, our deepest thanks.'

The portrait that Jackie had painted of herself for posterity is the picture she wanted the world to remember. She spent three years posing for this misty painting which now hangs in the ground floor of the White House. The muted portrait by Aaron Shikler shows an ethereally beautiful woman looking romantic, dreamy, and remote. She is standing in front of a carved fireplace in her New York apartment with fresh flowers and a bronze sculptured bust in the background shadows. Wearing a long pale peach Givenchy gown with a ruffled neck and long sleeves, she looks demure, almost childlike. There is no evidence of the gnawing inner tension, the emotional turbulence, the insecurity and restlessness which haunted her. The painter's brush has swept away all traces of torment and loneliness, leaving only a one-dimensional image of a wife-child with a whispery voice. It is an elegant understated vision of a twentieth-century American woman with a mind rooted in eighteenth-century France. The calm, serene exterior gives no indication of the contradictions and complexities beneath.

Even the elongated hands are unreal for a woman with rough, broad fingers and bitten-down nails. The painting focuses on an exquisite face and wide-set eyes which seem to be trying to find something in the undefined distance away from reality.

There are no strong primary colours in this portrait – nothing to indicate the driving essence of a woman who conquered and survived and succeeded at great personal cost. An elusive quality shines through the pink, mauve, and champagne brush strokes, but the woman behind the lady is lost in shimmers. The artistic deception is lovely, haunting, mysterious – but still deceiving. Yet this is the picture Jacqueline Bouvier Kennedy Onassis wanted to present to the world. This is the public image she superimposed on reality. 'I would have liked it even more lost in shadows,' she said, 'less specific, more impressionistic.'